IMAGE OF THE INVISIBLE

Image *of the* Invisible

The Visualization of Religion in the
Welsh Nonconformist Tradition

John Harvey

UNIVERSITY OF WALES PRESS
CARDIFF
1999

© John Harvey, 1999

British Library Cataloguing-in-Publication Data.
A catalogue record for this book is available from the British Library.

ISBN 0–7083–1475–9

All rights reserved. No part of this book may be reproduced, stored in a retrieval system, or transmitted, in any form or by any means, electronic, mechanical, photocopying, recording or otherwise, without clearance from the University of Wales Press, 6 Gwennyth Street, Cardiff, CF2 4YD.

The right of John Harvey to be identified as author of this work has been asserted by him in accordance with the Copyright, Designs and Patents Act 1988.

Typeset at University of Wales Press
Printed in Great Britain by Henry Ling Limited, Dorchester

For Sam and Kim

Contents

List of Illustrations		ix
Acknowledgements		xi
Introduction		1
1	God is Invisible: Word and Worship, Interdict and Image in the Reformation Tradition	6
2	Pit and Pulpit, Miners and Sinners: Sermonic Emblems in the Homiletic Tradition	26
3	Emblems and Emissaries: The Ministry of Art	45
4	'Seeing Him Who is Invisible': Visionary Emblems of the 1904–1905 Religious Revival	59
5	Images of God: Inspiration and Instrumentality	87
6	Cymro and Gomero, Pit and Pithom: The Bible in Wales	95
7	Work and Worship, Pit and Piety: Labour Transfigured	119
8	'The Shadow of Death': Mining and Mortality in the Paintings of Nicholas Evans	140
Conclusion		160
Appendices		162
Notes		170
Select Bibliography		204
Index		213

List of Illustrations

Between pages 90 and 91

Plate 1 Nicholas Evans, *Entombed – Jesus in the Midst* (1974)
Plate 2 Harold Copping, 'The Hope of the World' (*c.*1921)
Plate 3 'The Broad and the Narrow Way' (nineteenth century, second half)
Plate 4 'The Gospel Ship' (nineteenth century, second half)
Plate 5 Nicholas Evans, *Pit Closure – Miners Coming Up for the Last Time* (1977)

		Page
1	'Y Tabernacl a'i Gyntedd' (1862)	8
2	'Y Cysegr Sanctaidd a'i Gelfi' (1862)	8
3	C. B. Nicholls, Ark of the Covenant with Mercy Seat and Cherubim (1862)	9
4	John Thomas, Four Crosses (Calvinistic Methodist) Chapel (nineteenth century, second half)	15
5	Maesyronnen (Independent) chapel (1696)	16
6	Unidentified chapel interior, Wales (nineteenth century, second half)	17
7	John Thomas, Llanfair Caereinion Mynafon Church (nineteenth century, second half)	17
8	Book 4, Emblem 13 (1818)	22
9	Book 3, Emblem 11 (1818)	22
10	Book 3, Emblem 12 (1818)	22
11	'Great Drinkers Think Themselves Great Men' (1890)	25
12	'The "Penitent", or Fire-man, Igniting Fire-Damp' (1868)	33
13	H. Le Rolle, *The Nativity* [n.d.]	39
14	John Martin, 'Dedication of the Temple' (1835)	51
15	G. F. Watts, *Hope* (1886)	52
16	J. M. Staniforth, '"O! Marvellous Love! He Died for Evan Roberts!!!"' (23 January 1905)	56
17	J. M. Staniforth, 'A Result of the Revival. Then and Now' (*c.*1904–5)	56
18	Annibale Carraci, 'Crucifixion' [n.d.]	69
19	'Thou God, See'st Me' (nineteenth century, first half)	71
20	Book 2, Emblem 1 (1818)	72
21	Book 2, Emblem 14 (1818)	72
22	T. E. S. and A. M. W., 'An Empty Pulpit?' (16 January 1905)	75
23	John Thomas, two angels beside a deathbed [n.d.]	77
24	'Iesu Grist a'r Diafol' (1864)	78
25	Thomas Henry Thomas, 'Mary Jones and the Devil' [n.d.]	79
26	'A True Likeness of "Our Saviour"' (nineteenth century, second half)	82
27	*Gwlad Canaan; Ar Gynllun Gogledd a Deheudir Cymru i Blant* (nineteenth century, second half)	98
28	'Ebal a Garizim' (1844)	99
29	'The Pass of Llanberis' (1892)	99
30	'Y Nahr Quades Yn Mynydd Libanus' (1844)	100
31	'Pont Aberglaslyn' (1892)	100

32	'Mynydd Ararat' (1844)	101
33	John Sell Cotman, *Snowdon* (*c.*1809–10)	101
34	'Pyramidiau yr Aipht' (1844)	102
35	Unidentified chapel interior (nineteenth century, last quarter)	104
36	Baptist Chapel, Newtown, Powys (1881)	104
37	Sections and ornamentation of the Temple of Solomon (1732)	106
38	Bethel Welsh Baptist Church (1880)	107
39	'The Tabernacle' (1821)	107
40	'The Ark of the Covenant with the Mercy Seat' (1821)	108
41	Pulpit, Bethel Welsh Baptist Church (1880)	108
42	Tabernacle (1888)	109
43	Ground-plan of the Temple of Solomon by Prideaux (1847)	110
44	Pulpit and *sêt fawr*, Bethel Welsh Baptist Church (1880)	110
45	Table of Shewbread (1855–6)	112
46	Communion table (twentieth century, first half)	112
47	Nicholas Evans, *Strike – Gleaners on Slag Heap* (1978)	116
48	Nicholas Evans, *All Out – End of Shift* (1978)	116
49	Jean François Millet, *The Angelus* (1857–9)	120
50	Ford Madox Brown, *Work* (1852–65)	122
51	Nicholas Evans, *Coalface (2)* (1976)	123
52	Ainslie, 'A Colliery Explosion: Volunteers to the Rescue' (25 February 1882)	124
53	T. H. Thomas, underground service (1883)	126
54	J. M. Staniforth, 'A Changed Home. An Improvement' (9 January 1905)	127
55	'Revival Service in a Coal Mine' (22 December 1904)	128
56	J. M. Staniforth, 'The Religious Revival' (1904)	130
57	Rembrandt, 'Christ Preaching the Remission of Sins' (*c.*1652)	130
58	John Thomas, Capel Mair, St Clears [n.d.]	132
59	Engine-house no.5, The Prince of Wales Pit, Ebbw Vale (twentieth century, first quarter)	133
60	Gas engine, Bargoed Colliery (*c.*1913)	134
61	Mynydd Newydd Colliery, Forest Fach (1899)	136
62	Nicholas Evans, *Underground Chapel during 1904 Revival* (1977)	137
63	Nicholas Evans, *Standing a Post* (1976)	137
64	Nicholas Evans, *'Ashes to Ashes, Dust to Dust'* (1978)	141
65	Nicholas Evans, *'The Trumpet Shall Sound' – Resurrection!* (1978)	141
66	Nicholas Evans, *The Broken Rope* (1979)	144
67	Nicholas Evans, *Transport to the Far End* (1976)	146
68	Nicholas Evans, *Journey to the Far End* (1979)	146
69	Nicholas Evans, *The Last Bond* (1983)	147
70	*The Last Judgement* (detail) (*c.*1000)	147
71	John Petts, *The Cage* (1949)	148
72	Nicholas Evans, *Coalface – Tight Squeeze* (1980)	150
73	Nicholas Evans, *Candle-Men Carrying Out Dead* (1979)	150
74	Book 5, Emblem 8 (1818)	153
75	Nicholas Evans, *Ecce Homo* (1983)	157

Acknowledgements

I am grateful for the assistance of Tim Egan and Mark Evans of the Art Department, National Museum and Gallery, Cardiff; the staff of the Evangelical Library, London, the National Library of Wales, Aberystwyth, and South Wales Miners' Library, Swansea; O. C. Bowen, The Apostolic Church, Shrewsbury; George Canty, Miracle Gospel and Healing Crusades; Desmond W. Cartwright, Elim Pentecostal Church, Greenock; Bob Clarke; T. W. Walker, General Superintendent, Elim Pentecostal Church; Eifion Evans; Mark Owen, BBC, Radio Wales; Anona Clifford and Wil Petherbridge for translating Welsh texts, and Jacqueline, my wife, for her unerring support. I would also like to acknowledge the financial assistance I have received from the Sir David Hughes Parry Award, and the University of Wales, Aberystwyth.

Acknowledgement for permission to reproduce images is due to: Bethel Welsh Baptist Church, Aberystwyth for Plate 2; Castle Museum, Norwich for no. 33; Ceredigion Museum, Aberystwyth for Plates 3 and 4; the Revd Geoffrey and Mrs Iola Thomas for no. 19; Glynn Vivian Art Gallery for no. 69; National Library of Wales for Plate 5 and nos. 1, 2, 3, 4, 6, 7, 12, 13, 14, 15, 16, 17, 18, 22, 23, 24, 26, 27, 28, 29, 30, 31, 32, 34, 35, 37, 39, 40, 42, 43, 45, 49, 52, 53, 54, 55, 56, 58, 60, 61, 67 and 68; National Museum and Gallery, Cardiff for Plate 1, and no. 25; Newport Museum and Art Gallery, Monmouthshire for no. 71; Nicholas Evans for Plates 1 and 5 and nos. 47, 48, 51, 62, 63, 64, 65, 66, 67, 68, 69, 72, 73 and 75; Manchester City Art Galleries for no. 50; Rijksmuseum, Amsterdam for no. 57; Royal Commission on the Ancient and Historical Monuments of Wales for no. 5; Victoria and Albert Museum for no. 70.

Photographic credits are due to: Andrew Baldwin for nos. 8, 9, 10, 11, 12, 15, 20, 21, 59, 74 and 75; Castle Museum, Norwich for no. 33; Christopher Webster for no. 44; Glynn Vivian Art Gallery for no. 69; Victor Evans for nos. 47, 51, 62, 63, 64, 65, 66 and 73; Jacqueline Harvey for nos. 36, 41, 46, 48 and 72; National Library of Wales for Plate 5 and nos. 1, 2, 3, 4, 6, 7, 13, 14, 16, 17, 18, 22, 23, 24, 26, 27, 28, 29, 30, 31, 32, 34, 35, 37, 39, 40, 42, 43, 45, 49, 52, 53, 54, 55, 56, 58, 60, 61, 67 and 68; National Museum and Gallery, Cardiff for Plate 1 and no. 25; Newport Museum and Art Gallery, Monmouthshire for no. 71; Rijksmuseum, Amsterdam for no. 57; Robert Greetham for no. 19, 36, 41, 44 and 46; Royal Commission on the Ancient and Historical Monuments of Wales for no. 5; Rudy Lewis for Plates 2, 3 and 4; and the Victoria and Albert Museum for no. 70.

Note

All biblical quotations are from the Authorized Version (1611).

Dimensions are in centimetres, height × width.

The county names given in this book are those of the pre-1974 counties, by which the counties were known during the historical period to which much of this book refers.

[Jesus Christ] the image of the invisible God . . .
Colossians 1: 15

Faith speaks . . . in the language of one world, the world of sense and sight, concerning the things of another world, the world unseen and eternal.
John Caird, *The Symbolic Language of Religion* (1970)

Art should *interpret* industry as art once interpreted religion.
D. H. Lawrence, *Women in Love* (1920)

Introduction

Nonconformists were people of 'the Word'. They submitted to it as the inviolable, inerrant, infallible, and inspired revelation of God, as His authoritative rule in matters of faith and life. The Word revealed the glory and counsel of God, and regulated the Christian's character and the Church's conduct and polity. It was a lamp to illumine the benighted and a sword to arm believers in their offensive against sin and Satan (Psalm 119: 105, Ephesians 6: 17). Moreover, as John Elias (1774–1841), the foremost preacher in Wales, enthused, it was 'the palace in which they enjoy their delicious feasts and delightful music. Yea, this is their flowery garden, and shadowy walks in the heat of the day. Therefore their life and support are in the Word.'[1] The Word gave spiritual sustenance and solace, circumscribed their activities, animated their endeavours, interpreted their experience from the womb to the tomb, and formed their habitual mind-set. It so permeated the Nonconformist consciousness that its influence is evident in almost every aspect of the denominations' religious culture and social milieu.

Nonconformists were also people of the image, as preachers of the calibre of Elias, Daniel Rowland (1713–90), and Christmas Evans (1766–1838) demonstrated by their use of literary and rhetorical metaphor. However, this was not the only medium for picturing the Word. I have argued in *The Art of Piety* that, contrary to received opinion and a Calvinistic heritage, Nonconformity had made conspicuous use of visual representations. Congregations requisitioned a variety of visual artefacts to decorate chapel and home, to commemorate leaders and notable events in their history, and to convey the teachings of the churches. Inasmuch as these artefacts propagated the faith and aided worship and devotion they represent the religious art of the denominations. The Word governed the image, as it did all other departments of Nonconformist life; it became the subject, and often the substance, of the image, in illustrations of biblical stories and characters, pictures of pious behaviour, portraits of the pulpits' Wordsmiths, and typographical compositions of scriptural texts. Imaging the Word in these ways is one facet of a broader tradition of visualizing religion which is deeply rooted in the history and culture of Welsh Nonconformity. Within this tradition invisible religious concepts such as doctrine, biblical narrative, and spiritual experience, are given tangible expression in visual, literary, and conceptual imagery. A dominant motif throughout the book is the intermingling of the

Nonconformist life and God's Word which was stressed by Elias. This reflected a perception of the world suffused by the light of heaven, in which sensible things and common experiences emblematized and made concrete the realities of the unseen spiritual realm.

This book does not seek to give a comprehensive account of heaven cast in earth's mould or to pay equal attention to the whole history of Nonconformity. Rather, the aim is, by sufficient illustration and juxtaposition of ideas and imagery, to establish the general character of Nonconformists' visualization of the Word. The scope of the study is further constrained by what is, arguably, one of the tradition's most significant images – the painting entitled *Entombed – Jesus in the Midst* (1974) by the Welsh artist Nicholas Evans (b. 1907) (**Plate 1**). It depicts the aftermath of a coal-mining disaster: a section of underground roof has dropped like a guillotine, shearing two standing-posts and imprisoning four miners in the road. The men have gathered their water-cans and safety lamps in a curling-box and huddle around the low flame of the one lamp that remains alight. Two miners crouch, their faces buried in cupped hands in an attitude suggesting despair, while another pulls a jacket close about his shoulders to shield himself from the cold and damp. The fourth man kneels and prays fervently in the direction of the last member of the group who, according to the title, is Jesus. The subject-matter conflates the physical and spiritual realms, the everyday and biblical worlds, mining and religion, and work and worship. In these respects *Entombed* embodies some of the most salient themes and motifs of the culture associated with Nonconformity's visualization of religion. Furthermore it serves as a contemporary manifestation of and an important key to understanding this tradition. The picture typifies the strong association between coal-mining and Nonconformity prevalent in south Wales from the mid nineteenth century, and especially during the religious revival of 1904–5. Nonconformity was the religion of the coalfields. While miners often took their political language from the Bible, ministers, for their part, derived sermon illustrations and lessons from the harsh realities of coal-mining. In architectural terms, the association is evident in the formal similarities between chapel and colliery. It can also be seen in pictorial illustrations and religious writing of the period, in which labour assumes the status of a religious sacrament and the miner becomes an emblem for both sinner and saint (see Chapters 2 and 7). Interpreted as portraying a supernatural manifestation of Jesus, *Entombed* makes tangible the visionary experiences claimed by miners and their families during the revival and subsequently by Pentecostals in Wales (see Chapter 4). Furthermore, the picture represents a transposition of the biblical world into the contemporary world. As such, it restates a correspondence between Wales and Israel, and between the Old Testament Israelites and south Wales miners, which was established during the late nineteenth century (see Chapter 6).

Entombed also exemplifies a marriage of art and religion forged (in principle) by Nonconformists at the turn of the century. This emerged from two impulses:

a general belief that religion ought properly to permeate every legitimate sphere of life, and a recognition that art could perform a positive role in promoting and illustrating religious values. More specifically, the painting fulfils a manifesto proposed by some Nonconformists at the time, that Welsh art should serve religion and reflect the spirituality of the Welsh as expressed in their preaching (see Chapter 3). The sermonic dimension of *Entombed* derives from the association of its subject with the tradition of homiletic illustration in south Wales. This combination of preaching and painting also typifies the union of the Word and image fostered by the Protestant Reformation and nineteenth-century evangelical traditions of emblemature. Emblematic images externalized religious concepts without recourse to traditional Roman Catholic imagery and were thoroughly biblical in their sentiments. *Entombed* and Evans's later paintings share these characteristics.

In addressing Nonconformity's visual tradition within the wider field of Protestantism and art, the study heeds what F. Buchholz saw as the dangers of such an approach: 'Protestantism "as such" is not conceivable for the historian. He is always dealing only with particular denominations, which themselves again are limited within a time frame. To write on the position of Protestantism "as such" on art would mean to publish a book of blank white pages.'[2] The particular denominations that are dealt with here include the Calvinistic Methodists or Presbyterian Church of Wales, the Baptists, the Congregationalists or Independents, and the Apostolic Church, a branch of the Pentecostal movement. It is impossible to discuss Nonconformity in Wales in isolation from its English counterpart since denominational unions, such as the Baptist and Congregational, were national, and many Welsh ministers wrote for journals published in both countries. The articles on art and other issues in these magazines, while not constituting official pronouncements, have by virtue of their inclusion in the denominational journals been sanctioned by the churches' leaders. In the context of this book 'Nonconformity' refers to Welsh Nonconformity, unless otherwise stated.

In discussing religious art, one is also dealing only with particular definitions. I have adopted an interpretation of 'religious' consonant with the biblical sense of that term (Greek *threskeia*), meaning the outward expression, as opposed to the content, of belief (James 1: 26, Acts 26: 5, and Galatians 1: 13). Since Nonconformists, including Nicholas Evans, espouse a strictly bibliocentric theology, this is their understanding of the term too. In the chapters dealing with the connotative significance of Evans's paintings the term 'biblical' is introduced to describe the content of belief. In addressing the theological milieu, the study focuses on the doctrinal distinctives of Nonconformist revivalism, the cultural background to Pentecostalism in Wales, and the root of its theology. The timeframe ranges from the early eighteenth century to the present, with a focus on the religious revival of 1904–5 and the beginning of the Apostolic Church in 1909. A strong cultural continuity exists between the societies of biblical times on the one hand and Pentecostalism and Nonconformity on the other. Thus, in reading late-twentieth-century paintings in the context of the typology and symbolism of the biblical age, of eighteenth- to early-twentieth-century sermon illustrations, and of revivalist visions, the study does not perpetrate an anachronism.

Nicholas Evans

Nicholas Evans is a former miner and a Pentecostal lay preacher for the Apostolic Church in Wales, a Nonconformist denomination which grew out of the religious revival of 1904–5. After a brief period as a pitboy, Evans spent his working life employed by the Great Western Railway.[3] He started to paint in retirement, and in the course of fifteen years produced a considerable body of paintings, the majority of which are predominantly black, square, and made by using fingers, rags, and sponges. Evans's ability has not been informed by a life of diligent application to the rules and principles of art; likewise, his individuality of style has developed, for the most part, in isolation from artistic tradition. His paintings also perpetuate the visionary tradition insofar as the artist believes them to be divinely inspired, mediated in the form of a vision which he realizes in paint. The majority of these works depict scenes from the history of coal-mining from the late eighteenth century to just after the mid twentieth century. Within his subject Evans has concentrated on the themes of mining disasters, mass funerals, miners and pitgirls working underground and on the surface of the pit, the camaraderie among the colliers and between colliers and their pit ponies, the piety of the pitmen, the plight of the unemployed, the hardships of the lock-out and the 1920s depression, the militancy of the strikers, and important developments in the history of mining technology.

Mining and religion meet in his work as they do in his life. *Entombed* provides a paradigm for the integration of the concepts in these paintings.[4] While describing scenes of coal-mining many of Evans's paintings also evoke the biblical world. These evocations are an operation of the paintings themselves, performed by their subject-matter and compositions in conjunction with certain types of aesthetic and cultural knowledge.[5] They yield connotations of biblical imagery when a cultural knowledge of the Bible, mediated through a knowledge of both western religious painting and the Nonconformist tradition, is brought to bear on them. The application of this cultural knowledge does not involve arbitrarily ransacking the Bible for subjects, themes, images, or motifs. On the contrary, the paintings connote only particular stories, characters, and people in the Bible. That which directs the spectator to 'read' the paintings in terms of certain aspects of the Bible and not of others is the interpretative tradition of the Nonconformist idiolect. Viewed within this context, the scenes of mining take on a typological dimension and acquire the status of a biblical iconography:

some refer to this imagery directly, while others allude to a biblical ethos. Thus, by the same virtue of visualizing religious concepts, Evans's paintings are another manifestation of the religious art of Nonconformity (see Chapter 8).

1

God is Invisible: Word and Worship, Interdict and Image in the Reformation Tradition

Historians of Nonconformity's architectural expression distinguish two phases in its development. The first phase, spanning the late seventeenth and eighteenth centuries, was characterized by the use and adaptation for worship of existing buildings, such as farmhouses and barns, followed by the construction of simple, purpose-built meeting-houses in the vernacular style. The second phase coincided with the early decades of the nineteenth century, when buildings increasingly reflected the grandeur of prevailing architectural tastes, so much so that by the end of the Victorian age the chapel had ceased to be a place of relative obscurity and had become a palace of maximum visibility.[1] There are parallels in the development of other manifestations of Nonconformity's visual expression. The nineteenth century saw a corresponding increase in the use of visual artefacts to embellish the contexts and pursuit of religion. In all these respects, the progress towards visualization represented a radical departure from the simple, unadorned piety of Nonconformity in the eighteenth century.

Writers have often interpreted the absence of religious embellishments and images during that century as evidence of a dour spirit, rabid austerity, and picture-phobia in Nonconformity. However, mistrust of the trappings of worship by Reformers, Puritans, and Calvinistic Nonconformists was entirely rational. Advocates of reformed theology regarded the visualization of religion in a theocentric light. Accordingly, they founded their apologetic against ecclesiastical furnishings, architectural elaboration, and images of the Deity not on the danger of idolatry, as is often supposed, but in the nature of God. Their theology (in the proper sense of the science of God) profoundly shaped the appearance of proto-chapels in the first phase, and enabled Nonconformists to visualize religious concepts in the second.

The Invisibility of God in the Old Testament

'God is a Spirit' (John 4: 24). Consequently, the theologian Charles Hodge (1797–1878) concluded, 'He is not . . . visible, or tangible. He has neither bulk nor form.'[2] For Protestants in the Reformation tradition, the invisibility of God logically and ethically excluded the ascription of corporeity to the Almighty in thought or by deed.³ In the seventeenth century, the Puritan preacher Thomas Watson (*c.*1620–86) applied this argument to confute the Roman Catholic practice of representing God, along with other unseeable, supernatural entities. Citing Ambrose's (*c.*339–97) assertion 'Quod invisible est, pingi non potest' ['What is invisible cannot be painted'], Watson deduced: 'It is impossible to make a picture of the soul, or to paint angels, because they are of a spiritual nature; much less can we paint God by an image, who is an infinite, uncreated spirit.'⁴ Thus reasoned the biblical expositor Matthew Henry (1662–1714) too, for even on the rare occasions when God was manifest to the naked eye, His visible glory exceeded the power of human imagination to depict; whatever Moses, Aaron, Nadab, Abihu, and the seventy elders of Israel saw of God on Mount Sinai (Exodus 24: 9–11), 'it was certainly something, of which no image or picture could be made'.⁵ To prove the illegality of imaging God, Reformers and Puritans appealed to the physical phenomenon that accompanied His manifestation at Horeb (Mount Sinai) as often as to the second commandment prohibiting idolatry: 'Take ye therefore good heed unto yourselves; for ye saw no manner of similitude on that day that the Lord spake unto you in Horeb out of the midst of the fire: lest ye corrupt yourselves, and make you a graven image' (Deuteronomy 4: 15). That God had not revealed Himself in any palpable form other than as a voice indicated both His desire to a uphold His interdiction against fashioning cultic objects and false worship and a determination to remain unseen.⁶

The Reformers and their successors realized that, notwithstanding God's invisibility and prohibitions on image-making, Old Testament religion was far from being invisible. The Israelites had a diverse visual expression which was ordained and inspired by God, a conduit for relevation, and integral to their sacrificial rites and corporate worship. Dreams and visions were means of prophecy and direct encounters with God. Those of Joseph, Ezekiel, and Daniel demonstrate a symbolic visualization of religious concepts of extraordinary complexity and vividness (Genesis 37: 5–11, Ezekiel 1). In one of Daniel's visions, God appears in theophanic form as 'a certain man clothed in linen, whose loins were girded with fine gold of Uphaz' (Daniel 10: 5–21).⁷ Thus while censuring man's attempt to visualize Deity, God was free to represent Himself in temporary creaturely semblance. God made natural and numinous phenomena the external concomitants of His glory and terror, such as the bush that 'burned with fire . . . and was not consumed' (Exodus 3: 1–5); thunder and lightning, fire and smoke, and earthquakes and clouds accompanied the Lord's descent on Mount Sinai (Exodus 19: 16–18), and pillars of cloud and fire went before the Israelites to guide them on their journey through the wilderness (Exodus 13: 21).

The most sublime visual emanation of God is the Shekinah, or cloud of His radiance, associated with Israel's places of worship during their wanderings and settlement (Exodus 36–40, 2 Chronicles 3–4). The Tabernacle of Moses and the Temple of Solomon were the most tangible visualizations of Israel's religion **(1)**. The Nonconformists' visual conception of the Tabernacle and its furnishings

1 'Y Tabernacl a'i Gyntedd' ['The Tabernacle and its Vestibule'], steelplate engraving, *Trysorfa y Plant* (1862).

2 'Y Cysegr Sanctaidd a'i Gelfi' ['The Holy of Holies and its Furniture'], steelplate engraving, *Trysorfa y Plant* (1862).

3 C. B. Nicholls, Ark of the Covenant with Mercy Seat and Cherubim, steelplate engraving, *Trysorfa y Plant* (1862).

was informed by pictures derived from eighteenth- and nineteenth-century studies of biblical antiquities and archaeology. These were popularized in books such as John Kitto's *Pictorial Bible* (1847). From the mid nineteenth century onwards, Nonconformist literature (including the Calvinistic Methodist magazine *Trysorfa y Plant* ['The Childrens' Treasury']) borrowed liberally from these sources to illustrate articles on Old Testament worship (see Chapter 6). Theologically the Tabernacle and Temple were God's peculiar dwelling-place and the context of Israel's sacrificial system. The structures' ground-plans, compartmentalization, decorations, and furnishings gave spiritual meanings visual form, often explicitly as with the Ark of the Covenant, Mercy Seat, Altar of Incense, and veil (Exodus 25: 10; 16–17, Leviticus 16: 16–17, Psalm 141: 2). Both sanctuaries bore the hallmarks of conspicuous craftsmanship and elaborate ornamentation, and made use of sensuous and costly material, a physical token of the beauty and grandeur of Yahweh: 'The house which I build is great', declared Solomon, 'for great is our God above all gods' (2 Chronicles 2: 5). The Temple was decorated with figurative elements taken from the natural world: palm trees, pomegranates, lilies, flowers, and 'the similitude of oxen' (twelve sculptures which supported the huge bronze laver (1 Kings 6: 29, 2 Chronicles 3: 16; 4: 3–5)).

The supernatural world was represented by cherubim. These were embroidered on ten of the Tabernacle's curtains and the veil of the Temple, engraved on the walls of the Temple's Holy of Holies; and in both sanctuaries they were sculpted and set up on either end of the Mercy Seat (Exodus 25: 18; 36: 8, 2 Chronicles 3: 7, 10–4) **(2, 3)**. The Decalogue's stricture on making a 'likeness of any thing that is in heaven' would normally preclude making a graven image of cherubim, an order of angels. However, those that adorned the Tabernacle and Temple were not artefacts of the human imagination but fashioned after the pattern that God had prescribed (Exodus 25: 9, 2 Chronicles 3: 3). Therefore they were an exception to God's injunction, not a general rule (Exodus 20: 4).[8] Nevertheless, the cherubim sculptures proved to be problematic for the Reformers and Puritans as they had been for the Early-Church divines. Clement of Alexandria (*c.*155–*c.*220) could not believe that they were to be understood literally, for no heavenly creature had a shape capable of being rendered in a sensible form; thus he considered the term cherub to be a *symbolical* reference to the rational soul.[9] Henry concurred and forwarded an opinion, accepted by many reformed theologians then and subsequently, that the sculptures were not 'any effigies of an angel, but some *emblem* of the angelic nature' (my emphasis).[10]

The Reformers' repudiation of a literal interpretation of the cherubim was part of their general assault on the Roman Catholic advocacy of icons. The Congregationalist preacher and theologian John Owen (1616–83) was quick to preclude the construction that these sculptures represented the similitude of cherubim. Nor, moreover (given that they were set up in Israel's sacred places), were they a precedent for either worshipping images or placing them in a church. In his view, the scriptural reference substantiated neither the form nor the function of the sculptures:

> I desire to know what the cherubs were images of, and that they would show he ever appointed them to be adored, or to be the immediate objects of any veneration, or to be so much as historical means of instruction, being always shut up from the view of the people, and representing nothing that ever had real substance '*in rerum natura*' ['in the nature of things'].[11]

The cherubim were, to all except the priests who ministered behind the veil, invisible images. Therefore, the Reformers' axiom that one should not represent what cannot be seen remained intact.

The Image of God in the New Testament

The New Testament inherited the Old Testament doctrine of God's invisibility but not its culture of sacred buildings and imagery. The root of the decisive break with Israel's forms of worship was in Christ's incarnation and atonement, the theological implications of which apostolic writers expounded using typology. This is a system of interpretation in which Old Testament people, places, events, and things prefigure people, places, events, and things in the New Testament. Typologically, the New Testament conceived of the Tabernacle as an 'example and shadow of heavenly things', a figure or type foreshadowing, first, the true tabernacle, which is in heaven (Hebrews 8: 5), and, secondly, Christ, the new dwelling-place of God on earth. In Christ, 'The tabernacle of God is with men, and he shall dwell, as in the tabernacle, with them,' reflected the Welsh theologian Thomas Charles Edwards (1837–1900).[12] In this way, Christ made the requirement of a physical tabernacle obsolete.

Through His sacrificial death and heavenly intercession Christ (the antitype) embodied the Tabernacle's priestly and sacrificial functions, and in these respects also superseded the type:

> But Christ being come an high priest of good things to come, by a greater and more perfect tabernacle, not made with hands, that is to say, not of this building; neither by the blood of goats and calves, but by his own blood he entered in once into the holy place, having obtained eternal redemption for us. (Hebrews 9: 11–12)

Moreover, Christ's work not only effected a dissolution of the Tabernacle and Temple but also, more importantly, reconciled believers to God and secured immediate access to Him. No longer was there the need (or justification) for an intermediary in the form of a priest performing rites with the aid of outward signs and tangible symbols (Romans 5: 10, 1 Timothy 2: 5). For this reason, the Reformers argued, the accessories of Roman Catholic worship – the statues and pictures of Christ, saints, martyrs, angels, and Mary (which Catholics believed were able to bring the worshipper into direct contact with the persons depicted) – were not only superfluous to worship but also a denial of the sufficiency of Christ's high-priestly role.

Christ was not the only personification of a place of worship. Insofar as God abode in individual Christians through His Holy Spirit (as He had filled the Tabernacle and Temple with his Shekinah), their body was His temple (1 Corinthians 6: 19). Likewise, the Bible applies the image to the community of believers, 'builded together for an habitation of God through the spirit' or as a 'spiritual house' (Ephesians 2: 19–22, 1 Peter 2: 5). The New Testament reiterates the metaphor, as Arthur Penrhyn Stanley observed, in the expression ' "edification" . . . derived almost literally from the stones, silently fitted together, and rising stage above stage, in a sacred edifice'.[13] In affirming that God dwelled in the assembled congregation, and believing that the only prerequisite for worship was the promised presence of Christ (where two or three gathered in His name), New Testament Christians had no need of sacred buildings. They were free to congregate anywhere: in the open air, the humble surrounds of a believer's house, or an upper room (Matthew 8: 20, Romans 16: 5, Acts 1: 13).

Though Christ had abolished the appurtenances and ceremonies of the Tabernacle and Temple, New Testament Christians did not forget their significance (one fully appreciates the relevance of the antitype only with reference to the type). The sensible forms and functions survived in simile and metaphor. To convey the privilege of direct access to God that each Christian possessed, the apostle Peter refers to Christians as a 'holy priesthood', alluding to the Levitical order of priests who attended the functions of the Tabernacle. Likewise, drawing on the language of animal oblation in Judaism, the apostle enjoins them 'to offer up spiritual sacrifices, acceptable to God by Jesus Christ' (1 Peter 2: 5). In contrast to Old Testament worship ritual, the substance of the Christian's sacrifice was not shed blood, slain beasts, libations, and the first-fruit of harvest, but the 'fruit of our lips' – the 'praise of God continually', and the body, soul, and mind yielded in holy living (Hebrews 13: 15, Romans 12: 1–2). In these ways New Testament theology converted the sensuous and tangible externals associated with Israelite Tabernacle and Temple culture into inner realities and motions of the spirit.

Worship was now spiritual and therefore, like God, invisible. It did not require the aid of objective representations, other than the symbols Christ had ordained (baptism, and bread and wine). Seeing was no longer the basis of believing (John 20: 29). Henceforth, the apostles enjoined Christians to 'walk by faith, not by sight' (2 Corinthians 5: 7, Hebrews 11: 1). Therefore the impulse to visualize the invisible and appeal to the physical senses in worship was, in the Reformers' view, manifest faithlessness and a denial of the Church's true nature:

> men, being not able, by the light of faith, to discern the glory of things spiritual and invisible, do make images of them unto themselves, as gods that may go before them; and these they are affected withal: but the worship of the church is spiritual, and the glory of it is invisible unto the eyes of the flesh. So both our Saviour and the apostles do testify in the celebration of it: 'We are come unto mount Zion, and unto the city of the living God, the heavenly Jerusalem, and to an innumerable company of angels, to the general assembly and church of the first-born, which are written in heaven, and to God the Judge of all, and to the spirits of just men made perfect, and to Jesus the mediator of the new covenant, and to the blood of sprinkling, that speaketh better than that of Abel,' Heb. xii. 22–24. The glory of this assembly; though certainly above that of organs, and pipes, and crucifixes, and vestments, yet doth not appear unto the sense or imaginations of men.[14]

The transition from the Mosaic to the Christian dispensation was thus a passage from physical to spiritual, mediate to immediate, outward to inward, and seen to unseen. However, while Christianity dematerialized Israelite worship, it simultaneously made the object of worship more tangible. In Christ, God becomes visible (Colossians 1: 15, Hebrews 1: 3). The apostle Paul called Christ 'the image of God' (2 Corinthians 4: 4). Here 'image' (Greek *eikon*) is the same word used in Greek thought to describe a likeness, more often a plastic equivalent, such as a statue of a noble person. Iconodules (advocates of icons) appealed to the incarnation to justify the objectification of God in images. Given that those who met Christ during his sojourn on earth actually saw God, Roman Catholics considered it lawful 'to represent in a Picture to one man's eye, what hath bin seen by another's', the Puritan Abraham Woodhead observed.[15] The Anglican archbishop William Laud (1573–1645), who provoked the Puritans' ire against his advocacy of images and ornamentation in churches, also upheld the legitimacy of picturing Christ, but stopped short of the depiction of Christ 'as God . . . for the Deity cannot be portrayed or pictured, though the humanity may'.[16] For their part, the Puritans contended that Christ's visible humanity and invisible deity were inextricable so that it was impossible to consider one nature in isolation from the other:

> It is Christ's Godhead, united to this manhood, that makes him to be Christ; therefore to picture his manhood, when we cannot picture his Godhead, is a sin, because we make him to be but half Christ – we separate what God has joined, we leave out that which is the chief thing that makes him Christ.[17]

Only the gospel presented a complete and authentic portrait of Christ, and the Reformers also insisted that the only proper way to set Him forth before the eyes of men was to proclaim Christ crucified (Galatians 3: 1). 'Of what use, then,' wrote John Calvin (1509–64), 'were the erection in churches of so many crosses of wood and stone, silver and gold, if this doctrine were faithfully and honestly preached.'[18] The Reformers considered the preaching and hearing of the Word to be the exclusive and sufficient means of expressing religious ideas, a conviction which they derived from New Testament principles: 'how shall they believe in him of whom they have not heard? and how shall they hear without a preacher? . . . So then faith cometh by hearing, and hearing by the Word of God' (Romans 10: 14, 17). The apostolic Church never conceived of visual images as an adjunct to or substitute for oral proclamation, or as a means of inculcating faith. The only references to religious images are in the context of teaching about pagan idols, which the apostolic writers, inheriting Mosaic law, unequivocally disavow (Acts 19: 23–41, 1 Corinthians 8: 4, 1 John 5: 21). Preaching represented Christ through the medium of the Bible – the Word. In this way it was closer in essence to the eternal and pre-incarnate status of Christ as the 'Word' (Greek *logos*) than material images were to His incarnate form (John 1: 1).[19] Since preaching made Christ present to His people, material representations betrayed a loss of faith in the efficacy of this means and in 'an experience of the [spiritual] representation of Christ in the gospel'.[20]

New Testament and Reformed Theology in the Nonconformist Meeting-House

> Jesus, where'er thy people meet,
> There they behold thy mercy-seat;
> Where'er they seek thee, thou art found,
> And ev'ry place is hallow'd ground.[21]

William Cowper's (1731–1800) hymn gave devotional expression to the liberation of worship from architectural requirements. These sentiments would have been a source of consolation and encouragement to the early Dissenters who had seceded from the Established Church and all its pomp to gather in the decidedly unecclesiastical surroundings of a converted cow-house. Like New Testament Christians, Dissenters and early Nonconformists conducted their worship in a domestic context. After the Act of Toleration (1689), they abandoned their clandestine gatherings in fields and woods and convened instead in kitchens and barns owned by members of the congregation.

The bare-board, lime-washed homeliness of these buildings and the later barn-chapels stands in stark contrast to the other-worldly splendour of Israel's sanctuaries, churches, and indeed of chapels erected during the second half of the nineteenth century. Nonconformists did not consider the meeting-house or early chapel to be sacred and never consecrated them. Consecration was a practice which Nonconformists considered to be a remnant of popery and to express the superstitious belief that holiness could be imputed to buildings.[22] This is not to say that they thought the meeting-places unworthy of respect, or that the buildings were without religious significance. New Testament theology moulded the character of the early meeting-house as much as the congregations' limited resources. The New Testament spoke of Israel's holy places and their furnishings – the fine embroidered curtains, statuary, and cunning workmanship – as 'figures of the true', imperfect and destined to 'vanish away' at the establishment of a second and better covenant (Hebrews 8: 5–9: 28). Architectural grandeur, ornament, and images – the 'sensible pledge and tokens of God's presence', as Owen described them – comprised a system of signification made inferior and obsolete by the reality they foreshadowed.[23] For example, the Mercy Seat, above which God communed with Moses, was no longer confined to the Holy of Holies. It was present, as Cowper wrote, amid the gathering of His people, as the grace of God (Exodus 25: 22, Leviticus 16: 15, Romans 3: 25).

This gathering was the most important feature of the meeting-house, for it was the congregation and not the building that comprised His temple. However,

4 John Thomas, Four Crosses (Calvinistic Methodist) Chapel (nineteenth century, second half), photograph.

the vast majority of photographs of meeting-houses and chapels show peopleless pews and empty pulpits. The photographs of the Welsh Calvinistic Methodist John Thomas (1838–1905) provide a rare glimpse of congregational life. His chapel interiors often include a select representation of camera-conscious worshippers, principally the assembled occupants of the pupit and *sêt fawr* and attendant organist and officiaries, adopting a formidable pose **(4)**. Photographers and historians more usually record chapels in a state of disuse, dereliction, or during weekday vacancy. Thus one is apt to forget that, far from being bare, these interiors were once thronged with worshippers. Against the backdrop of the meeting-room's naked simplicity the congregation assumed a visual prominence greater than its Roman Catholic counterpart, lost amid the embellishments and grandeur of a church. The unobtrusiveness of chapel 'architecture' in this way realized the new covenant's high view of the worshipping community.

The layout of the interior was also an appropriate analogue for the pared-down elementalism of Calvinistic Word-orientated worship. The Reformation emphasized the Word of God as the primary basis for worship. Preaching, praying, hearing, and singing (together with observance of the Lord's Supper) were the essential building-blocks of the service. In this sense, J. S. Whale observed, Protestant worship summons up associations with the 'Word-Service of the Synagogue rather than the "Mystery-Service" of the Temple and of

5 Maesyronnen (Independent) chapel, Glasbury, Radnorshire (1696).

Eastern and Western Catholicism'.[24] The clearly audible declaration of God's Word, read in the vernacular language (rather than in the Vulgate), coupled with congregational singing, extempory prayer, and vivid sermon illustrations (see Chapter 2) comprised an auditory, oratory, and imaginative presence that compensated for the absence of visual embellishments.

However, it was the congregation who most significantly mitigated the lack of images made by hand. According to the creation account in Genesis chapter 1, verses 26–7 man is made in the 'image' (Hebrew *selem*) and 'likeness' of God. Reformation theologians argued that this resemblance extended beyond an ethical and cognitive identification to include, in some small measure, a physical identification. Calvin believed that 'the divine glory is displayed in man's outward appearance'.[25] While true of all mankind, the doctrine of the *imago dei* in the New Testament had particular pertinence to Christians. 'God is to be admired in his saints,' wrote Calvin (echoing the words of Bishop Theodore (*c*.602–90)).[26] In them God progressively restored the divine similitude, obscured and distorted by the effects of the Fall, to its original glory (2 Corinthians 3: 18, Romans 28: 1, Colossians 3: 10). Therefore, when believers gathered for worship, the meeting-house or chapel was resplendent with God's images.

The chasteness of the meeting-house was a visual analogy for the modesty of spirit that was to colour every aspect of the Christians' behaviour, or 'conversation' (1 Peter 3: 2, Philippians 1: 27). This disposition was to be a distinguishing

6 Unidentified chapel interior, Wales (nineteenth century, second half).

7 John Thomas, Llanfair Caereinion Mynafon Church, Montgomeryshire (nineteenth century, second half).

mark of their private and public conversation with God especially. The Nonconformist hymnist Isaac Watts (1674–1748) provided a volume of practical advice on this in his *Guide to Prayer* (1715). In the following excerpt, substitute the concept of prayer with that of building or architecture, and Watts could be describing the décor of a meeting-house:

> Let your Language be grave and decent, which is a Medium between Magnificence and Meanness. Let it be plain, but not coarse. Let it be clean, but not lofty and glittering.
>
> The Language of a Christian in Prayer, is the clothing of his Thoughts, or the Dress of his Soul, and it should be composed like the Dress of the Body, decent and neat, but not pompous or gawdy; simple and plain, but not careless, uncleanly or rude.
>
> An excessive fondness of Elegance and Finery of Stile in Prayer, discovers the same Pride and Vanity of Mind as an Affection of many Jewels and fine Apparel in the House of God: It betrays us into a Neglect of our Hearts, and of experimental religion.[27]

Among the finest examples of this poise and propriety are Maesyronnen at Glasbury in Radnorshire (1696), the oldest surviving meeting-house chapel in Wales **(5)**, Capel Beilheulog (*c*.1740), Gwenddwr in Breconshire, and Capel Newydd (*c*.1770s) on the Llŷn peninsula. If the language of architecture expressed the thoughts and soul of the congregations, these buildings spoke of the probity, seriousness, pragmatism, and single-mindedness of the Nonconformist at worship, and of the moderation which Christians were commanded to make 'known unto all men' (Philippians 4: 5) **(6)**.

In the third paragraph Watts alludes to the apostle Peter's injunction that Christian wives prefer the 'ornament' of the mind and soul to that of the body:

> Whose adorning let it not be that of outward adorning of plaiting the hair, and of wearing gold, or putting on of apparel; but let it be the hidden man of the heart, in that which is not corruptible, even the ornament of a meek and quiet spirit. (1 Peter 3: 3–4)

The typological identification of the Christian's body with an 'earthly . . . tabernacle' or 'building of God' suggests that Nonconformists may have considered the injunction to have had implications for the adornment of places of worship (2 Corinthians 5: 1). A fondness for the outward splendour of architectural ornament and images would have savoured of worldly ostentation, ill-befitting those who, fallen, humbled, and redeemed by God's grace, cultivated the inward, invisible, and imperishable adornments of the soul.

Like Christians in the New Testament, early Nonconformists looked 'not at the things which are seen, but at the things which are not seen' (2 Corinthians

4: 18). The spartan interior of the meeting-house offered little appeal for the 'eye of the flesh' and, therefore, no distraction from the contemplation of spiritual and heavenly things. The interior drew no attention to itself, comprising furnishings, forms, and materials that were only too familiar to the worshippers' everyday experience and ordinary habit. In this respect, the context of worship was effectively transparent. The literal transparency of the windows enabled the congregations to look beyond the realm of the meeting-house. Unlike the Roman Catholic and Anglican churches and nineteenth-century chapels, which employed stained, etched, or frosted glass, meeting-houses used clear glazing (if the windows had glass at all). In stained-glass windows God was visualized either anthropomorphically or symbolically; through plain glass windows God's invisible attributes, 'his eternal power and Godhead', could been seen visibly in the created order beyond the building's walls (Romans 1: 20). Stained and translucent glass obscured a view beyond the walls of churches. They hermetically sealed worshippers from all but the light of the outside world. The context of religious worship was in this way a discrete, self-contained, and almost wholly artificial environment, save for the attempts to import the creation via the traceries, vaulting, and foliation of Gothic. The windows of the Nonconformists' buildings, conversely, established a continuity and actual (as opposed to representational) relationship between the interior and the natural world, the 'hallow'd ground' of the congregations' first assemblies.

For all its divine splendour, the creation and all other 'things which are seen [were] temporal', destined to pass away on the 'day of God' along with the dissolution of the heavens (2 Corinthians 4: 18, 2 Peter 3: 10–12). The impermanence of the visible world is central to the eschatological prospect of New Testament and Reformed theology. It constrained Christians to live lightly regarding the present and to direct their attention to things above (see Chapter 3). Having 'no continuing city', they saw themselves as sojourners passing through this world *en route* to heaven (Hebrews 13: 14, 1 Peter 1: 17). In this respect Christians were the antitype of the Israelites making their way to the promised land through the wilderness. The portability of the Tabernacle underlined the transience of the Israelites' existence. New Testament Christians expressed the concept by refusing to establish permanent places for worship. Having founded buildings in which to gather, Nonconformists had less scope to express this belief. But perhaps the absence from the meeting-house of all but the most essential furnishings and design was as eloquent a testimony to their vision of a more glorious and abiding Tabernacle to come, and to their conviction that the meeting-house was, at best, only temporary accommodation.

The starkness of the meeting-house interior resulted not only from the absence of elaborations but also from the presence of its most distinguishing and austere characteristic – whiteness. From a practical point of view, white maximized the reflectivity of the walls (and in some instances the ceiling too) and significantly enhanced the artificial illumination of the oil lamps and the natural light that entered by the windows. The brightness and extent of the tone also mitigated the sense of darkness and gloom associated with parish church interiors, caused by their grey stone walls and the obstruction of natural light by stained glass **(7)**. Thus it was a simple but effective means of distancing the meeting-house from any association with Established Church architecture. The practice of whitewashing interior (and exterior) walls was, like the structure of the meeting-house and early chapel, derived from agricultural and domestic buildings, such as the Welsh long-house. The congregation's experience of white walls would therefore have been commonplace. However, for congregations steeped in the Word, the colour could hardly have been neutral, theologically speaking. White has an explicit spiritual significance throughout the Old and New Testaments. It describes the garments of God in Daniel's vision of 'the Ancient of days', of Christ in the disciples' vision of His Transfiguration, and of the redeemed and holy angels in John's vision on Patmos (Daniel 7: 9, Luke 9: 29, Revelation 7: 9; 15: 6). The associated concepts are divinity, purity, cleanliness, and holiness. While not an intentional visual symbol, the white interior was, in this way, an apposite expression of the Puritan spirit. Moreover, the Nonconformists' theocentric sensibility was likely to have concluded that since 'God is light', light is an image of God, and the luminous interior of the meeting-house an enveloping manifestation of His presence (1 John 1: 5).[28] The interior of seventeenth- and eighteenth-century meeting-houses and chapels was thus a potent visualization of New Testament and Reformed theology, an emphatic metaphor for the invisibility of God and the spiritual nature of worship and the church.

The Image of the Word: Protestant Emblem Books

By refusing to pander to the sensual aspect of human nature and focusing the congregations' attention on the spoken and written word, the meeting-house interiors expressed a highly conceptual attitude to Christian worship and instruction. This is not to say that Nonconformists always conceived of and conveyed the truth abstractly. While rejecting the plastic arts in the context of worship, preachers and writers were not averse to visualizing religious concepts using concrete literary imagery. John Bunyan's (1628–88) Puritan classic *The Pilgrim's Progress* (1678) is the prime example. The book conveys in vivid allegory the Calvinistic theology of irresistible grace, the perseverance of the saints, and the idea of the Christian life as a constant battle between the forces of light and darkness. Roger Sharrock established a pictorial lineage for Bunyan's visual imagination, contending that, in all likelihood, the writer was familiar with the popular emblem books of Geffrey Whitney (?1548—?1601), George Wither (1588–1667), and Francis Quarles (1592–1644). The emblem book prospered particularly in the Protestant countries of Europe during the sixteenth and seventeenth centuries. A number were composed by writers with Protestant sympathies and used to spread Reformation ideas.[29] The emblem book was both a pictorial and a literary genre, the format comprising symbolic images as engravings to which mottoes, verses, and epigrams were attached. Of the many religious examples published in the seventeenth century, the *Emblemes* (1635) of Quarles were the most popular in Great Britain. Quarles's influence on Bunyan is evident in the use of emblems as a literary device in *The Pilgrim's Progress*, and in the relationship between particular illustrations in Quarles and the 'emblem theatre' of Interpreter's House.[30]

Bunyan is also indebted to Quarles's use of allegorical figures to represent the Divinity. At Interpreter's House the 'man with a vessel of oil in his hand' is an emblem of Christ. In the *Emblemes*, Christ is figured as a Cupid. As Karl Höltgen points out, 'Quarles had to take account of the Protestants' iconophobic sensibilities' and their determination to root religious practices in the Scriptures.[31] In the preface to the *Emblemes*, Quarles reassures his readers accordingly: 'Let not the tender eye check, to see allusions to our blessed SAVIOUR figured in these types. In Holy Scripture he is sometimes called a Sower; sometimes a Fisher; sometimes a Physician: And why not presented so, as well to the eye as to the ear.'[32] In casting God as a metaphorical character in a visual allegory ('a silent parable', as he called it) Quarles did not imply an actual resemblance between the appearance of the image and that of the person depicted. By this means emblems visualized the Deity without compromising the sanctity of God's invisibility or the prohibitions of the second commandment.

Two other factors enabled the Reformers to countenance using this type of religious image. First, emblems represented religious concepts without recourse to the traditional pool of Roman Catholic imagery; therefore they were untainted by association with the papacy. Secondly, as Huston Diehl has cogently argued, the Reformers objected not to the use but, rather, to the abuse of religious images. They rejected only those images that might by their physical and material attributes seduce individuals into believing in the visible and carnal rather more than the invisible and spiritual. Like meeting-house interiors, emblem pictures possessed little by way of a sensuous aspect. The scale, schematic convention, and peculiar conjunctions divest the engravings of an illusory dimension or attachment to the world of appearances that might otherwise confuse image and reality. Furthermore, the manner in which the images represent angels and demons indicates a clearly symbolic rather than actual relationship to their subjects. The symbolic visualization of invisible spiritual entities had a precedent in the Bible. Henry conjectured that the cherubim over the Ark were an 'emblem of the angelic nature' and not a similitude of the real. Likewise, emblems visualized religious concepts in a memorable and figurative manner, and operated as signs that pointed towards the spiritual reality with which they shared only a metaphorical relationship. Just as God did not intend the cherubim for adoration or to be a medium for worship, so emblems did not command veneration or

8 Book 4, Emblem 13, steelplate engraving, *Emblems, Divine and Moral* (1818).

9 Book 3, Emblem 11, steelplate engraving, *Emblems, Divine and Moral* (1818).

10 Book 3, Emblem 12, steelplate engraving, *Emblems, Divine and Moral* (1818).

possess intrinsic spiritual potency. Emblems functioned only as mnemonic aids, in which the images were 'internalized as the vehicles of spiritual recollection'.[33] Because the nature and use of emblematic images were distinct from those of icons and idols, the Reformers considered them to be safe and acceptable.

The practice of representing spiritual things using visible signs had a further biblical antecedent in typology. Christ referred to Jonah's three-day captivity in the belly of the whale as a sign of His resurrection (Matthew 12: 39–40). The Israelites' crossing of the Red Sea was interpreted by the apostle Paul as a type of baptism (1 Corinthians 10: 1–2).[34] Like antitype and type in the Bible, word and image are interdependent in emblem books. As the 'shadow' is subordinate to the 'true' so the image is merely instrumental to meditation upon the Word. In and of themselves the images are not self-explanatory; indeed at first sight their meaning is cryptic. They are significant only when viewed in conjunction with the text(s). The reader can interpret the image's meaning variously, since it is not an illustration of any one of the accompanying texts. The texts not only elucidate but also maintain the image's meaning within the bounds of biblical doctrine. This leash restrains any proclivity the image might have to present a distorted or erroneous view of its subject. True to the principles of Calvinism, the word and not the image was the arbiter of truth. Therefore, unlike an icon, the emblematic image had no autonomy.

The concept of dependency and subservience was central to the Protestant ideal of the permissible sacred image. It is evident in Henry More's (1614–87) polemic *An Antidote against Idolatry* (1647). While rejecting high Calvinism, he agreed with the Reformer that images ought not to be set up in churches.

Nevertheless, More conceded, where churches allow pictures they ought to be as an edifying adornment and not for worship, that is, with

> some proper *Inscriptions* also adjoined: As upon the Picture of the *Resurrection* and *Ascension* of Christ some such Inscription as that of *St. Paul, If ye be risen with Christ, seek those things which are above* . . . And thus every piece, which are not to be many, should have their proper *Inscriptions*, without which they should not be permitted in the Church, as being fit for nothing but to arrest and detain idle Eyes of Men longer than is convenient.[35]

Fundamental to this outlook is Calvin's persuasion that spiritual and moral benefit derives exclusively from hearing and reading the Scriptures.[36] At best the image is an embellishment of the Word, while the Word enables the image to rise above the level of a lure and mere distraction.

Although originally written for a Puritan (and predominantly Anglican) audience, in the following two centuries Quarles's work contributed significantly to the visual and literary culture of Dissenting and Nonconformist communities.[37] Perhaps the most popular and widely disseminated spin-offs from his emblem book were 'the broad and the narrow way' posters of the nineteenth century **(Plate 3)**. These, as E. H. Gombrich established, had their antecedent in the genre of ancient moral subjects, the most famous and influential being the *Tabula Cebetis*, a dialogue which described a panoramic painting depicting human life in allegorical terms.[38] The posters comprised a compendium of emblematic incidents depicting the consequences of a good and evil life set, like Quarles's emblems, in a landscape. Representatives of the two types of people referred to in Christ's parable (Matthew 7: 13–14) were shown. The wicked indulge in and receive punishment for great sins, such as pride, vanity, and gluttony, as well as the most iniquitous social vices of the day. Prominent among these at the end of the nineteenth century were card-playing, theatre attendance, Sabbath-breaking, and lotteries (see Chapter 3). The poster represented a telling pictorial document of changes in evangelical scruples and censoriousness about low culture. Conversely, the righteous heed the admonition of preachers, flee temptation, and reap the blessing of eternal life. The incidents of vice and virtue take place on two roads along which the sinner and saint walk to their respective destinations. The device recalls Bunyan's metaphor of life as a journey in *The Pilgrim's Progress*.

Together with Bunyan, Quarles helped nurture a tradition of allegory and emblematic which influenced the imagery of both hymns and sermon illustrations (see Chapter 2). The influence was often very direct in the case of hymns. The hymn beginning 'Will your anchor hold in the storms of life', by Priscilla Owens (1829–1907), has a clear debt to the maritime emblemature of Book 4, Emblem 13 **(8)**. The image depicts Cupid bearing a child-figure (representing humanity) and an anchor (the biblical symbol of hope (Hebrews

6: 18–19)) on his back. Behind them others perish in the storm-tossed sea, victims of the shipwreck on the horizon:

> Will your anchor hold in the straits of fear,
> When the breakers roar and the reef is near?
> While the surges rave and the wild winds blow,
> Shall the angry waves then your bark o'erflow?[39]

Owens's allegory is also an evangelistic adaptation of Quarles's self-reflective verse accompanying Book 3, Emblem 11 which elaborates on the metaphor: 'The world's a sea; my flesh a ship . . .' Emblematically, the visual image portrays God reaching out to the sinner in peril. Cupid kneels by a large rock, the Pauline metaphor for Christ and an antitype for the rock God gave to nourish the Israelites in the wilderness (1 Corinthians 10: 4; Numbers 20: 8–11) **(9)**. In Owens's hymn, the rock secures the anchor. In this way the emblem accrues the additional significance of stability, strength, and safety – characteristics ascribed to God when referred to as a rock in the Psalms (Psalms 18: 2; 27: 5; 31: 2). Augustus Toplady's (1740–78) hymn 'Rock of Ages, cleft for me' draws on this metaphor, as well as Book 3, Emblem 12, which shows the child-figure hiding in the entrance to a cavern from a vengeful Cupid **(10)**.[40] The recurrence of similes and metaphors based on seafaring in the eighteenth and nineteenth centuries was, to a large extent, due to the British Isles being surrounded by water and having to rely on sea, wind, and sail to conduct trade with, and to travel to, other countries in the expansion of the Empire.

Toplady led Calvinistic Methodist ministers in sponsoring the reissue of Quarles's work in 1778 under the title *Emblems, Divine and Moral*.[41] He commended the work for its evangelical tenor and potential 'to convey the most important lessons of instruction into youthful minds'.[42] This association of the genre with young readers increased significantly among Nonconformists in the nineteenth century, a development anticipated by Bunyan's pictureless emblem book entitled *A Book for Boys and Girls* (1686).[43] Originally emblem books were written for a mature and well-educated readership. The Latin legends and copious quotations from the Early-Church Fathers, not to mention the gruesome and morbid tone of some images, rendered Quarles's work singularly unsuitable for children. The implicit assumption that emblem books were inappropriate for adult Nonconformists reflected a long-established suspicion that a dependence on images was incompatible with spiritual maturity. The Reformers regarded the visual symbols and paraphernalia of Temple worship as a divine concession to the Church in its state of infancy. With the advent of the gospel, they believed, God expected His people to 'put away childish things' and apprehend the things of the Spirit unaided.

Nineteenth-century emblem books acquired not only a new audience but also a fresh emphasis. In the seventeenth and eighteenth centuries the books were principally a vehicle for the contemplation of the invisible God and sacred truths.

11 'Great Drinkers Think Themselves Great Men', steelplate engraving, *John Ploughman's Pictures* (1890).

Inasmuch as meditation on God aimed to affect ethical improvement, the 'divine' and 'moral' aspects of the emblem were inseparably yoked. However, after 1800 the lofty devotional purpose of the emblem book receded and it became pre-eminently a means of ethical instruction for the young. Like 'the broad and the narrow way' posters, the moral issues addressed in the emblem books often pertained to prevailing social vices. For example, in the preface to one of a series of emblem books collectively entitled *John Ploughman's Pictures*, the Baptist preacher Charles Haddon Spurgeon (1834–92) declared: 'To smite evil – and especially the monster evil of drink – has been my earnest endeavour.'[44] The books' proverbial sayings expose a variety of other popular temptations and follies by way of pictorial and literal illustrations, rhymes, and homely anecdotes **(11)**. While they were not written specifically for children, Spurgeon's use of accessible images, and a simple, pseudo-rustic language assured a wide audience for the emblems.

While the tradition of emblem books ended with the nineteenth century, Nonconformist emblemature persisted in various forms until the second decade of the twentieth century. The following chapters will examine five expressions of the tradition: the religious and ethical interpretation by Nonconformist preachers of famous and popular paintings; the adaptation of images taken from everyday life to serve as sermon illustrations; the emblematic visions of the religious revival of 1904–5; the evolution of the chapel as a type of Tabernacle or Temple; and the social and religious construction of the coal-miner as a representative sinner and saint.

2
Pit and Pulpit, Miners and Sinners:
Sermonic Emblems in the Homiletic Tradition

Nonconformists worshipped in meeting-houses and early chapels that were constructed of local materials and by native skills. In this way, their religion was fused with everyday circumstances. Likewise preachers in these chapels combined the heavenly and the mundane by fashioning their sermon illustrations from the stuff of everyday existence and adapting the congregations' common experience to visualize religious concepts. People, places, and events acquired a parabolic dimension, and the visible world became a vast dictionary of emblems. Quarles declared 'the Heavens, the earth, nay every creature' to be emblems of God's glory.[1] Thus construed, objects from nature, and indeed varieties of human experience, provided an unlimited source of types, metaphors, similes, and allegories, for which sermons were the equivalent of the interpretative epigrams, poems, and mottoes. Whereas in the emblem book signs and symbols were mediated by pictorial illustrations, in nature they could be experienced directly. Accordingly, the world represented a vernacular and ever-present continuity of images for Nonconformists to meditate on. 'This little landscape of [their] life', to quote a nineteenth-century hymn, assumed spiritual redolence and became the place where the believer took on the role of the child-figures in Quarles's devices.

The Emblem Book of Life

In a lecture prescribing the characteristics of preaching during times of revival, W. B. Sprague (1795–1876) recommended that, in order for there to be an 'intelligent conviction of sin', hearers be given not only a clear and rational sermon but, in addition, one which was adapted to their surroundings and lives, and closely and personally applied.[2] Both he and the revivalist Charles G. Finney (1792–1875) enjoined preachers to avoid declaring the truths of the gospel as abstract propositions and to address congregations 'in the *language of common life*'.[3] Sermon illustrations were, thus, to be fashioned out of the surroundings, events, and objects that the congregation knew intimately, a principle deduced from the parables of Christ,

who always illustrated his instructions by things that were taking place among
the people to whom he preached, and with which their minds were familiar . . .
He talked about the hens and chickens, and children in market-places,
and sheep and lambs, and shepherds and farmers, and husbandmen and
merchants.[4]

Welsh preachers were exemplary in this respect. William Williams of Wern (1781–1840) was distinguished for

the quickness with which he detected the analogies existing between human and spiritual operations . . . Never, perhaps, since the days of the Great Teacher, did any preacher lay the objects of nature and the pursuits of men under greater contributions for the exposition and enforcement of religious truth.[5]

Daniel Rowland too illustrated sermons 'by pertinent scriptural allusions, and by similes from those objects, which happen to be nearest at hand'; while Christmas Evans was credited with 'a great power of imagination in drawing pictures from scenes of real life for practical purposes'.[6] Having been brought up in a rural environment where he later also preached, Rowland, like others who ministered in the agricultural communities of the eighteenth century, turned to nature and the material culture surrounding work and life on the land for his illustrations. Nature was not only the context of the people's common experience, but also God's means of providing them with a livelihood and physical sustenance. Had the land been difficult to work and the weather a constant adversary the congregations might not have been so favourably disposed 'to receive such lessons as Nature might give, to aid and illustrate the deeper lessons of Divine Grace'.[7] The concept of nature as a potential instructor in divine truth was deduced from Christ's practice of correlating aspects of the natural world with religious ideas and experience. As James Buchanan explained in *Analogy Considered as a Guide to Truth* (1864):

Our Lord evidently regarded nature as a Symbol, whose literal meaning might have a spiritual application; and hence he spoke of knowledge under the name of light, – of spiritual renovation as a birth, – of faith as a mental eye-sight, – of the Spirit's agency as similar to the influence of the unseen wind.[8]

So grounded were the illustrations of Christ's parables in everyday life that both nature and the labour of the land were a constant reminder of the transcendent spiritual reality they symbolized.[9] The scenes and conditions of farming and village life in rural Wales would have resembled the pastoral settings of Christ's parables sufficiently to endow the preacher's illustrations with a strong biblical resonance; his references to trees, birds, streams, pastures, seeds, and ploughing would have evoked in the minds of his hearers not only the things themselves, with which they would have been familiar, but also the same images used in the Scriptures. In this way not only were the contemporary and biblical worlds intermingled but also, more specifically, the lands of Israel and Wales (see Chapter 6).

Another form of homiletic illustration involved the derivation of emblems from objects not found in the Bible, but which shared certain characteristics with biblical images. A prime example of this is the emblem of a lighthouse. One is featured in the background of Book 4, Emblem 13 of Quarles **(8)**. Here, as in the context of sermon illustrations, it connotes several interrelated concepts associated with its functions and with those ascribed to the Bible as the Word of God – guidance, warning, and illumination. The following stanzas, intended for children (as was most nineteenth-century emblemature), provide an exposition of these themes:

> The lighthouse! the lighthouse! it shines from afar,
> Brilliant and clear as an evening star;
> It gleams o'er the ocean's deep blue wave,
> A friendly beacon to guide and save.
>
> . . .
>
> The Bible! the Bible! o'er life's rough sea,
> It guides mankind to eternity;
> In grief or in gladness, in age or in youth,
> There is light for all from the Lamp of Truth.
>
> It warns of the dangers which near us lie,
> It shows us the path to joys on high;
> It points us to Christ as the only way,
> Which can lead to the realms of endless day.[10]

The reference to 'the Lamp of Truth' derives from the Old Testament image of the lamp as a metaphor for the spiritual knowledge, wisdom, and illumination contained in the Scriptures, which can rightly direct the course of the believer's life (Psalm 119: 105). The lighthouse also serves as a symbol for Christ as 'the light of the world' (John 8: 12); Christ is also referred to in the New Testament as the Word made flesh (John 1: 14), and is therefore closely identified with the Scriptures. The lighthouse was an apt illustration of the eternal misery and loss awaiting those who ignored the warnings in the Bible; for people living in Welsh coastal towns, the foundering of vessels that failed to heed the lighthouse signal would have been a frequent and living parable.

A variant form of the emblem occurs in an allegory by Christmas Evans, in which the lighthouse stands for the Ten Commandments. (The significance of the image in homiletic illustration, as in emblem books, varied according to the context or, more specifically, the accompanying text.) Evans sought to demonstrate by it the inability of the law of God to provide salvation for those apart from Christ. It was

> said that birds on dark and stormy nights, having neglected to nest before the approach of night, lost their way in the dark, and scores of them flew towards the Lighthouse light, knocking themselves against its glass, and were strewed about the place on the following morning. It is similar with thousands of some that know not Jesus, and that have not nestled in the tree before night, and that are overtaken by the storm of death, and knock themselves against the great Lighthouse of the Law of Sinai, expecting to get a refuge there, but it is too weak through the flesh to impart life to a single sinner.[11]

As in Bunyan's allegory *The Pilgrim's Progress*, each element of the illustration taken from the real world has its spiritual counterpart. Thus birds are emblems for souls, dark and stormy nights represent death, and the tree (as he goes on to explain) is the kingdom of God. The last is a simile derived from Christ's parable of the mustard seed which 'becometh a tree, so that the birds of the air come and lodge in the branches thereof' (Matthew 13: 32). In bringing invented and biblical similes together, Evans transplanted the tree from Israel to the landscape of Wales, but its didactic significance remains the same. The illustration was adapted from a story told by the keeper of the Skerries lighthouse, situated between Ireland and Anglesey, where Evans grew up and where he preached from 1802 to 1826.

In ministering to congregations on the island, many of whom would have been mariners and shipwrights, Evans frequently resorted to maritime imagery to illustrate his sermons. Sails, rigging, the wind, and the ebb and flow of the tide became an interrelated network of symbols capable of conveying biblical teaching:

> The soul is a great ship with its sails spread out for eternity . . . laden with treasure; the sea along which it sails is salvation; the breeze that wafts it along is the Holy Spirit. Weigh anchor, sinner, and you will ride in safety over the last billows . . . It is a sad sight to see a ship that has lost its anchor driven before the hurricane, but far more sad to see an immortal soul driven into eternity before the hurricane of God's fury, having lost its hope.[12]

Outside the homiletic and hymnological traditions the ship was an emblem of the Church chiefly by way of an association with Noah's ark in its capacity as a sanctuary (Genesis 6: 11–8: 19). Quarles identified the ship with the biblical concept of the 'flesh', in other words the natural body corrupted and decaying as a consequence of sin (1 Peter 1: 24), in which the soul was 'the passenger, confus'dly driv'n' (see Chapter 1).[13]

The tradition of the ship emblem or allegory was pictorialized in *The Gospel Ship* **(Plate 4),** a cheap and populist chromolithograph published by M'Lay and Company of Cardiff. A commercial sailing vessel is shown in profile, as in the genre of maritime painting. Written on its sails are various phrases associated with seafaring concepts. Each is allied to a biblical text; for example 'Berths Secure' (John 6: 37), 'Captain' (Hebrews 2: 10), 'Captain's Cry' (Genesis 3: 9), 'Ballast' (James 1: 17), and 'Passengers' (1 Timothy 1: 15). 'Time of Sailing' is accompanied by the quotation from the second book of Corinthians, chapter 6, verse 2 commending that 'now is the accepted time . . . now is the day of salvation'. The ship floated in the 'Sea of Time' (Revelation 18: 6). The print would have served as a visual tract used in the evangelization of the port communities and seamen's missions of south Wales during the second half of the nineteenth century.

Industrial Emblems

Rowland and Evans also gleaned illustrations from Welsh industry. Minerals and metals had been mined in Wales since the Middle Ages.[14] Coal began to assume importance in the fourteenth century in Flintshire and at Kilvey, near Swansea; it expanded from the fifteenth century onwards so that by the eighteenth century, there were coalfields extending across the breadth of south Wales from the eastern valleys to Pembrokeshire.[15] In the Tudor period the mining of minerals developed alongside the coal industry.[16] Rowland compared the believer's search for the hidden depths of truth and wisdom in the Scriptures with mining for gold: 'O what miracles of grace are here! How many golden veins contained in this rich quarry! Through thy help O Lord, I will dig some of them, and bring them to light.'[17] However, gold was not exploited in Wales until the discovery of auriferous veins in Merioneth in 1843, over fifty years after Rowland's death.[18] This would not therefore have been an illustration drawn from the common experience of the people. Its message would probably have been understood, if not from an awareness of gold-mining elsewhere, then certainly from the Scriptures, where wisdom, truth, and the blessing of God are compared to buried treasure to be unearthed by those who diligently seek it (Deuteronomy 33: 19, Proverbs 2: 4–5, Matthew 13: 44).[19]

Christmas Evans on at least one occasion used the analogy of iron-ore mining and smelting to describe preachers who pressed their hearers to perform religious duties, with little regard for the faith that should accompany such works. They were like

> an iron ore worker, who would go to the quarry where the ore is being raised, taking his hammer in his hand and attempt to make bars of iron out of the stones in their natural state, without a furnace to melt them, or rolls to push them and press them under.[20]

Here, iron represents the unbeliever whom the preacher vainly tries to fashion into a righteous person without first softening him with the grace of God. An intriguing emblem, derived in part from the process of mining, appeared in the middle of Christmas Evans's dramatic portrayal of the crucifixion, where he compared a green tree with Christ, and dry trees with 'the world lying in wickedness'.[21] As the green tree falls and is thrown into the fire, signifying Christ's death, the scene changes, whereupon Evans – as though, he said, in a vision –

> beheld the beam of a great scale; one end descending and the other ascending. The end containing the weight of the atonement I saw descending as low as the grave: the other end ascended, and in it were the prisoners of the tomb. There also I saw the basket of Mercy, full of pardons; and all the essentials of eternal life rising up from a pit of unmeasurable depth.[22]

The description is like that of a very basic machine used in early mining, balanced upon a pivot or fulcrum, with a weight attached to each end.[23] Its function is not to weigh but rather to hoist men and women – accompanied by the blessings of salvation – out of the pit in which they are entombed. This is achieved by the action of a counterbalance, symbolizing the propitiatory sacrifice of Christ's death, descending 'as low as the grave' – an oblique reference to His burial.

Evans used a complex mining allegory in a discourse on Zechariah, chapter 3, verse 9:

> Look at the rock whence ye are hewn, and the hole of the pit whence ye are digged. Many have quitted hewing stones from an old hard rock because it was more cost than profit. For the same reason, I know some gentlemen who have given up digging iron ore because it was so deep in the earth. Their ropes are too short, they have not sufficient quantity of timber to hold up the roof; and worse than all, there is such a *deadly damp* in the bottom, that no man can live there. Look at the quarry that I have opened in the flinty rock, and look at the depth of that horrible pit that I dug out, saith the Lord. This is the pit of corruption, enmity, and death. The Son of God went down to the bottom of it in the basket of the promise, and sucked the inflammable gas into himself; and by the rope of the commission, he hung the basket of the Gospel, for his servants to go down into the pit to dig stones for this spiritual building, while he is standing by the wheel of intercession, on top of the pit, drawing all to himself. Notwithstanding the rock is so hard, and the expense so great, the atonement of the cross is more than equivalent; the hammer of the gospel is well tempered, and is sufficiently heavy to break the rock in pieces. The chisels of conviction are in the hands of him who is able to convince the world of sin, of righteousness, and of judgement to come.[24]

The illustration is in essence the same as the one above. Preachers frequently adapted the same illustration to the expositional demands of different doctrines. On one occasion it might serve as a straightforward simile, while on others the preacher pressed the analogy in greater detail, characters, elements, and events being changed or introduced and different applications emphasized, as in this instance. Here, the principal elements of the illustration have been drawn from the Scriptures, beginning with the verse in Zechariah and parallel and related metaphors in the New Testament: Christ is the foundation stone of a spiritual temple, which is the Church, made up of 'living stones' who are believing men and women (1 Peter 2: 4–5). Every element in this allegory has its spiritual counterpart. In the illustration Christ also takes on the dual identity of a miner who digs for 'living stones', and of a surface worker who draws the baskets of ironstone to the surface of the pit and sends down other miners (the preachers of the gospel) to hew stone after him. The mason who chisels the rude stones into shape represents the Holy Spirit. The principal intent of the illustration is to enhance the believer's appreciation of the cost of his redemption and the suffering that Christ willingly endured to secure it.

Evans used the pit as a metaphor for several concepts: 'corruption', a term synonymous in the Bible with physical death, putrefaction (Psalm 16: 10, Acts 2: 27), and the soul's infection by evil (Romans 8: 21, 1 Corinthians 15: 50); 'death', which is also a synonym for the absence or cessation of spiritual life (Romans 7: 24); and 'enmity', that is the natural man's hostility towards God (Romans 8: 7, Ephesians 2: 15–16). The pit thus represents the spiritual condition of mankind apart from Christ. Elsewhere Evans compared the spiritual world, were it to be deprived of the influences of the Holy Spirit, to an airless and uninhabitable pit.[25] The application of the notion of the pit, therefore, admitted a considerable latitude.

The 'deadly damp' at the bottom of the pit is a reference to pockets of noxious and explosive marsh gas that iron-ore miners and coal-miners encountered.[26] (Deposits of iron ore and coal were frequently found together in Wales.)[27] In the allegory, Evans makes this hazard of mining, which in part gave the pit such a strong association with death, the means of Christ's sacrifice, the contemporary equivalent of a Roman gibbet. Christ's act of sucking 'the inflammable gas into himself' reflects his willingness to 'taste death for every man' (Hebrews 2: 9). Incidentally, the sacrifice of an individual to save the lives of others was also a concept associated with mining in France in the eighteenth century. An illustration in Louis Simonin's *Mines and Miners* (1868) entitled *The 'Penitent', or Fire-Man Igniting the Fire-Damp* **(12)** shows a man who

> came every evening to set fire to the gas in the mine – to provoke the explosion, in order that the working stalls should be accessible again the next day ... he crawled on the ground before firing the explosive mixture ... In one hand he held a long stick, with a lighted candle fixed at the end of it, and he went alone,

12 'The "Penitent", or Fire-man, Igniting Fire-Damp', steelplate engraving by Fritz Hildebrandt, *Mines and Miners; or, Underground Life* (1868).

lost in this poisoned maze, causing explosions by advancing his lamp, and thus decomposing the noxious gas . . . He was called the *penitent*, on account of the resemblance of his dress to that of certain orders in the Catholic Church; and this word seemed at the same time to be dictated by a bitter jest, for frequently the penitent, a victim sacrificed beforehand, was blown away by the explosion, and never returned alive.[28]

With the expansion of the coalfields in the nineteenth century,[29] the potential of the mining industry as a source of homiletic illustration was exploited more widely and applied more closely to the living and working conditions of the south Wales communities. By the mid nineteenth century, 'Welsh Nonconformity had almost swallowed Wales', not only because of its position as the dominant religious expression of the people, but also because it touched Welsh life at so many points, through chapel-based entertainments, journals, and other literature.[30] Such was Nonconformity's influence that it became 'the religion of the coal-field in the halfcentury or so preceding the great expansion of coalmining which began in mid-century'.[31] The culture of the collier was thus largely that of the chapel. Theology became a topic of conversation among working men underground, and preachers addressed colliery politics from the pulpit.[32] Miners and ministers shared a further connection in that some colliers made the journey from pit to pulpit to become preachers, a process facilitated by the provision of religious education through the Sunday schools. Prominent among these in the nineteenth century were Nathaniel Thomas (1818–88), Benjamin Evans (1816–66), Benjamin Evans (1844–1900), and Watkin H. Williams (1844–1905). The foremost examples of this transition in the early part of the twentieth century were the revivalist Evan Roberts (1878–1951) and Daniel P. Williams (1882–1947), founder of the Apostolic Church in Wales.[33]

The pit was an obvious source of illustration when preaching to congregations which included a large contingent of colliers and their families. It fulfilled the requisite conditions of a familiar and common experience capable of conveying aspects of the truth without drawing attention to itself. Not only was it the dominant and unifying motif of the community, grounded in its corporate consciousness, but it also evoked its counterpart in the Old Testament, with which it both shared the same name and had a close formal correspondence. This was particularly true during the early years of mining when the pit was basically a deep hole in the earth, which is what the term denotes in the Old Testament.[34] The disparity between the two types of pits lay in their respective functions. The biblical pit included holes dug in the ground where prisoners were incarcerated (Isaiah 24: 22), dead bodies were cast (Jeremiah 41: 7, 9), and wild animals prowled (2 Samuel 23: 20), besides wells of slimy bitumen (Genesis 14: 10). The associations of the pit in its literal sense were therefore captivity, punishment, death, and putrefaction.

These connotations were transferred to the metaphoric use of the word in, for instance, the prophecy of the Messiah, where releasing his people from captivity to their enemy was likened to sending 'forth thy prisoners out of the pit wherein is no water' (Zechariah 9: 11); the dead were called 'they that go down to the pit' (Isaiah 38: 18). The word also described the afterlife as an underworld or 'the nether parts of the earth' (Ezekiel 32: 24), where God assigned the spirits of the departed: 'I shall bring thee down with them that descend into the pit, with the people of old time, and shall set thee in the low parts of the earth, in places desolate of old, with them that go down to the pit' (Ezekiel 26: 20). In other texts the pit is strongly associated with the region to which God assigned the spirits of the wicked. Ezekiel, for example, made descent into the pit synonymous with going down to hell (Ezekiel 31: 16). Viewed as a whole the metaphorical applications of the pit in the Old Testament fall into two classes: as a correlative of death, it evokes hopelessness, calamity, darkness, the grave, decay, and separation from the land of the living; and it describes the physical or spiritual captivity of believers to circumstances, a tangible enemy, personal sin, or trials. The subterranean infernos that frequently raged after explosions were often likened to hell by rescuers or colliers lucky enough to have escaped.

The coal-pit itself possessed many of the same connotations for the miner. The writer Jay Gee, a Calvinistic Methodist, established the correlation strikingly in his overtly evangelistic serial based on the exploits of a Christian miner called Collier Jack, and published in the Calvinistic Methodist magazine, the *Children's Treasury*, in 1913. The stories and characters are fictitious, but probably had a basis in real-life experiences. One episode describes a young boy's Bible class: 'One Sunday afternoon Jack addressed his scholars on "The Pit", for he worked at a local colliery, and unfolded to them its wonders, and made simple illustrations to impress their youthful minds. His text was "He brought me out of the horrible pit . . ."'[35] In another episode the hero relates his close escape from death near the bottom of the pit, when with the colliery manager he walked into a pocket of black damp (marsh gas). He tells of how, having prayed for help, they managed to reach the mouth of the pit and safety. The story prefaces Jack's testimony of his deliverance from vices to which he had become captive and from which he had beseeched God to release him. The connection between the recount of his escape from the pit and his escape from vice is made clear by his application of Psalm 40, verse 2: 'I cried, "God be merciful to me a sinner," and he brought me up out of an horrible pit (the pit of sin and death), out of the miry clay, and set my feet upon a rock.'[36] The incident at the coal-mine becomes a parable for the dangers and consequences of sin from which God will save those who pray to Him. Within the illustration Gee symbolized the presence of death in the palpable form of noxious black damp, as Evans had done in his illustration from ironstone-mining. In the story of his conversion Jack emphasizes deliverance from old vices: the pit from which he had been hoisted was one not only of death but also of sin. The dark and malignant gas might therefore also serve as an emblem for sin, since sin and death are also linked in a causal relationship in the Scriptures (Romans 5: 12; 6: 23).

Mining disasters served both as a context in which to address issues of life and death, and as a parable of man's spiritual plight. The bond of humanity is for all individuals at best temporal. For the miners it was particularly insecure: colliery disasters often separated hundreds of them from their comrades and families. Intimations of their mortality were an ever-present reality as they worked in the mine, sensed in every creak of timber, fall of stones, or flicker of the lamp. The following report demonstrates the way in which preachers turned a colliery explosion into an evangelistic tract aimed at pointing out the sobering realities of mortality and eternity. The incident took place at Cwmtillery Colliery, near Abertillery, Monmouthshire on 18 December 1876. The realization of 'twenty-three precious souls being hurled into another world', most of whom had not made their peace with God, filled the townsfolk with a dreadful sense of awe. Among the dead had been some of the notorious sinners of the town, which itself had a reputation for gross ungodliness. Far from being just another mining accident, the commentator concluded that 'God had visited the locality in a fearful manner': the disaster was an act of divine judgement, a warning to the locality regarding His displeasure over sin.[37] The colliery and its environs became a latter-day Sodom and Gomorrah, a byword for iniquity that had had its just punishment rained down upon it. The funeral sermon for the dead miners took as its text 'Prepare to meet thy God'. A précis of its content appears at the close of the report. The lessons this disaster ought to strike home were:

(a) *Death awaits us all* . . . God has spoken with great emphasis that death awaits every son and daughter of Adam . . . Job strikingly compares this life to a weaver's shuttle. How thin the partition is between this world and the world to come! Death can and will sever the connection in a moment in the twinkling of an eye!

(b) *The Necessity of being prepared when death comes*. It frequently comes very suddenly. These twenty-three men had not a moment's warning! When the collier leaves his wife and family in the morning, he knows not but that death may overtake him before night. All these men expected to return home the same evening, but they were in another world, soon after they had descended into the pit! Oh! how important it is to be ready to meet the Son of Man![38]

Thus, because of the unusually precarious nature of his work, the miner's lot epitomized the insecurity of everyone's lives, and the miner came to symbolize all people in their need to prepare for death (see Appendix 1). Here too the association of descent into a pit with entering another world recalls the image of the pit as a gateway between the material and spiritual domains.[39]

Gee echoed the same sentiments in 'Collier Jack'. During a sermon delivered to a gathering of miners in his Sunday school class, Jack recalls an explosion at a mine close to his home. He chooses the incident to illustrate man's inability to rescue himself from his spiritual calamity by his own effort:

Many of the poor sinkers were called to eternity at a moment's notice. A few, however, were still alive, at the bottom of the wrecked shaft, and the pit was full of deadly gases. Their cries were heartrending as they shrieked for help. Now, poor sinners, you are just in as bad a plight as those poor miners. They couldn't help themselves; neither can you . . . If they must be saved, help must come from above; entirely apart from themselves. Willing hands soon got to work, and improvised a temporary means of descent. Stout hearts entered that hoppit, and down through the deadly gases, without light, they went, at the risk of their own lives, and brought to bank safely several of the bruised and bleeding men. Now, dear friends, I want to apply the illustrations. You are at the bottom of the pit of sin and death, and 'when you were yet without strength, in due time Christ died for the ungodly,' and such you are – helpless, ungodly – there's no denying the fact. 'The Good Shepherd' looked down from Heaven, and saw your pitiable condition . . . His own eye pitied, and His own arm brought salvation to us.[40]

The miner amid devastation and carnage is a picture of the spiritual condition of the miners Collier Jack is addressing and, by extension, of sinners from all walks of life. In describing the work of redemption Gee, like Evans, represented Christ as a miner descending into the pit to draw out those trapped in it to safety. The metaphorical significance of the descent in Gee's illustration is ambiguous, conveying the sense both of Christ coming into the world, through His incarnation, to face death, darkness, and the sacrifice of His own life, and of His descending into the lower parts of the earth, a biblical metaphor for Christ's death and burial. If the surface of the colliery represents heaven, then the pit beneath is the world, and those in it are all individuals in their spiritual plight. Jack, like other preachers of this period, mixes metaphors with complete indifference: one moment Christ is figured as a miner, in the next He is a shepherd (Psalm 23: 1, John 10: 11).

In the 1904–5 religious revival one of the most characteristic emblems of mining, the safety lamp, was invested with several biblical connotations. The services of preaching and prayer conducted underground in many south Wales collieries during this period often concluded with an invitation to the unconverted to repent, and to signify their having done so by raising their lamp (see Chapter 7, **(55)**).[41] The darkness of the pit may have been so profound as for it to have been the only clearly visible gesture. It may, in addition, have been an outward sign of an inward spiritual change. The biblical metaphors of the believer as light (Matthew 5: 14), and of light as spiritual life (John 1: 4), would have encouraged a strong identification between the miner and the lamp he carried. John Henry Newman's (1801–90) hymn 'Lead, kindly light' was one of the anthems of the revival, sung both in the chapel and down the mine:

> Lead, kindly Light, amid th' encircling gloom,
>   Lead Thou me on;
> The night is dark, and I am far from home;
>   Lead Thou me on.
> Keep Thou my feet; I do not ask to see
> The distant scene; one step enough for me.[42]

At the outset of a service at Penrhiw Colliery, Pontypridd, Glamorgan, the visiting preacher remarked that he considered it most appropriate to be sung underground, 'where all was gloom, and where there were toil and danger'.[43] The hymn had particular poignancy for the miner whose working environment was an apt metaphor for the 'dark night' of the soul, to which Newman alludes, or the dark world of sin.[44] He had constantly to rely on his light to dispel 'th' encircling gloom' and to illuminate his every step through the mine. In this way the miner was a metaphor of the believer as pilgrim through the world, who has only the light revealed in Christ and the Scriptures to guide his steps.

This analogy was given greater definition in R. D. Edwards's 'The Collier's Lamp', a short essay written for children describing the author's first visit underground. The account of his progress through the pit and of its conditions illustrates several lessons:

No man is allowed down into a coal pit without a lamp. And each man must have his own lamp.

God, who knew that we, too, on our journey through the world, would need light; has prepared a lamp for each one of us. 'Thy Word is a lamp unto my feet, and a light unto my path.'

Don't try the journey without the lamp, boys and girls, and see to it that each one carries his own lamp. Make the Truth of God your very own, and its light will help you on life's way.[45]

Edwards emphasized the inadequacy of relying on another person's knowledge of God to see one through this world, and the dangers facing those who set out on the journey without that light, thus enjoining the necessity of personal faith and extolling the practical usefulness of the Bible.

The association of particular mining terms with biblical concepts also arose naturally out of the environment of the pit. At an underground prayer meeting of Bwlfa and Nantymelyn Collieries in 1904, one miner had prayed: 'Oh, Lord, . . . Jesus Christ was born in a stable, and here are we in this old stable underground praying to Him and singing His praises.'[46] Notwithstanding its quaintness, the expression demonstrates that, for this miner at least, the conditions of work underground bore a striking resemblance to images in the Bible. The same connection is evident in the newspaper illustrator J. M. Staniforth's (1863–1921) drawing of the underground service (see Chapter 7, **(56)** and H. Le Rolle's (exh. 1910) *The Nativity* **(13)**, which formed the basis of one of James Burns's homilies in *Sermons in Art by the Great Masters* (1908)). Like the colliery stable depicted by Staniforth, 'The interior is represented as a large cave, the roof and sides of which are supported by heavy trunks of trees.'[47] For this one collier, the association of the stables bridged the gap of nearly two thousand years and over two thousand miles. In their conflation of Bwlfa and Bethlehem, the miners worshipped Christ in their stable as the wise men and shepherds had done in their day; and were also identified with Christ in His state of humiliation: both had known known the lowliness of the stable in the company of animals. To their mind, Christ was able to sympathize with them in their circumstances.

'Entombed – Jesus in the Midst' and the Homiletic Tradition

Entombed – Jesus in the Midst **(Plate 1)** is the pictorial corollary of the tradition of sermonic emblems. Christ is represented as a miner, following in the iconographic tradition initiated by Christmas Evans's industrial allegory. Unlike allegory, the painting does not supply a narrative explicating the spiritual significance of the image as a whole and in its various parts. The image is an emblem with only a title as an accompaniment. However, the title, as Roland

13 H. Le Rolle, *The Nativity* [n.d.], oil on canvas.

Barthes reasoned, operates as a text.⁴⁸ When interpreted according to the biblical allusions summoned up by the title, the painting yields several related narratives.

The archaic expression 'in the midst', denoting Christ's presence in the painting, is taken from the Authorized Version of the Bible. There are two references in the Gospels to Christ being 'in the midst'. The first occurs in a discourse on prayer, where Christ promised His disciples: 'For where two or three are gathered together in my name, there am I in the midst of them' (Matthew 8: 20). The promise, as Henry commented, is of the assured presence of Christ where believers assemble for an act of Christian communion:

> By his common presence he is in all places as God, but this is a promise of his special presence; where his saints are, his sanctuary is, and there he will dwell . . . he is in the midst of them to quicken and strengthen them, to refresh and comfort them, as the sun in the midst of the universe. He is in the midst of them, that is, in their hearts; it is a spiritual presence, the presence of Christ's Spirit with their spirit, that is here intended.⁴⁹

Henry interpreted the covenantal presence of Christ as something that was apprehended spiritually, as an internal and invisible communion of the divine and human spirit. The painting objectifies the experience: 'Jesus in the midst' becomes a palpable phenomenon.

The second reference to Christ 'in the midst' occurs in John's Gospel and its parallel texts, when Christ returned to His disciples on the day of the resurrection (John 20: 19–20). The account draws attention to the door of the room being shut, yet unable to bar Christ from access. The implication is that the resurrected Christ was able to pass through solid objects unhindered. On a second and similar appearance eight days later, the disciple Thomas was invited to place his fingers in the nail prints and thrust his hand into the wound in Christ's side, thus evincing, among other things, that Christ was neither ghost nor vision but flesh and blood (John 20: 27).

The scene in the mine represents a similar circumstance. The tons of coal that obstruct the miners' way of escape have not prevented Christ from entering and ministering comfort. A nail print is visible on the back of His left hand, and a rip below the breast pocket of His shirt reveals a wound in His left side.[50] This is not to suggest that Christ was crucified in these clothes, even though there are iconographic precedents for depicting Him fully dressed on the cross. As in the homiletic tradition, Christ is a miner only in the secondary world of the illustration: historical reality is suspended for the purpose of the lesson. In every other respect Evans has painted the risen Christ in the same way as he has the miners: He appears fully incarnate, possessing a corporeality co-substantive with that of the others. The representation of Christ as 'in fashion as a man' (Philippians 2: 7) stresses the earthly humanity of the God-man, and thus His ability to participate in the sufferings of men.

Entombed also reads as a contemporary transposition of another instance of Christ 'in the midst', recorded in the Old Testament. This is the story of the fiery furnace into which Nebuchadnezzar cast Shadrach, Meshach, and Abednego. Here a theophany, or pre-incarnation of Christ, miraculously appeared to accompany and preserve the three in their trial (Daniel 3: 24–5). Gee, in an episode from the serial 'Collier Jack', applied this text in an obituary to a believing miner killed underground in a colliery explosion. His body was found, like one of the figures represented in the painting, kneeling in an attitude of prayer, an image intended to convey the miner's faithfulness unto death. The episode drew attention to the consolation Christians know *in extremis* and served as an evangelistic tract to unconverted colliers who daily faced the possibility of sudden and violent death. Its sentiments were a commendation of the benefits of salvation and a warning about the fearfulness of dying without Christ:

Real Christianity is a good thing to live with, and a good thing to die with. 'Though I walk through the valley of the shadow of death, I will fear no evil, for Thou art with me.' What a comfort to realise the blessedness of the divine presence of the Son of God in the fiery furnace![51]

Here Christ's attendance is conceived as an inward reality comprehended by faith rather than an actual physical presence, as in Daniel's account.

No one interpretation of the Christ-representation completely accounts for the many nuances and allusions that the painting evokes. What we perceive may be the unification of Christ's emblematic, visionary, and real presence in such a way as to transcend an exclusively symbolic or anecdotal interpretation. Similarly, the theme of the work is a confluence of biblical references rather than the representation of one particular narrative, and thus it resists being reduced to a latter-day illustration of the promised companionship of Christ in answer to prayer and in times of trouble, or of evidence either for the resurrection of Christ or for the persistence of visionary encounters with Him. Instead, the interpretations amalgamate to form an image that evokes all of them simultaneously, harmonizing the discontinuous biblical references. This corresponds to the preacher's method of cross-referencing texts to exegete one by juxtaposition with others.[52]

The choice of the emotive word 'entombed' – commonly used to describe the fate of miners trapped underground after an explosion – also summons up biblical narratives that either include the word or imply the concept. The fall has prematurely interred the miners. Among them stands one who has also known the sealed sepulchre from the inside (Matthew 27: 60), yet could not be contained by the great stone that covered its entrance. His presence in the tomb may thus signify His authority over their entombment. Though in this instance the obstruction may never be removed from the road, this grave will give up its dead at the day of resurrection. The association of the miners' entombment with that of Christ is strengthened by the text that Nonconformists generally interpret as referring to Christ's burial: 'he also descended first into the lower parts of the earth' (Ephesians 4: 9).

Beyond the title, the painting's interrelated symbols suggest a further narrative significance. To begin with, Christ wears the shirt, breeches, and cap of a colliery-rescuer rather than the period costume of New Testament times. Evans's departure from traditional iconography serves to signify Christ's identification with the miners. Preachers in the nineteenth-century revivals had stressed that Christ died to save even the lowly miners. Eli Ginzberg wrote:

> Their dramatic sermons, especially their elaborate pictures of heaven and hell, of angels and devils, of resurrections and days of judgment, inspired the ignorant workmen. The ministers preached so that even the most ignorant could understand, and one point above all others they hammered home: the Lord was as much concerned with poor, hard-working, ignorant folk as He was with kings, statesmen, and coal owners.[53]

In representing Christ in the clothes of a miner, Evans takes this message a step further: Christ is shown to be not only concerned for the miners but also willing to associate with them and, indeed, to be taken for one of them. The image is consonant with Isaiah's concept of the Messiah as one who would be 'numbered with the transgressors' (Isaiah 53: 12), a prophecy, in part, of Christ's willingness to be ranked with publicans and sinners, with whom He habitually kept company. In portraying Christ as a lowly miner Evans provides a metaphor for the incarnation of Christ as one abased to lowliness and anonymity (Philippians 2: 7). He is 'made in the likeness of sinful flesh' (Romans 8: 3), and in his human frame He is indistinguishable from them. Christ has entered the miners' world on their terms, submitting Himself to its perils and trials and experiencing their infirmities, thus enabling Him to sympathize with their condition.[54]

Nicholas Evans translates Christmas Evans's conceptual emblem of Christ the miner into a perceptual image. In *Entombed* Christ is portrayed as a long-haired, bearded, philosopher-type of traditional Christian iconography; the relationship between reality and image is no longer metaphorical but implies an actual resemblance. The painting constitutes a mode of representing God distinct from that used in sermonic emblems and Quarles's engravings, and disregards the Calvinistic prohibition. Nicholas Evans alludes to Christ's divinity by means of a nimbus formed by the incandescence surrounding the lamp on Christ's cap. The symbol inhabits the scene as a native element which has been invested with spiritual significance. In *Sacred Themes and Famous Paintings* (1885) the Welsh minister David Davies commended William Holman Hunt's (1827–1910) *Shadow of Death* (1873), in particular, for symbolizing Christ's divinity by means of a natural part of the scene rather than the contrived device of a golden disc or luminous circle associated with the Roman Catholic tradition. In *Shadow of Death* a nimbus is intimated by the placing of the arch of a window behind Christ's head. Similarly, the shadow of Christ's outstretched arms cast on to the rear wall of the workshop conveys the premonitory emblem of the cross.[55] In the same way, the brilliance of Christ's heavenly glory, conveyed at the transfiguration by the 'white and glistening' appearance of His clothes (Luke 9: 29), is suggested in *Entombed* by an element indigenous to the scene. The stratification of the wall of coal which blocks the miners' escape comprises two blocks of parallel forms moving outwards from either side of Christ, appearing like rays emanating from His body. The emblem of the cross is alluded to by the intersection of the vertical form of the figure of Christ with the horizontal timber that traverses the upright posts on either side of Him. The miners become like the figures often portrayed gathered around the base of the gibbet in scenes of the crucifixion.

Evans depicts Christ lifting up a safety lamp over the despondent group of miners. As we have already seen, the lamp or candle had various religious connotations for the miner. Here the lamp, like the one He holds in Holman Hunt's *Light of the World* (1853–6) (to which Evans's painting bears more than a passing resemblance), symbolizes Christ Himself. Following Johannine symbolism, Christ is made the source and dispenser of spiritual light and the life it brings to those it illuminates: 'I am the light of the world: he that followeth me shall not walk in darkness, but shall have the light of life' (John 8: 12). Charles Wesley (1707–88) amplified the metaphor in a verse of his hymn 'And can it be':

> Long my imprisoned spirit lay,
> Fast bound in sin and nature's night:
> Thine eye diffused a quickening ray;
> I woke, the dungeon flamed with light!
> My chains fell off, my heart was free;
> I rose, went forth, and followed thee.[56]

Like Wesley, Evans pictures the sinner in his unconverted state in terms of physical incarceration in a dark, subterranean hold.

While Christ holds out light and life in one hand, He holds out hell and death, symbolized by the two keys, in the other. The precise interpretation of this is not clear. The implied meaning may be that Christ possesses dominion and power over life and death. The sentiment expressed may be that the miners' destiny, one way or the other, is in His hands. Or, again, Christ may be holding out two alternatives to the miners: life if they turn to Him in faith, death and hell if they stubbornly refuse to repent. The miners' lamps also connote a metaphoric significance. Christ's lamp burns like a sun, while their one remaining source of illumination is nearly exhausted. In the Old Testament the life of the individual was likened to a lamp; snuffing out the flame was equivalent to extinguishing life (Job 21: 17, Proverbs 20: 20; 24: 20). The miners' lives are, symbolically, almost spent.

Were it not for the presence of Christ among the miners, the painting would be no more than a representation of a mining disaster. With Jesus in the midst, the image connects with the homiletic tradition to become the visualization of a spiritual allegory, a network of interrelating symbols and allusions of varying degrees of complexity which one can read in a variety of ways simultaneously. It becomes a repository of sermonic lessons, few of which are explicit, all of which can be inferred. Two basic narratives have been suggested. First, the miners face the loss of their mortal lives: thus Christ may symbolize the object of their prayers, the God who hears and answers, and who will sustain them in their imprisonment and bring release. Secondly, interpreted according to Christmas Evans's allegory, Christ is in the midst as rescuer-redeemer: He is present to save the miners from physical captivity and peril, a parable for Christ's mission to rescue helpless sinners from their captivity and appalling destiny.

In these ways homiletic emblems conflated not only the sacred and mundane but also the biblical and contemporary worlds, the lands of Israel and Wales, and the spheres of religion and labour. Accordingly, they reflected and contributed to a complex of amalgamations undergirding Nonconformist culture from the eighteenth to the early twentieth century (see Chapters 3–7). In contrast to the pictorial images in emblem books, congregations perceived the verbal icon (to borrow W. K. Wimsatt's term) of the sermon illustration not with the eye of flesh but with the mind's eye.[57] In this sense it constituted the Protestant ideal of the sacred image – one that was able to convert the obscure and abstract into a vivid and concrete image while possessing neither substance nor sensuality. The desire for a tangible and visual, as opposed to conceptual, embodiment of religious concepts, which emblem books had previously provided, re-emerged at the end of the nineteenth century. In the context of a broader conception of common experience and of the legitimate arena of Christian participation, preachers adorned their sermons with illustrations drawn from the world of art.

3
Emblems and Emissaries: The Ministry of Art

The Tabernacle and Temple represented irrefutable evidence that art had a place in the divine order of things and, moreover, that it had served religion as a means of honouring God and symbolizing eternal and intangible realities. But the history of Israel and of the church also taught the Reformers that outside the bounds of permissible usage images had given rise to false worship. Furthermore, during periods of gross apostasy, even artefacts made under God's imprimatur had become objects of idolatry (2 Kings 21: 3–5, 7; 18: 4). Consequently, the Reformers maintained an ambivalent attitude towards art and its relation to religion. While cautioning against the excesses of image devotion, most of them conceived of art as charged with divine dignity and as having the potential for religious utility.[1]

While Nonconformists in the late nineteenth century were wary of the vices of religious representation, they were nevertheless keen to exploit its virtues. Public enthusiasm for art and religion was growing. Religious commentators realized that both aimed to maintain the 'higher aspirations of the soul' and to 'lessen the appetite for lower sensuality'. For this reason, they were keen to conscript art as an instrument in the churches' campaign for moral and spiritual reform.[2] Painting and sculpture came into the churches not as objects to be venerated but, rather, emblematized, as images typifying the virtues and attributes of the Christian character.

Christian Culture

Nonconformist attitudes to art during the last quarter of the nineteenth century ranged from holy indifference through circumspect acceptance to missionary enthusiasm. The former attitude was, according to one minister, symptomatic of an excessive interest in the culture of the soul and of the world to come; furthermore, it reflected an unhealthy preoccupation with the fallenness of the present world, and a misunderstanding about the extent of the Christian's participation in it. The practical consequences of this position were:

> As regards the present life, it appears to look coldly if not actually frown upon, some of the most reasonable and ennobling hopes and aims of humanity. It

requires its followers to take their amusements lightly and half-heartedly. Art, poetry, science and statesmanship, the cultivation of the varied and marvellous tastes and faculties with which man has been endowed – these it seems to tolerate rather than heartily recognise and hallow.[3]

Advocates of this position conceived of the Christian's interest almost exclusively in terms of preaching and developing spiritual character.[4] The pressing need to 'prepare to meet thy God' and of the passing nature of this present world made even the most legitimate 'things of earth . . . grow strangely dim' (to quote the sentiment of a well-known hymn). The incomparably more worthwhile endeavour of cultivating Christian virtues was often contrasted with the striving of the artist:

> The artist is engaged with his canvas for months, perhaps for years; the sculptor plies at his marble, but none of their works can follow; for the picture and the statue together with their fame must all be left behind. But the man of God is engaged upon works that will follow him when time is no more; the lines and the strokes and the chisellings which he has wrought upon himself will remain indelible when the rocks will melt with fervent heat; and the impressions he has carved into the characters of others are so deeply engraved that they will be legible in the Day of Judgment.[5]

Nonconformists who positively affirmed the value of art were no less concerned with the issues of time and eternity. What distinguished them was their belief that art could be conscripted to promote spiritual ends. The serviceability of art was usually discussed in the context of deliberations about culture. Culture at the time was perceived to be high culture with an emphasis on the intellectual aspect of civilization: the training, development, and refinement of mind, taste, and manners. This sense of culture overlapped with Nonconformity's spiritual, ethical, and social agendas.[6] Culture was considered efficacious in delivering the working class and the intellectually indolent from their dissipation in base, wasteful, and self-seeking preoccupations. These included popular forms of entertainment and leisure. To this end too, Nonconformists regarded art as a salutary and preservative force – in the words of Robert Downes, 'a potent antidote to low sensuality, purifying the thought as tragedy purifies the passions. By cultivating the imagination they also prevent cruelty. That proneness to materialism which is the constitutional infirmity of our nature is also checked by the influence of art.'[7]

While commending the advantages of art and culture, Nonconformists fiercely resisted excessive claims regarding the scope of its efficacy. In an address of 1898, the Calvinistic Methodist minister David Jones roundly challenged the view, advocated chiefly by Matthew Arnold's (1822–88) *Culture and Anarchy* (1869), that culture was a panacea for society's troubles. Jones remarked:

> We live at a time when there is a high premium put upon culture, especially the culture of the intellect; and doubtless we shall all agree that culture is capable of doing very much for the human race. But culture cannot do everything. Culture cannot produce life; its function is to strengthen and enrich life. There is no life for sinful man save in union with Him who is the Fountain of Life.[8]

Such convictions also ran counter to the claims of aestheticism, a nineteenth-century German Romantic theory of existence which Arnold had vigorously championed in Britain. It sought, according to the evangelical theologian Archibald Alexander, 'the highest value of life in the realm of the beautiful', and endeavoured to promote 'the supreme good of the individual through devotion to art'.[9] In contrast, the Christian theory of existence insisted that devotion to anything other than God was futile and idolatrous: 'Far be it from me to disparage art', remarked the Revd Daniel Hughes;

> nay, I plead for more artistic homes and places of worship. The influence may be good and elevating, but when it is contended that art can wholly save, and so the Cross is discounted, I remember that some of the finest palaces have been homes of immorality, and that from a moral point of view they were, and are, refuse heaps.[10]

Likewise, Abraham Kuyper (1837–1920) concluded in his discourses on Calvinism delivered in 1898, that regardless of its many benefits art was not to be placed on the same level as a religious movement.[11]

Ministers also cautioned against an inordinate affection for the arts, a counsel endorsed by secular publications. The entry for 'Art' in the *Popular Encyclopaedia*, for example, observed that while the influence of the arts had

> on the whole been beneficial by withdrawing men from sensual and selfish pleasures, it must be admitted on the other hand, that an intense devotion to one art has a tendency to destroy a healthy balance of mind in the devotees, and make them negligent of the duties they owe to society, careless of moral and political corruption, so long as they can enjoy art for its own sake.[12]

'Balance' became the watchword of the age. Evangelical journals perennially discouraged their readers from an excessive preoccupation with cultivating cerebral virtues and artistic taste at the expense of neglecting their spiritual responsibilities and growth.[13] Christians were also encouraged to participate in culture circumspectly and discriminatingly. On the apostle Paul's injunction 'be not conformed to this world: but be ye transformed by the renewing of your mind, that ye may prove what is that good, and acceptable, and perfect, will of God' (Romans 12: 2), D. Gwynfryn Jones commented: 'Enjoy life, the text seems to say, share its commerce, partake of its struggles, its art, its poetry, its science;

but resist its obscenity, its narrowness, its covetousness, its licentiousness, its materialism. Walk in all the paths and avenues of life, but keep your garments white.'[14]

However, there were broad roads which some Nonconformists considered Christians to have little hope of walking while remaining undefiled. These were the new forms of leisure pursuits and amusements (with their attendant social vices), which had taken a strong hold on the working class and proved a serious competition to the attractions offered by the chapels. Ministerial invectives were directed in the main against gambling, theatre-going, novel-reading, and athletics. Published denunciations were rarely a blanket condemnation or an expression of insensitive piety. Each activity was judged according to its merits and demerits, the reasons for a prohibition being clearly explained. These articles, as a whole, reveal four basic criteria for assessing the legitimacy of participation. The first criterion was whether the activity was inherently bad,[15] secondly, whether it led one into sin.[16] A third condition was that the activity be spiritually edifying, enriching the soul and quickening the Christian for spiritual service.[17] Fourthly, did the activity demand an excessive amount of time, love, energy, and money that might otherwise be spent on the serious business of life? Thus moderation was implored.[18]

Art passed at the bar of all four of the criteria. Nonconformists regarded it as neither intrinsically bad nor sin-inducing, and possessing few of the worldly circumstances concomitant with other pastimes and professions. Unlike theatre-going and drama – contempt of which was due as much to the context of bawdy playhouses as to the plays' content – art could be viewed in the rarefied and civil atmosphere of the museum and gallery.[19] Nonconformists' only objection to art was the exhibition of indecent pictures of immodestly dressed men and women.[20] Art depicting nakedness failed the second criterion; it incited impure imaginations and lust, and was thus incompatible with holiness. 'What a grand sight it is', the Revd D. Gwynfryn Jones wrote,

> to see the young and cultured youth in the dawn of his manhood turning aside with a mixture of scorn and pity from the counsel of the ungodly, closing his eyes lest the nude, carnal pictures, which contaminate and curse the city walls, should enter his soul.[21]

The artist could also avoid the disorientation of identity assumed to be attendant in the acting profession. 'A man', argued the Revd Elwyn Thomas, 'may describe evil or portray it in . . . sculpture, without putting himself into the exhibit of evil, without merging his personality with another personality.'[22] The only criticism of the moral integrity of the artist's profession concerned incidents of impropriety and immorality which sometimes took place in the studio between the artist and his model.[23] The classical argument for art as an elevator of the mind and spirit and as a civilizing influence on life enabled it to qualify at the bar of the third criterion. This required that a pursuit be spiritually and morally edifying before a Christian could enter into it with a good conscience. Since visiting an exhibition consumed less time, energy, and money than attending a theatre, Nonconformists considered enthusiasm for art to be neither profligate nor tending to excess.

These criteria reveal not only a cautious advocacy of cultural participation but also a desire to subject culture, in all its forms, to the spiritual and moral precepts of the Bible. Many considered Christianity to be 'a governing principle that guides the whole of life'.[24] This implied the redemption of every facet of the so-called 'secular' world through the application of Christian ethics.[25] Thus sanctified, the desire and capacity for art and culture, together with the means for its satisfaction, became gifts from God for the enrichment of mankind. Advocates of cultural rehabilitation were not all of the same theological persuasion. Some espoused the conservative and orthodox doctrines of the Reformed tradition and others the theology of the 'social gospel'. The latter were the most vocal protagonists of the cause. The social gospel owed much to the new theology of higher-critical scholarship, and both had gained a hold on the minds of many Nonconformist ministers and church members by the end of the nineteenth century.[26]

The social gospel conceived of the kingdom of God not first as a spiritual realm but as 'a perfect Commonwealth or universal brotherhood wholly of this world'. This was a regenerated social order where justice, righteousness, and peace prevailed, and salvation was a communal, not an individualistic, experience.[27] Some believed that the churches' commission was to reform the social order. The idea constituted a socialization of Christianity which in turn motivated a programme for the Christianization of society. It entailed the redemption of all aspects of life for edifying service. The principle of 'Christ in every realm' became the motto of this movement:

> There is no doubt that Christ means to recover the whole of our present life from the dominion of evil and annex it as part of His Kingdom. The corporate life of man here and now is claimed by Him. The home, the school, the factory, the market, the polling booth all are His. The worlds of art and nature, poetry, music, science, painting and sculpture – He claims them all.[28]

The Art of Preaching

Many interpreted Christ's claim on the world of art in terms of allying it to the mission of the churches. From its inception, Nonconformity had hallowed poetry and music in the service of the kingdom of God.[29] While, at the turn of the twentieth century, the conscription of drama to this end was a divisive issue, art, in contrast, provoked comparatively little public debate as to its moral and religious utility (see Appendix 2). Nonconformists annexed art to the kingdom by pressing it into the service of preaching. They did this by deconstructing emblematically the subjects of popular art works to convey a spiritual significance. The practice reflected a revival of enthusiasm for emblemature, typology, and allegory during the Victorian age. This had been fostered, in part, by the works of Cowper and other evangelical hymnists of the previous century.[30] Ministers, moralists, and critics of the arts turned to the Bible, nature, art, and human experience for visible emblems or types of invisible and otherwise incomprehensible truths.[31] The emblematic spirit enabled Victorians to interpret all of life in religious terms. In this way emblemature contributed to a more widespread endeavour on the part of Nonconformists at the end of the nineteenth century to integrate religion with every legitimate sphere of human activity and the cause of morality in particular. Art was conceived as not only a beneficiary of this union but also an instrument of religious and ethical reform. With the tradition of emblem books proper almost extinct, the adaptation of art in this way represented the last expression of the tradition of Protestant emblemature.

The genre arose at the beginning of the Victorian age with works such as *Illustrations of the Bible by Westall and Martin* (1835) by the Anglican clergyman Hobart Caunter. Image and text were coupled, much as they had been in emblem books. Engravings of paintings by Richard Westall (1765–1836) and John Martin (1789–1854) accompanied an exposition which served as the interpretative medium reconciling the illustrations to the biblical texts **(14)**. The works chosen were Protestant in spirit, inasmuch as they provided a faithful visual description of the incidents recorded in the Scriptures. The episodic structure and brevity of the texts suggests that the book was a companion to daily Bible-reading and meditation, a customary practice among evangelicals in the nineteenth century. Fifty years later *Sacred Themes and Famous Paintings* (1885), a series of discourses by David Davies, maintained the minister as intermediary but allied to Caunter's descriptive flair a Puritan penchant for pointing out art's infidelity to biblical history. The book focused on paintings 'illustrative of the passive suffering aspects of our Lord's life on earth, and of the relation which they bear for all time to human sorrow and Christian endurance'.[32] Davies provided a commentary on the paintings, rather as Henry had on the Bible, which sought not only to elucidate but also to apply their significance to the believer's experience by way of warning and encouragement. The pastoral approach to preaching pictures was further developed in *Sermons in Art by the Great Masters* (1908) and *Illustrations from Art for Pulpit and Platform* (1912) by the Scottish minister and historian of religious revivals James Burns. The texts proceed by way of observation, description, and interpretation of the image to address its significance to the heart (and thereby induce either affirmation, resolution, or personal commitment). Like Quarles, Burns was finally evangelistic in his aims. At the end of an exposition of Holman Hunt's depiction of Christ at the door in *The Light of the World*, Burns asked: 'And

14 John Martin, 'Dedication of the Temple', steelplate engraving, *Illustrations of the Bible by Westall and Martin* (1835).

what of ourselves? Comes there no message to us? . . . One, Whom have we kept long without, is even now knocking.'[33]

The Light of the World, along with Jean François Millet's (1814–75) *The Angelus* (1857–9), was among the paintings most often chosen as the basis of sermonic interpretation (see Chapter 7 **(49)**).[34] Burns's approach to Holman Hunt's painting was largely indebted to John Ruskin's (1819–1900) typological decoding of the painting's themes and incidents. For example, the door was a type of entrance to the heart; that it appeared not to have been opened for a long time signified the mystery of sin – the heart shut up against goodness and Christ. The weeds that choked the door were a visual symbol of 'neglect', reminding the viewer 'of the law which holds in the things of the soul as well as the things of nature'. The absence of a handle on the door taught that it could be opened only from the inside (an observation designed to invoke a personal response).[35]

Davies and Burns inspired many imitators. At the beginning of the twentieth century, Welsh Nonconformist ministers poached from their books both examples and interpretations to form the basis of short, pithy articles. These they more often published in denominational magazines for children with the explicit aim of instilling ethical rather than strictly religious values. The articles reflected a redirection of emblematic literature away from an adult audience (for whom Davies and Burns wrote) and from a preoccupation with devotional subjects during the nineteenth century.

15 *Hope*, photolithograph of a painting by
G. F. Watts (1886).

A disquisition on the capacity of painting to teach moral principles appeared in 'How a Painter Can Preach', published in the Calvinistic Methodist magazine *Monthly Treasury* in 1903. The article took as example William Frith's (1819–1909) series of five paintings collectively entitled *The Road to Ruin* (1878). The subject, wrote Frith, was 'the evils of gambling . . . I desired to trace the career of a youth from his college days to his ruin and death – a victim to one of the most fatal vices.'[36] The description of the paintings in the article follows approximately that given by Frith. However, it not only brings to the reader's attention the vice but also presents a gloss on the things that attend and foster it: 'It is supposed that there is no harm in Cards, no harm in Races, no harm in Drinking, no harm in Betting, provided all is done in moderation.'[37] The painting (like Spurgeon's book of emblems) became also a tract advocating abstinence from a variety of undesirable social habits. Paintings like these became surrogate biblical texts; Frith's paintings, for example, provided a narrative comparable to the story of the prodigal son.

The practice of taking 'secular' art works and baptizing them with a Christian significance was demonstrated with tiresome regularity in relation to G. F. Watts's (1817–1904) *Hope* (1886), prints of which were often hung on the walls of Sunday schoolrooms **(15)**. 'The unbroken string is Christ. He is the world's hope. Through Him the world will recover its lost heritage,' interpreted the Revd Evan Williams.[38] Watts intended a less pronounced optimism, which was humanist rather than specifically Christian.[39] The image's capacity to accommodate a variety of interpretations derives from its emblematic character and the generality of the painting's title. The iconographic precursor of *Hope* is Quarles's Book 5, Emblem 6, which depicts a figure sitting upon the sphere of the earth looking upwards to God. Williams imbued the concept of hope in Watts's work with the consolation and sense of certainty expressed in the biblical text and verse that accompanied Quarles's emblem.[40] Hope and Christian perseverance were, likewise, emblematized by a hermeneutic transfiguration of the *Laocoön* (c.25 BC). The story conveyed by the sculpture is of Laocoön, the Trojan hero and priest of Apollo, and his sons vainly resisting strangulation by the serpents that encoiled them. Christianized, its meaning became: 'Life is so encoiled, and the conflict is long protracted, only to end, however, under Christian courage, in conquest for parent and child.'[41]

Burns acknowledged the criticism that in such cases the interpreter 'puts more into the work than the author meant to convey'. He nevertheless believed that it 'in no way invalidates the truth of the interpretation. In the work of those who see visions there is always more in the vision than they understand, and all the prophets speak better than they know.'[42] Downes had written in similar vein in 1895, emphasizing that the perceived meaning was proportional to the spiritual stature of the spectator – a 'picture flashes out a message which all may read, though he who is greatest will see most on the canvas'.[43] For example, in the following exposition of Holman Hunt's *The Awakening Conscience* (1852) the preacher assumes a profound spiritual insight into the heart of the startled woman: 'She starts up, her eyes are full of terror, she sees herself, her sin, her doom, but not only that; she feels that the eyes of Christ are upon her, she sees her saviour also – never one without the Other.'[44]

The appropriation of paintings reflected a utilitarian view of art popular among Protestants during the second half of the nineteenth century. Watts's contemporary Frederic Leighton (1830–96) reproached the mentality in his Second Discourse, delivered in 1881:

> it is asserted that the first duty of all artistic production is the inculcation of a moral lesson, if not indeed of a Christian truth; and that the worth and dignity of a work of Art are to be gauged by the degree in which it performs this duty. Unless it preach, as from a pulpit, the cardinal doctrines of the Faith, or declare – whether by ambiguous symbolism, or by definite embodied example – the loftiness of virtue and the deadliness of sin; unless a very gospel made more

eloquent by form and colour cry aloud to us from the canvas or from the marble – then, we are told, the artist has laboured in vain, for his work fails in the fulfilment of the highest function of Art.[45]

For Nonconformists also, the chief end of art was the visualization of ethical and spiritual values. However, their esteem for art was not wholly in proportion to its ability to communicate the values they approved. They recognized the importance of beauty in art, but considered it as subordinate to and dependent on the potential for moral and spiritual service. (To be fair, attention to the aesthetic merits of art was irrelevant to the purpose of illustration: paintings, in the Nonconformists' view, served only the need for pressing home a point or lesson.) For this reason they disdained the idea of art for art's sake and the 'sensuous French type' of painting typified by Impressionism.[46] Ideally art should, like the fruit of the tree of knowledge, be both 'good for food, and . . . pleasant to the eyes' (Genesis 3: 6).

Revivals: The New Century

We have in our midst the mountain of the Lord's house, we have as guardian angel that fair child of God, the spirit of religion; and so long as our art, science, commerce, trade, literature, politics, like fair maidens in the house, minister and subserve their interests to her, all will be well with us, and triumph and success is assured, our peace shall flow forth as a river, and our righteousness shall go forth into the ends of the earth.[47]

The Revd W. Jenkins's psalmodic rhapsody encapsulates the spirit of *fin de siècle* optimism, national buoyancy, and heady expectation prevalent during the latter part of the nineteenth century. This was a period of real and hoped-for renaissance in the fortunes of Welsh culture. Nonconformists longed for a consolidation of the religious enthusiasm at the time in the shape of 'a spiritual revival of religion [to] mark the beginning of the twentieth century'.[48] They also expected the new century to usher in a revival of Welsh art and its fruitful collaboration with the nation's religion.

In a lecture delivered less than a fortnight before the beginning of the 1904–5 religious revival, the Revd Iona Williams outlined his expectation that, in the future, Welsh art would minister to the needs of religion, while religion would be characteristic of the nation's art, as it was of the Welsh people. Religion and morality, he argued, would preserve Welsh art from descending into the abyss of mere aesthetic indulgence. Imbued with these qualities, Welsh art would demonstrate an 'imaginative power, as often manifested in the discourses of our preachers', and serve to express 'lofty morals and spiritual ideas'.[49] Williams's imagination had been captured by the idea, as G. F. Watts had put it, of expressing 'in the Language of Art, Modern Thought in things ethical and spiritual', a monumental art of formal integrity and vehement moral purpose which would serve not only religion but also the state by reconnecting art to the nation's aspirations and interests:[50] 'In Watts we have something more than mystic poetry. He is a prophet of righteousness and his work speaks, not merely to the sense of the beautiful, but also to the mind and conscience, and in this he indeed suggests the Welsh character.'[51]

For the most part Williams's appraisal of Watts, and the Nonconformists' convictions regarding art's ethical, spiritual, and national utility, were derived wholesale from Ruskin.[52] Nonconformist enthusiasm for Ruskin was due partly to his evangelical upbringing, even though he eventually abandoned many of the tenets of his parents' faith in preference for a type of social Christianity.[53] During the period when his faith was most robust, Ruskin had contended that a mere aesthetic or sensual apprehension of art and nature (what he termed *aesthesis*) diminished both the thing perceived and the percipient. *Theoria*, being a moral response to beauty, must accompany sensual cognition.[54] Art cultivated to appeal only to man's sensual instincts, he deduced, 'contributed to the destruction of the nation practising it', whereas 'wherever Art has been used *also* to teach any truth, or supposed truth – religious, moral, or natural – there it has elevated the nation practising it, and itself with the nation'.[55] Such art would clearly be expedient to the advancement of national aggrandizement in Wales at the beginning of the twentieth century.[56]

Ironically, by the time Wales had espoused Ruskin's doctrine of beauty and utility, England was already abandoning it in favour of an extreme form of aestheticism known as formalism. Its principal advocates were Roger Fry (1866–1934) and Clive Bell (1881–1964). Fry had been instrumental in introducing Post-Impressionism to Great Britain in 1910, a movement which, along with Impressionism, Ruskin had condemned as an exercise in pure *aesthesis*, and from which he had insulated the British during his lifetime. In 'An Essay in Aesthetics' (1909), Fry advocated the emancipation of art from any ulterior purpose, be that moral, political, or religious: 'we must . . . give up the attempt to judge the work of art by its reaction on life, and consider it an expression of emotions regarded as ends in themselves'.[57] Art was no longer an instrument for affecting ethical improvement but rather the object of 'disinterested contemplation', apprehended by feeling in response to the 'significance of form'.[58]

By the end of the 1920s, some commentators in Wales responded to this turnabout in aesthetic theory. As the marriage between virtue and vision dissolved, so also did their conviction that art's chief end was to direct 'man's being towards Truth and Goodness'.[59] 'True art never preaches,' wrote a contributor to the *Welsh Outlook* in 1914. 'Its duty is to represent and to reveal, not to moralize.'[60] In England, the writings of Fry and Bell, and later those of R. H. Wilenski and Frank Rutter, had inspired the beginnings of an intelligent appreciation of art's formal qualities. In Wales, wrote Ifan Kyrle Fletcher in 1927, this 'attitude is

16 J. M. Staniforth, '"O! Marvellous Love! He Died for Evan Roberts!!!"', pen, ink, and wash, *Evening Express* (23 January 1905).

17 J. M. Staniforth, 'A Result of the Revival. Then and Now' (*c.*1904–5), pen and ink, 21.5 × 25.5.

proceeding with far more delay . . . Few, indeed, are those who think twice about the pictures which adorn their walls, and so the purple sunsets of Victorian sentimentalists continue in undisputed sway.'[61] With regard to both artistic taste and theory, Wales was stuck in the nineteenth century. Nearly twenty years after Ruskin's death commentators in Wales were still holding to ideas that Ruskin himself had partly abandoned in his lifetime. It reflected, not so much their esteem for him, but rather a lack of direction after he died.[62] Bereft of an authoritative interpreter of the works of man and God, and of a bridge between the worlds of art and religion, Nonconformists no longer had someone to tell them what to think. (Modern movements received not so much as a passing mention in denominational magazines.) Enamoured with only the aspects of art that overlapped with its interests, Nonconformity had no use for 'true art'.

Revivals in art, as in religion, wrote Burns, exhibit 'a return to simplicity and naturalness'.[63] The religious revival of 1904–5 represented a casting-off of the formal conventions of the Nonconformist liturgy in favour of spontaneous religious enthusiasm (see Appendix 3). This was accompanied by the renunciation of all actvities that were perceived as either detrimental or without appreciable utility to the development of the soul. Cultural activities generally took a poor second place to the concerns of the revival and were altogether abandoned by some. As one journalist wrote: 'The revival absorbed all secular subjects and superseded all other functions.'[64] The revival emphasized the urgent need for the unconverted to get right with God and to withdraw from the entanglements of the world. Evan Roberts, the revival's figurehead, advocated abstinence from all activities on the basis of the four criteria outlined above **(16)**. But even those practices that were not clearly prohibited or frowned upon, which he called 'doubtful things', were to be jettisoned in order that no obstacle remain in the way of God's continued blessing and the Church's rise to a higher plane of spiritual experience. Football fixtures were reported cancelled and teams disbanded because of a lack of interest. 'Many concerts . . . had their programmes changed for psalms, hymns and spiritual songs, the temper of the audience being unable to endure secular music.' University students missed lectures, preferring to attend prayer meetings; eisteddfods were postponed. Public houses were almost emptied, and serious crime reduced to a negligible level **(17)**. The Welsh press also published numerous testimonies of those working in entertainment and sport who gave up their profession when they were converted.[65] Sydney, Evan's brother, set theatre-going in clear antithesis to spirituality, deeming it incongruous with loving God.[66] Evan Roberts polarized cultural pursuit and religious affection with respect to the novel, for example: 'Once I liked novels. Now it is peace that I love most of all, for the Spirit has baptised me.'[67] The writer Hall Caine's (1853–1931) analysis of this remark discerned two attitudes which reflected a contempt for the novel that is less innocuous than is at first apparent:

> It means not merely that novels may be of pernicious influence (although of course it includes that idea), but also, and mainly, I think, that fiction as such is a trivial thing to occupy the mind of man in the face of the stern facts of life. It says in effect, 'With all the burning realities of time and eternity confronting him, how can a man waste his interest on the shadows of people who have never existed and incidents which have never taken place?' That is an attitude towards imaginative art which dates back to the birth of it.[68]

The preoccupation with 'the burning realities of time and eternity' may to some extent have dulled the general enthusiasm for national cultural revival by concentrating attention on the higher culture of the soul. Thus the long-awaited religious revival, which some believed would be the consummation of the cultural renaissance in Wales, turned out to be the greatest obstacle to its development.

While working-class entertainment and the literary forms of the play and the novel were spurned, poetry and painting appear to have been exempt from the revivalists' disdain. Poetry was held in high esteem in the culture of Welsh Nonconformity: many preachers were also bards, their poems being a vehicle for spiritual devotion, and some of them even being used as hymns.[69] Painting, which, according to one newspaper report, was appreciated by Roberts, may have found favour because of the moralizing tone of many Victorian works and their potential for sermonic exposition.[70] Though painting did not contribute to the revival's progress, images in the form of visions were a principal means of its promotion. They were emblems of religious experience, and a potent if ephemeral realization of the Nonconformist aspiration for an art of both spiritual utility and homiletic vision.

4

'Seeing Him Who is Invisible': Visionary Emblems of the 1904–1905 Religious Revival

The major religious revivals in Wales in 1739 and 1859 were both furthered by preaching. However, in the revival of 1904–5, which many predicted would eclipse the achievements of its predecessors, the central and predominant position hitherto occupied by preaching was assumed by music (see Appendix 3) and a variety of paranormal phenomena including visions.[1] The visions were significant in that they became a feature both of the ministry of Evan Roberts and in the furtherance of the revival. They represented a tendency unprecedented in the history of Welsh Nonconformity to visualize spiritual concepts – providing Nonconformists with incorporeal emblems of religious experience.

The Visionary Tradition

Accounts of visionary experiences form an integral part of the Judaeo-Christian tradition. Visions were one of the means by which God communicated with the prophets and apostles, written accounts of which were later incorporated into the Old and New Testament Scriptures. The completion of the canon of Scripture, so Protestants have generally believed, did away with the necessity for visions, since all one needed to know about God and the way men should live was contained in the Bible.[2] Consequently, while the Roman Catholic tradition is replete with testimonies to visions of God, Christ, the Virgin Mary, deceased saints, and supernatural beings, Protestant history boasts comparatively few. The best-known is probably the vision of the devil that appeared to the Reformer Martin Luther (1483–1546) while he was translating the Bible in the solitude of his room at the Wartburg.[3]

However, visionary experiences, as H. Elvet Lewis remarked, have been a feature, for better or worse, in every revival.[4] Jonathan Edwards (1703–58), in his discourse on *The Distinguishing Marks of the Spirit of God* during the eighteenth century revival in New England, wrote of some people who were subject to a 'kind of vision' when under the 'vehement and intense exercises and affections of the mind'.[5] Edwards believed that such experiences were no more than the effusion of an exalted imagination. They were not divine revelations or significations from heaven of what should come to pass, as Evan Roberts believed his visions to be.[6] Writers contemporaneous with Roberts understood the visions to be merely the demonstration of an extraordinary visualizing power.[7] Roberts himself conceived of his visions as mental pictures but would not concede that they were other than divinely inspired.[8]

Even if their origin was human rather than divine, many considered the visions to be remarkable in their influence upon Roberts himself and the congregations to which he recounted them. The prominence and widespread acceptance of the visions by Nonconformists during the revival may have been due to a number of factors. From the outset of the revival descriptions of visions experienced by Roberts and members of the meetings were published in both the *Western Mail* and *South Wales Daily News*. The newspapers helped spread an awareness of the visions not only as a general phenomenon but also in terms of their imagery and mode of perception. These provided precedents with the potential to shape and influence the visions of others.[9] The concept of visionary revelation would have been an attractive doctrine to the working class, which made up the greater proportion of the revival congregations. As Hugh McLeod wrote, it had been so for the Anabaptists, Quakers, and Primitive Methodists before them: 'for here was a form of religious experience that was accessible to a completely illiterate person as to the greatest theologian or biblical scholar'.[10]

The visions were also popular because they provided a form of immediate and comprehensible religious imagery appropriate to the mental disposition of the congregations. In *Primitive Traits in Religious Revivals* (1905) Fredrick Davenport observed that crowds, such as those at a revival meeting, think in 'emblems or symbolic images, such as the flag, the native land, the Church, the Scripture', and 'that appeals to the imagination have paramount influence'.[11] From the eighteenth to the mid nineteenth century sermons and hymns had provided a ready supply of emblems, symbolizing common ideals like the prosperity of the Church, the victory of Christ, and the vanquishing of the devil. However, by the end of the nineteenth century, Welsh preachers were deemed to have lost the ability to use concrete and easily understood images, together with the fervour, lucidity, and homeliness of expression that had characterized the preaching of previous generations.[12] Roberts's visions, in part, supplied the arresting images that contemporary preaching was failing to deliver. The majority of the visions were not, however, supernatural sermon illustrations, that is designed to explicate the precepts, principles, and incidents of Scripture. In the absence of anything that could be described as a sermon (Roberts did little by way of conventional preaching), they illuminated the phenomena of the revival itself – the spiritual battle, the progress of the revival, and its glorious destiny.

The Biblical Tradition

Many believers in the congregations were reluctant publicly to criticize the visions. This may have reflected their desire to use to them to provide evidence for the supernatural, miraculous, and revelatory nature of Christianity. The Independent minister Edmund Jones (1702–93) had similarly conceived his *Relation of Apparitions of Spirits in the Principality of Wales* (1780). Jones wrote his book in order to confute the detractors who did not believe in spiritual realities, 'to confirm others in the belief of Eternity and the World to come, and incline them the more to a preparation for it'.[13] Belief in these doctrines had been severely undermined by late-nineteenth-century liberal and higher-critical theology.[14] The visions also attested to the veracity of biblical prophecy. Many Nonconformists believed Roberts's visions to be one of the outworkings of Joel's prediction, 'the fulfilment of God's promises to the Church':[15] 'And it shall come to pass afterward, that I will pour out my spirit upon all flesh; and your sons and your daughters shall prophesy, your old men shall dream dreams, your young men shall see visions' (Joel 2: 28). That God had poured out His Spirit was evident from the thousands who were being converted; therefore, Roberts reasoned, the prophecy was a direct reference to the present revival.

For D. M. Phillips the divine origin and inspiration of these visions was also authenticated by their connotation of and resemblance to those of the Old and New Testaments. Reflecting on them, he wrote: 'Pan yn myned drwy y rhai hyn teimlwn ein bod yng nghanol prophwydoliaethau Ezeciel neu lyfr y Datguddiad.'[16] ['While going through these we felt that we were in the midst of the prophecies of Ezekiel or the book of Revelation.'] Roberts's visions do not evoke the grand manner of the biblical visions (they lack the formal majesty, symbolic complexity, and other-worldliness of these, as well as the eschatological intent which significantly determined their character). Nevertheless, they have in common with the visions of Ezekiel and the apostle John images, themes, development, and style of description. Sun, moon, and stars undergo a supernatural metamorphosis to become vehicles of awful spiritual significance.[17] For instance, in one vision Roberts stared up at a star in the sky and it appeared to him to open in a strange way: 'deuai y pelydrau mawrion allan i gyfeiriad y ddaear a chadwyn fawr yn uno eu godreuon, yna ymsaethai pelydrau allan o'r gadwyn drachefn'.[18] ['the large rays came out in the direction of the earth with a large chain joining their border, then rays would shoot out from the chain again'.] In recounting his vision, he took pains to convey the unusual arrangement of light and geometry, as had Ezekiel in the description of the formation of the wheels within wheels in his vision (Ezekiel 1).

Many of the visions were traditionally biblical, inasmuch as their imagery was derived from Scripture rather than being innovative. However, biblical imagery was adapted to circumstances familiar to the visionary. For example, the two horses, one red and the other white, seen galloping together in a vision at Moriah

Chapel, Loughor, Glamorgan represent the most direct reference to apocalyptic imagery (Revelation 6: 2, 4).[19] Here, however, they appear pulling a contemporary carriage.[20] (A chariot, seen moving upwards with speed into the sky in a vision in Swansea in 1905 was interpreted by Roberts as one which would finally take converts to heaven.[21] This may allude to the incident where Elijah ascended to heaven in a chariot of fire (2 Kings 2: 11).) In another vision seen on several occasions, a hazy figure hands the revivalist a piece of paper with '100,000' written clearly upon it (indicating the number of people who would be converted during the revival). This must have been derived from the image of the apostle John receiving the angel's declaration that 144,000 would be set apart to receive mercy from God (Revelation 7: 4).[22]

The fiery pit of the apocalypse (Revelation 9: 2) features in Roberts's vision of hell, which he received one evening while sitting in his room at Newcastle Emlyn:

> Gwelodd ddyfnder anferth, a chafodd ei hun wrth y drws arweiniai iddo, yr hwn a agorai tuag allan. Pydew tanllyd annesgrifiadwy oedd y dyfynder yma, ac yr oedd ei faint yn annirnadwy bron. O'i gwmpas yr oedd muriau mawrion, fel nad allai neb ddianc allan.
>
> Gwelai y preswylwyr yn eu poenau yno; ond y lle adawodd argraff ryfedd arno, ac nid y preswylwyr.[23]

> [He saw a great depth, and found himself at the door which led into it, and which opened outwards. This depth was an indescribable fiery pit, and its size was almost incomprehensible. Around it were large walls, so that no one could escape.
>
> He saw its inhabitants in torment there; but it was the place that left a strange impression on him, not the inhabitants.]

Roberts had himself narrowly escaped a pit explosion as a collier. The image of the colliery pit-bottom on fire thus strongly informed his conception of hell (see Chapter 2).

Other visions involved creative syntheses of biblical imagery. In a vision perceived at a chapel in Swansea in 1905, Roberts saw a large column of candles in union but without light. This he interpreted as the converts yet to be lit and to give light to others, using the metaphor of believers as 'the light of the world' (Matthew 5: 14) as the basis of a unique image prophesying the future success of the revival.[24] The symbol of a lighted candle is also used in the New Testament to refer to the church (Revelation 1: 12, 13, 20; 2: 1, 5). It is employed in this sense in the vision of the candle and sun he described in a letter to Florrie Evans dated 6 November 1904: 'In front of me I could see a candle lit; in the background a Sun rising in divine splendour. What is the interpretation? The Revival is now only as candle light to what it will be.'[25] In the Bible, however, the radiating sun, which sometimes represents spiritual illumination and whose rays are healing for those who believe (Malachi 4: 2), is never represented together with a candle as it is in Roberts's vision.

A further instance where symbols are brought together from different parts of the Bible is a vision Roberts perceived on a Sunday afternoon in October or November 1904. Filled with despair over the state of the Church, he walked in the garden, where

> in the hedge on his left, he saw a face full of scorn, hatred and derision, and heard a laugh as of defiance. It was the Prince of this World who exulted in his despondency. Then there suddenly appeared another figure, gloriously arrayed in white bearing in hand a flaming sword borne aloft. The sword fell athwart the first figure and it instantly disappeared. He could not see the face of the sword bearer.[26]

Roberts recognized Christ by the brilliant white raiment in which He appears in the account of his transfiguration (Matthew 17: 2). The vision sets up a contrast by juxtaposing the two opposing figures, who represent the dualism of the spiritual realm. The account of the temptation of Christ in the wilderness (Matthew 4: 1–11) provides the only biblical precedent for such a confrontation, although the narrative gives no indication that the devil took on physical form. In this incident Christ wields not a literal weapon against the adversary but 'the sword of the Spirit, which is the word of God' (Ephesians 6: 17). Roberts depicted Christ with a sword, which possibly also alludes to the flaming sword God placed east of the garden of Eden 'to keep the way of the tree of life' (Genesis 3: 24). In the context of his vision the sword does not read as a deterrent, but as the power of God wielded against the enemy of the Church. Roberts's 'art', therefore, consisted in creating new conjunctions of images drawn from the Bible. These in turn generate fresh symbolic readings and associations expressing his own ideas. This particular vision was not a 'mental picture', but perceived as part of the external world.[27] Roberts suggested that visions may also be spiritual or physical.[28] Accordingly, D. M. Phillips, Roberts's biographer, divided the visions into those that were 'fewnol' ['subjective'], which Roberts perceived only in his mind, and 'wrthddrychol' ['objective'], which manifested themselves externally.[29]

Phillips might as accurately have compared Roberts's visions with those of the prophet Zechariah. In one vision, Zechariah sees the devil standing at the right hand of Joshua to accuse him (Zechariah 3: 1). Roberts also visualized satanic opposition in an anthropomorphism of the devil on one other occasion. He saw Satan on his left side once while he was leading a prayer meeting.[30] Visions of Christ and the devil, perceived either together or independently, were by far the most common experienced by Roberts and other Nonconformists. The figures were very often construed as physical manifestations of the persons. One young man at a revival meeting at Ynyslwyd declared that he had actually perceived

Christ in bodily presence.[31] Mary Jones, the 'Welsh Seeress', saw the devil appear to her in the road as she drove her trap home, while another woman recounted seeing the devil sitting by her in chapel while at a revival meeting and urging her not to make an exhibition of herself.[32] ('Real' and imaginary encounters with the devil had also been a phenomenon of the 1859 revival in Ireland.)[33] Such visions objectified the twin spiritual forces that fought for the souls of men and women and often served as emblems of personal religious crisis, as in the case of Roberts's vision in the garden and in another, published in the *Forward Movement Torch*, experienced by an old lady in January 1904:

> Last night, just after I had gone to rest, and while still awake I beheld two forms approach my bed.
>
> Whoever can these be, thought I. As I gazed upon them, I saw that the foremost had the most beautiful countenance I had ever seen; and I noticed his lovely fair hair was parted in the middle. Glancing at the other form, I saw he was black and ugly. 'O, that is the devil,' I said, and guessed the other was Jesus.
>
> Just then the Saviour spoke to me, and said, 'whom will thou serve this day?' 'Thee blessed Lord', I quickly replied, and immediately the Saviour came nearer, and stood by my side. The devil tried his best to come between us, but he failed, and then he slunk away.[34]

The *South Wales Daily News* also recorded that 'A boy said he had seen Satan in a vision. He was tempting him to do wicked things, and while the conflict was going on another figure appeared, and the boy's face beamed with joy as he recognised him as Jesus Christ.'[35] While the contrast of elements in all three is the same, the crises they represent are different. In Roberts's vision it is one of temptation to discouragement; in the old lady's vision it is a crisis of allegiance and in the young boy's it is a temptation. All three illustrate the nature of spiritual conflict and the triumph of Christ over the temptations that assail the Christian.

The visions were given to Zechariah to encourage him in the work he was undertaking for God and to dispel the despondency into which he and God's people had fallen. Roberts clearly believed that many of the visions he had perceived were for the same purpose, to assure him of the great ingathering of converts and that God supported his cause. In his vision of Christ and Satan, Roberts interpreted Christ's vanquishing of His adversary as Satan put to flight, a reading that he believed was substantiated by the number of men and women being converted in the revival.[36] Phillips recounted another of Roberts's visions:

> Ar ei ffordd i Aberdâr, Tachwedd 13eg, gwelodd beleni hirgul duon yn ymdreiglo allan o'r haul. Yr oedd y peleni yn anferth o fawrion, ac yn ymdreiglo allan gyda nerth a chyflymder . . . Teyrnas y goleuni yn bwrw allan deyrnas y tywyllwch a

awgrymai yr olygfa iddo. Dywedai wrth y cwmni nad oedd eisieu digaloni, oblegid gwyddai wrth y weledigaeth fod Duw o'u plaid y dydd hwnw.[37]

[When on his way to Aberdare, on 13 November, he saw black elongated balls rolling out of the sun. The balls were enormous, rolling out with strength and speed . . . The kingdom of light casting out the kingdom of darkness was what the vision suggested to him. He told the company that they need not be disheartened, since he knew from the vision that God was on their side that day.]

The Hymnological Tradition

Hymns too were a means of articulating personal religious experience. As in the visions, concepts such as faith, repentance, conversion, assurance, and forgiveness were visualized in vivid metaphors based on, or derived from, biblical imagery, or adapted from everyday life.[38] Death, the believer's passage from this world into the next, was usually expressed in hymns by the crossing of a great river which lay between earth and heaven. William Williams (1717–91) wrote:

> When I tread the verge of Jordan,
> Bid my anxious fears subside;
> Bear me through the swelling current,
> Land me safe on Canaan's side.[39]

The precursor of this theme is Israel's journey out of the wilderness, through Jordan, into the promised land (Joshua chapters 3 to 4). The event was adapted as an allegory for conversion, the believer's translation from the kingdom of darkness into the kingdom of light. The concept was visualized in the following report of a testimony given by one of the congregation at Brynteg Congregational chapel, Llanelli, Carmarthenshire on 11 November 1904. Like Roberts's vision (see below), it features a landscape of considerable beauty, full of people:

> One of the most remarkable utterances of this remarkable night was that of a woman who gave a vivid description of a vision which she had seen on the previous evening. 'I saw,' she said, 'a great expanse of beautiful land, with friendly faces peopling it. Between me and this golden country was a shining river, crossed by a plank. I was anxious to cross, but feared that the plank would not support me. But at that moment I gave myself to God, and there came over me a great wave of faith, and I crossed in safety.'[40]

As in many of Roberts's visions, the elements of the Old Testament record are here transfigured into everyday equivalents. The promised land becomes the 'beautiful land', the Jordan is reduced to a shining river, narrow enough to be spanned by a wooden plank. The people of Israel were enabled to cross the river when 'the waters which came down from above stood and rose upon an heap' (Joshua 3: 16); the visionary imagined a more mundane and familiar means to convey her from one side to the other. The vision is an allegory for the crisis of conversion. The visionary represented to herself, in a tangible and immediate image, what is essentially an unobservable event, together with the concomitant movements of her spirit – faith in God and submission.

In a vision perceived at Moriah, Loughor, Roberts described a rural genre scene in which

> gwelodd gae o yd eithriadol o eang. Yr oedd y cae y peth mwyaf addurniadol ag a welodd ef erioed. Ynddo gwelai luaws mawr o ferched a gwragedd a rhai dynion, yn ymdrechu am eu bywyd i gasglu ysgubau yng nghyd. Yr oedd pawb yn y cae wrth eu bodd, ac yn cyflawni eu gwaith gyda llawenydd.[41]

> [he saw an exceptionally vast field of corn. It was the most ornate field he had ever seen. In the field was a multitude of girls, women, and some men exerting themselves for their very lives gathering in the sheaves. Everyone in the field was delighted, fulfilling his work with joy.]

The vision signified the great ingathering of converts during the course of the revival. In harvest hymns, for example Henry Alford's (1810–71) 'Come, ye thankful people, come', thanksgiving for the fruit of the land is often merged with the image of the reaping of souls into the garner of heaven, following Christ's parable of the harvest, in which believers are likened to labourers in the field (John 4: 36):

> All this world is God's own field,
> Fruit unto His praise to yield;
> Wheat and tares together sown,
> Unto joy or sorrow grown.
>
> . . .
>
> Give His angels charge at last
> In the fire the tares to cast;
> But the fruitful ears to store
> In His garner evermore.[42]

The experience of conversion is figuratively visualized by Daniel P. Williams, the founder of the Apostolic Church in Wales, in a vision that came to him at a revival meeting. He was awaking from a black-out brought on by Evan Roberts having 'laid hands' upon him. The attendant circumstances of the experience had a bearing on the content of the vision's imagery. As he regained consciousness he heard a woman singing a line from a hymn, 'The gates of heaven opened wide, I see a sea of blood':

> It was then that Daniel had a vision of Jesus on the cross, His body streaming with blood, and underneath it a sinner's head, and as the blood of Jesus fell on the parts of the sinner's head, it became white – like snow. The sinner, Daniel realised, was none other than himself.[43]

The metaphor of the sea of blood would appear to have triggered off the visualization of the stream of blood which poured from Christ's body. A verse from a popular hymn of the time by William Cowper almost certainly exerted a direct influence on Williams's emblem for forgiveness:

> There is a fountain filled with blood
> Drawn from Immanuel's veins;
> And sinners, plunged beneath that flood,
> Lose all their guilty stains.[44]

The image is even more vivid in the vision, where Williams himself observes the dying Saviour. From the seventeenth century, hymns often enjoined worshippers to 'see', 'view', 'gaze upon', 'survey', or 'behold' Christ crucified. 'Looking' was generally conceived in the figurative sense of comprehending, reflecting upon, or considering with the eye of faith the death and atoning work of Christ as, for example, in the lines from a hymn by James Montgomery (1771–1854): 'When to the cross I turn my eyes / And rest on Calvary', and in the opening stanza of Isaac Watts's (1674–1748) hymn:

> When I survey the wondrous cross
> On which the Prince of glory died,
> My richest gain I count but loss,
> And pour contempt on all my pride.[45]

Such sentiments do not encourage a vivid mental conception of the crucifixion. In Bishop William How's (1823–97) 'It is a thing most wonderful' (a hymn popular among evangelicals of all denominations), the spectacle of Christ's suffering is described more literally – 'seeing', as in the visionary's experience, is a contemplative and conscious act of mental visualization:

> I sometimes think about the cross,
> And shut my eyes, and try to see
> The cruel nails and crown of thorns,
> And Jesus crucified for me.[46]

In the third stanza of Watts's hymn (quoted above), the hymnist moves from a general view of the crucifixion to particular scrutiny of Christ's wounds: 'See from His head, His hands, His feet / Sorrow and love flow mingled down.' The description evokes a more substantive image of Christ's suffering. Similarly, in How's hymn, the focus of the imagined scene is specific; however, here it is not the wounds but the instruments of Christ's torture that are the object of meditation.

Visions and Religious Pictures

The afflicted Christ is a recurring theme in the visions of the 1904–5 revival, which reflected the central position given to the doctrine of the crucifixion in the revival.[47] Throughout the revival there were reports of numerous visions of Christ on the cross, of His wounds, and of the means of crucifixion.[48] In a preamble to an address about Christ's suffering, Roberts recalled a vision in which he had seen: 'a Roman in the act of nailing my Saviour to the Cross. I could see him kneeling on his arm; see the nails being driven in; see the hammer falling.'[49] Rather like the salutary medieval exercise of contemplating the wounds of Christ, such visions focused the believers' attention on the intensity of Christ's suffering, and thereby stimulated their will and affections to holy living. Roberts's vision extended the range of religious images familiar to Nonconformists. 'Artists', he said, 'have pourtrayed Jesus nailed to the Cross; but I have not yet seen a picture of the actual nailing.'[50] Like many pictures of the crucifixion, the vision provided an illustration of an aspect of the event that is not described in the gospel narratives, but which, nevertheless, could be inferred as having taken place. Pictures depicting the crucifixion were rarely set up on the walls of either the chapels or Nonconformist homes during the nineteenth and early twentieth centuries. Such images would have had too strong an association with the idolatry and superstitious worship associated with Roman Catholicism. However, a few appeared as engraved illustrations in pulpit Bibles and family Bibles published by companies outside Wales **(18)**. Since they were not specifically tailored for a Nonconformist market and a Calvinistic sensibility, these Bibles contained images that were often at variance with the doctrines of evangelical Dissent.[51] The visions of Christ on the cross expressed an aspect of Nonconformist visualization that had hitherto been suppressed by Calvinistic theology. Such visions differ from religious paintings in that they were only momentary images of religious contemplation. By virtue of their supposedly divine origin, the visions were sacred images, but they were not venerated as such. As in the tradition of emblems, what appears to have been important to believers was not the image itself, but the message it conveyed. In these ways the visions were also a substitute for conventional religious representations – inner emblems of personal devotion.

18 'Crucifixion', steelplate engraving by S. P. after a painting by Annibale Carracci (1560–1609), *Bibl Yr Addoliad Teuluaidd* (London: London Printing & Publishing Co., [n. d.]).

Roberts's first recorded vision, experienced prior to the revival, was also a picture of Christ's suffering rarely represented in Nonconformist visual culture. In what may have been a subjective (that is, a mental or spiritual) vision, he witnessed Christ's agony in the Garden of Gethsemane (Matthew 26: 36–46). At the climax of a Sunday service in Abergwynfi, Glamorgan, on 2 November 1904, the revivalist was reported as saying how once, while listening to a preacher at Newcastle Emlyn,

> he received much more of the spirit of the Gospel from what he saw than from what he heard. The preacher was doing very well, was warming with his work, and sweating by the very energy of his delivery. And when he (Evan Roberts)

saw the sweat on the preacher's brow he looked beyond and saw another vision: his Lord sweating the bloody sweat in the garden (and then as Mr Roberts thought of the 'vision' he utterly broke down).[52]

He had experienced a sermon in the form of a 'picture' more striking and effective to him than that delivered by the preacher.

The incident at Newcastle Emlyn may have persuaded Roberts of the capacity of pictures to convey the essence of religious ideas immediately, dramatically, and emotively. It may also have motivated him at the very outset of the revival to have some of the visions reproduced and distributed in the form of picture-postcards.[53] A former collier, Roberts had had no formal training for the ministry; he was not gifted in oratory nor had he pretensions to eloquence.[54] The visions were an expedient, and possibly superior, alternative to rhetorical discourse as a means of drawing and holding sway over the immense crowds. Moreover, Roberts had been brought up in a cultural milieu which encouraged a pictorial conception of religion – a highly sentimentalized one – and in a context in which the Word of God and images were frequently found together, supporting and explicating each other. The walls of Roberts's home were described by one reporter as a veritable emblem book, being 'covered with pictures and mottoes'.[55] These would have included engravings, similar to those in the illustrated Bibles, and solemn Bible texts and pious verses beseeching God's blessing or commending godliness and industry, which were bespattered over domestic crockery, wrought in samplers, and writ large in brightly coloured and varied typography **(19)**. Collectively the artefacts served to enhance the religious ethos of the chapel and home by providing a pictorialization of spiritual and moral ideals, as didactic and evangelistic tools, and as a means of elevating the spiritual affections and ambitions.[56] They do not entirely explain his predisposition to visions as a mode of religious expression, but, given that so many of the revival's congregations had also grown up in a similar environment, they help us to understand further why the visions had such an appeal.

The potential of a religious picture to move and inspire a person's affections had been recognized on a number of occasions in evangelical literature since the latter part of the nineteenth century. The conversions of prominent Christians on seeing paintings, usually depicting Christ, were described without censure. An issue of *Christian Age* for 1900 published an anecdote of Nicolaus Ludwig von Zinzendorf's (1700–60) encounter with a picture of *Ecce homo* with the inscription 'This have I done for thee, what hast thou done for me?'[57] Zinzendorf's conversion was, arguably, a response to the verbal proposition, the poignancy of which was enhanced by the graphic representation of Christ's humiliation. (Some Puritans had believed that religious pictures were efficacious only when accompanied by an appropriate biblical text (see Chapter 1).) A similar construction could be placed on Roberts's account of the vision at Newcastle Emlyn, given that his perception of it was accompanied by the message of the

19 Ornamental plaque with text: 'Thou God, See'st Me', (nineteenth century, first half), probably Staffordshire ware.

preacher. The vision distilled the heart of the preacher's message – the suffering Saviour.[58]

Roberts's visions demonstrate a figurative attitude to religious concepts.[59] In this sense, comparisons can be drawn with the series of allegorical scenes that John Bunyan's Christian is shown at Interpreter's House (see Chapter 1). Both are revelations in the form of spiritual similitudes, identified by interpretation and designed either to cheer or to warn the spectator. In one scene, Interpreter shows Christian 'a place where was a fire burning against a wall'; the fire was a symbol for 'the work of grace that is wrought in the heart'. The devil cast water upon the fire while, at the back of the wall, another figure, identified as Christ, poured on oil. The emblematic representation of Christ and the devil in an adversarial relationship is a likely progenitor of the revivalists' visions of the same. Similarly, the incident of the figure 'arrayed in white' felling his sword athwart the devil in Roberts's vision is reminiscent of Christian's encounter with the demon Apollyon who was, likewise, vanquished by the sword. Among Nonconformists, Bunyan's allegory was second only to the Bible in popularity and familiarity, and would have exerted a significant influence on their visualization of religious concepts.[60] The identification between the Puritan dreamer and the Nonconformist visionary did not escape the Welsh press. During a period known as the 'Seven Days of Silence', the *Evening Express* published a cartoon by Staniforth, representing Roberts as Christian, determinedly walking through 'the valley of the shadow of death' (Psalm 23: 4), on either side assailed by demons, devils, and monsters.

20 Book 2, Emblem 1, steelplate engraving, *Emblems, Divine and Moral* (1818).

21 Book 2, Emblem 14, steelplate engraving, *Emblems, Divine and Moral* (1818).

Many of Roberts's visions could be described as emblematic in that they represent symbolic objects that, either individually or together, convey a spiritual message. One cannot be sure that Roberts, like Bunyan, was familiar with emblem books, though it is not unlikely. At least thirty editions of Quarles's book of emblems were published in the nineteenth century alone.[61] Toplady considered the book to convey spiritual lessons

> in the most pleasant and interesting manner – by hieroglyphics, or figurative signs and symbols, of divine, sacred, and supernatural things; by which mode of communicating knowledge the fancy is charmed, the invention is exercised, the mind informed, and the heart improved.[62]

The term 'hieroglyphic' could apply to Roberts's visions that comprise a single element or a conjunction of static elements, for example his vision of a key, signifying that God had given him the ability to open the hearts of men.[63]

There are specific iconographic similarities between the visions and emblems. Take, for example, Roberts's vision of the candle and sun, in which the light from the latter outshines that of the former. In Book 2, Emblem 1, Quarles depicts Cupid about to 'snuf and trim' a burning candle set upon an orb; to the right of the orb a boy blasts at the sun with a bellows **(20)**. Underneath the image is the legend 'Sic lumine lumen ademptum' ['Thus is light taken from light'] and the epigram 'So shines the sun in native splendour bright / Thy feeble ray eclipsing with its Light.' One of the lessons this emblem conveys is that the light of man's merit, desire, and knowledge pales in comparison to the glories of heaven. In Roberts's vision the contrast of these two lights was interpreted as indicating that the success of the revival in its latter days would greatly exceed that of its beginning. In another vision, witnessed by Evan Roberts and his brother Sydney while looking at the moon, Evan saw it swell, pulsate, and then fill with a divine presence. Sydney added: 'ac ymddangosai fel braich yn dyfod allan o honi i'r ddaear, ac yn myned yn ol a rhywbeth gyda hi'.[64] ['and there appeared as an arm reaching out of it to the earth and taking something back to itself.'] There is a superficial resemblance to a pictorial device Quarles uses in Book 5, Emblem 6, illustrating the text 'Whom have I in heaven but thee; and there is none upon earth that I desire beside thee?' (Psalm 73: 25). Here the divine presence fills an orb set above the clouds, which represents the heavenly sphere. Whitney represented God's intervention in the world by the visual metonym of an arm that reaches out – in this case from a cloud – to take up the reins of Francis Drake's ship and thus ensure its safe voyage.[65]

Roberts saw certain visions on more than one occasion. Among these was the vision of Christ holding weighing-scales in the sky, to weigh men. The scales here are a symbol of the standard of God's righteousness by which all men are to be judged. The metaphor occurs in the book of Daniel, where 'Tekel', one of the words God wrote on the wall at Belshazzar's feast, is interpreted as 'Thou art weighed in the balance and found wanting' (Daniel 5: 27), and in the book of Revelation, where the scales are held by the rider of the black horse (Revelation 6: 5). Roberts sometimes saw himself in one of the scales' pans and not weighing enough, which signified that he was wanting in righteousness. However, Christ's love would come and weigh to the floor the pan he was in, illustrating graphically the doctrine of Christ's merit being imputed to the repentant sinner.[66] Quarles represented the scales being held out by an angel in Book 1, Emblem 4. The angel figures in several of the other emblems, and in their accompanying texts is often designated 'Lord', which summons up an association with the 'angel of the Lord' mentioned in the Old Testament, whom Protestants often identify with God.[67] Roberts's visionary confrontation with Christ and Satan in his garden recalls the Quarles emblem of the 'just man' confronted by an angel holding an olive branch and the devil holding a feather. In this context they personify virtue and temptation **(21)**.

The visions also echo the fantastic aspects of the emblems. The symbols in the emblems have a material reality, yet, because of their abnormal scale, the transformations they have undergone, and the often odd conjunction of objects, they are rather disquieting. In another emblem, the heads of animals and beasts protrude from the surface of an orb, representing the created order. This is similar to another of Roberts's visions, which he saw on several occasions, in which four 'branches' shoot out from the moon towards the four corners of the earth, with rays undulating from them and turning back on themselves.[68]

An important distinction, however, must be made between the traditional Protestant view of emblematic images and the revivalists' use of visions. Huston Diehl has established that the Reformers allowed the use of images as commemorative aids, to 'function as vehicles that remind the viewer of what he cannot see, rather than become ends in themselves. The viewer may use a spiritual image to recall something else, something spiritual, invisible, and incorporeal.'[69] As mentioned in Chapter 1, emblems operated as signs pointing towards the reality with which they shared only a metaphorical relationship. There was always maintained a 'disparity between the visible and invisible'.[70] In visions such as those of the key and of the sun and candle, there is a distinction between the sign and the signified reality; but the sign has an inherent spiritual significance apart from the message it conveys which is derived from the belief that the visions were themselves spiritual. A vision such as that of Christ and the devil in the garden is even further removed from the nature of an emblem because the distinction between sign and reality is not clear; the image of the two figures could either have been a representation of Christ and the devil, or the actual persons in a visionary form.

One cannot be sure of the extent to which emblem books had a direct influence on the imagery of the visions. Nevertheless, some Nonconformist leaders certainly considered religious paintings to have induced the visionary experiences during the revival. It was supposed that visions could, in some instances, be attributed to the exercise of a vivid imagination under the influence of religious pictures or as a consequence of the intense contemplation of spiritual things. In a Methodist society meeting, a boy recounted a vision he had seen at an evening service on Christmas Sunday in 1904. He recalled seeing the apostle Paul in the pulpit, and John and Peter on the pulpit stairs. Then the vision changed, and in place of John and Peter he saw two hands bearing nail prints. There was no face or form, but he could also see the feet of Christ and the hammer driving in the nails. The boy was asked whether there was a picture of the crucifixion in his home, to which he answered no, but said that he had been reading for some nights before going to sleep the Gospel narratives of the crucifixion.[71] (Interestingly, the *Evening Express* published an illustration to accompany an article on the state of the Welsh pulpit which is remarkably similar to the boy's vision, in the revival edition of 16 January 1905 **(22)**. Instead of John and Peter, Moses and Christ appear suspended above the stairs of the pulpit, representing the law and grace respectively. In the pulpit, the place of Paul is taken by the Holy Spirit in the form of a dove hovering over an open Bible, as He is depicted in the emblem of the Calvinistic Methodist Church. It is not inconceivable that a newspaper reporter might have been present when the boy recounted his vision – throughout the revival the *Western Mail* and *Evening Express* daily published on-the-spot accounts of the meetings – and relayed the description to the newspaper's artist.)

That he had been reading the Gospel narratives does not explain how the boy could identify the figures in the vision as the apostles. He simply remarked that he somehow knew by instinct.[72] Nonconformists frequently appealed to intuitive

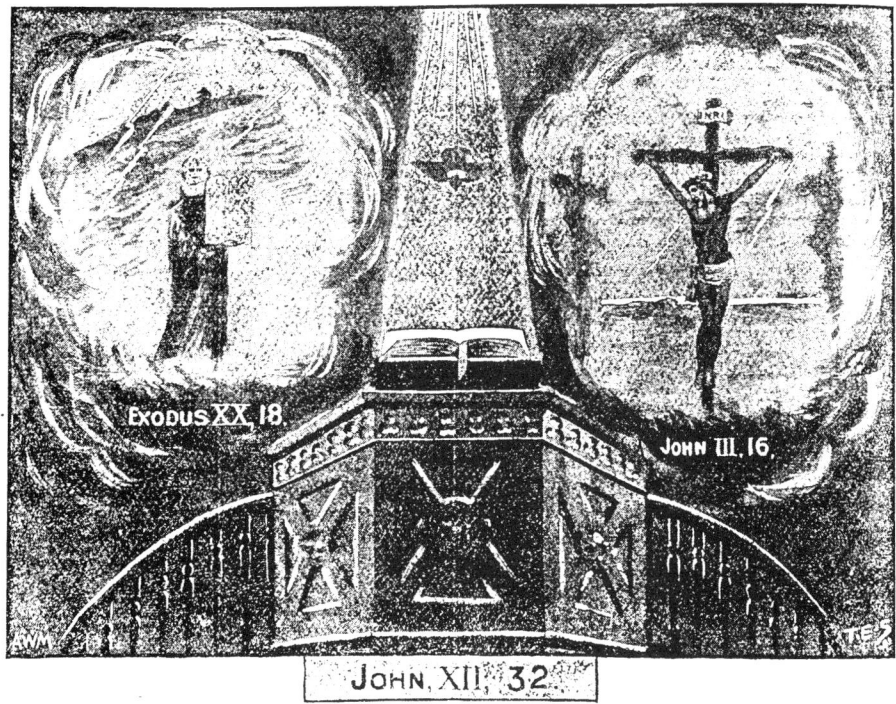

22 T. E. S. and A. M. W., 'An Empty Pulpit?', pen, ink, and wash, *Evening Express* (16 January 1905).

knowledge as the basis for their confident assertions as to figure-identification. An instance of this concerns the remarkable 'objective' vision of Christ witnessed at a Sunday evening service led by the Pentecostal evangelist Stephen Jeffreys at the Island Place Mission Hall, Llanelli, a fortnight before the outbreak of the First World War. The vision is unusual in that it was perceived by a large number of people simultaneously. The accounts of those who attested to the experience differ in some respects, possibly because each of them saw what accorded with their expectations. The following testimony sets out the features that are common to most accounts:

> While Pastor Jeffreys was preaching there appeared slightly above his head a lamb's face on the wall behind him. It looked like a living young sheep and beautiful too, and remained quite clearly for about a quarter of an hour, and then transformed into the Face of the Saviour. His eyes were deep set, alive and penetrating. They watched every movement of the Pastor as he went to and fro, this way and that way on the rostrum.[73]

W. J. Adams, in his investigation of the phenomenon, asked those who saw it how they could be sure that it was Christ's face. Summing up their answers, he wrote, 'All the children of God present knew instinctively, at once and without question, that He was the dear Saviour.'[74] However, when these testimonies are examined separately they reveal that the identity of Christ was established more by association with the traditional iconography of Christ-representation than by spiritual insight. According to the curator of the Mission Hall, the head of Christ was 'very similar to the portraits we see of our dear Lord Jesus Christ'.[75] Jeffreys remarked that 'the face was the one we usually picture in our minds when we think of Christ'.[76] In both these cases identification is based on a preconceived idea of what Christ ought to look like. His face, explained the evangelist, had

> a Roman nose and Jewish features. His hair was like wool, parted in the middle, and had a curl on each temple over his eyes and ears. His head was slightly leaning to the left and His expression was pitiful; and when I examined closer it looked as though His hair was streaked with white like that of a middle-aged man in grief.[77]

Some others claimed to have seen the head with a crown of thorns upon it.[78] All agreed that the vision showed Christ as 'a man of sorrows and acquainted with grief' (Isaiah 53: 3).[79] Christ's identity in this vision was also confirmed by the rationale of the transformation of the typological symbol, the lamb, to its antitype, Christ.

The principles by which visionary figures are recognized are, according to Joseph Runzo, analogous to those determining the recognition of figures in religious pictures: at its most rudimentary level, the identity of figures in visions, as in western religious painting, is established inferentially by the application of certain rules. These are rules of 'a game of make-believe . . . that all members of society knowingly participate in', by which a figure in a painting is deemed to represent a certain supernatural being or holy person by dint of certain expectations we have of how they should be represented.[80] These expectations are conditioned by a knowledge of the devices employed by artistic tradition to signify that a certain figure is, for instance, a representation of God and, conversely, that other figures in the painting are not. Thus identification is made on the grounds of recognizing the God-depicting signs which one figure possesses and which the others do not. Runzo believed that the identification of a figure in a particular vision is made with reference to an established tradition of interpretation.[81] As visionary experience is in general a rare phenomenon in the history of Welsh Nonconformity and Protestantism, there has not accumulated a body of interpretative precedents to which the revivalists could have appealed to identify the figures in their visions. In the absence of a long and established visionary tradition, the iconography of religious art supplied an alternative touchstone for figure identification.[82]

Illustrated Bibles, devotional books, and denominational literature formed a repository of religious imagery drawn from Protestant and Catholic art.

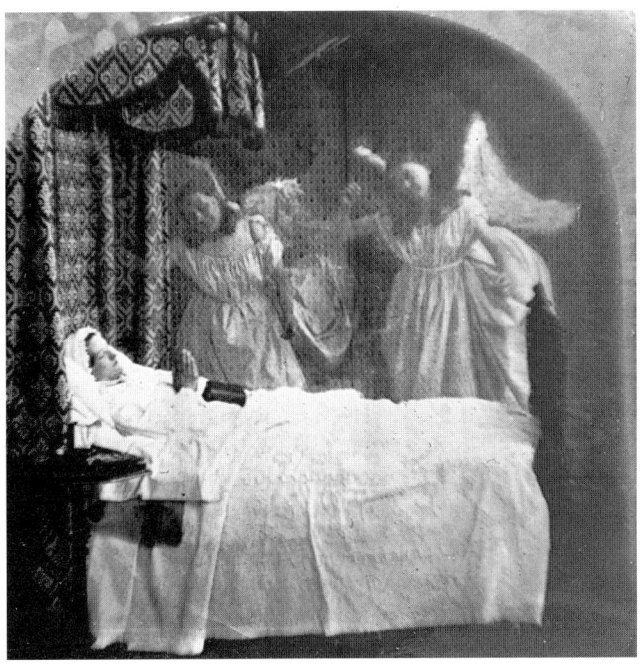

23 John Thomas, two angels beside a deathbed [n.d.], photograph.

Children's magazines, especially, often included illustrations of Christ, angels, and the devil. The pictorial evidence alone suggests that the injunctions of the Second Commandment were understood by Welsh Nonconformists in the nineteenth century to prohibit neither the visualization of religion *per se* nor the pictorialization of spiritual beings in particular. As was shown in Chapter 1, the Bible clearly demonstrates that the commandment did not censure all representations of things in heaven, for God had ordered the Israelites to embroider and sculpt images of cherubim. Illustrations reconstructing the appearance of these cherubim *in situ* appeared in Welsh Bible dictionaries and educational magazines of the denominations in the nineteenth century. John Thomas contrived an image of angels standing at what is presumably the deathbed of a believer to show the unseen comforters that attend the saint *in extremis* **(23)**. The human models are dressed in long white gowns, crowned with haloes, and fitted with wings. Thomas's conception of angels followed a tradition of representation that had persisted from early Christian art to the illustrations in the denominational literature of his own day.

The devil was invariably depicted as a spindly, dark figure with horns and tail, very often in the form of a cartoon caricature personifying evil. Satan was seldom represented as a real person in the illustrated literature of Welsh Nonconformity, with the notable exception of depictions of the temptation of

24 'Iesu Grist a'r Diafol' ['Jesus Christ and the Devil'], steelplate engraving, *Trysorfa y Plant* (1864).

25 Thomas Henry Thomas, 'Mary Jones and the Devil'
[n.d.], etching and aquatint, 10.2 × 7.

Christ in the wilderness **(24)**. In an undated etching entitled 'Mary Jones and the Devil', presumably depicting one of the supernatural encounters of the 'Welsh Seeress', the Welsh artist and Baptist Thomas Henry Thomas (1839–1915) followed the traditional stereotype **(25)**. Perhaps this is to be expected, since the Bible describes the devil only in terms of metaphor, such as a roaring lion (1 Peter 5: 8) and an angel of light (2 Corinthians 11: 14). It was in this latter guise that Evan Roberts conceived of the devil in a vision at a Swansea chapel during his mission there in 1905: Satan appeared as a silver seraph turning before him.[83] In other revival visions, Satan is described or implied as having anthropomorphic form, though the percipients do not relay details about his physical characteristics apart from generalities such as his darkness, demeanour, or personality, as in the old lady's vision above. This is not without precedent. Luther spoke of Satan in terms of his 'threatening attitude, exulting with a bitter and hellish sneer, and gnashing his teeth in fearful rage'.[84] The description resembles Roberts's vision of the devil's face in the bush.

The appearance of Christ in the visions was, in contrast, recounted in significantly greater detail. The disproportionate attention given to Him was, in one sense, a psychological symbol for His pre-eminence in the affections of the visionary, and of His superiority over the adversary. The Bible, after all, speaks of Satan as one who is not to be entertained (James 4: 7). The scant detail with which he is described in the visions reflects this depreciation in visual terms. Sensitivity to the symbolic connotations of inappropriate visualizations of Satan is illustrated by the following quotation from a letter to the editor of the Calvinistic Methodist magazine, the *Treasury*, in 1916. The correspondent relates an experience at one of the denomination's magic-lantern services:

> a picture of 'The Temptation' was shown, and Satan was represented as a huge black being bigger than the Saviour. Two children . . . were anxious to know how the devil could be bigger than their Master, whom, they had been taught, was all powerful . . . I know you would object to such a picture from your remarks in the Treasury, and yet I am told such slides are fairly common.[85]

The ability of visionaries to see Christ with comparatively greater clarity was not because the Bible provided them with a comprehensive picture of what He looked like. Indeed it gives no details of Christ's physical attributes beyond those prophesied of the Messiah by Isaiah, to which the members of the Island Place Mission Hall alluded in their vision: 'he hath no form nor comeliness; and when we shall see him, there is no beauty that we should desire him. He is despised and rejected of men; a man of sorrows, and acquainted with grief' (Isaiah 53: 2–3). Other sources offering a putative description were passed down from antiquity, derived from artefacts like the Turin Shroud and the Veil of Veronica, which, according to legend, had the image of Christ's face miraculously printed on it. Many such relics, because of the extreme reverence with which they were regarded, were carefully guarded by the Roman Catholic authorities and could not be seen by the public. In *The Face of Christ* (1933), C. C. Dobson describes how the artist Thomas Heaphy (1813–73) managed to ingratiate himself with members of the Roman Catholic hierarchy and thereby obtain an opportunity to see the veil and other such relics.[86] Heaphy devoted many years of his life to producing accurate copies of the earliest known likenesses of Christ, for example those on the cloths but principally the portraits in the frescos of the SS. Nereo ed Achilleo catacombs, of which he published unillustrated descriptions in the *Art Journal* during 1861. A critical appraisal of these so-called representations of Christ was published in Heaphy's *The Likeness of Christ* (1880).[87] Thomas Henry Thomas included an illustrated talk on the 'Representations of the Saviour in Art' in his syllabus of lectures delivered around 1870. A favourable appraisal of the discourse appeared in the *Somerset and Wiltshire Journal* of 4 February 1871:

Mr Thomas commenced with an observation on the necessity of prosecuting the study of his subject with seriousness, touching as it did upon matters of great religious importance. He then referred to the desire which had been manifested by every section of the church (except the Puritans and their successors, the Dissenters of England) to represent the Saviour in art. He then gave the results of a careful inquiry and investigation as to the probable existence of authentic portraits of the Saviour, the claims of which he considered rested on very insufficient evidence.[88]

The quest for an authentic portrait of Christ surfaces in articles published in evangelical newspapers many times towards the end of the nineteenth century and in the early years of the twentieth century.[89] In 1887 the *Evangelical Magazine* published a story in which reference was made to two pictures of Christ on the wall of a living-room. One was a reproduction of the Veil of Veronica, the other a photograph of a supposed likeness of Christ which, the author added, was familiar to the public.[90] This was most probably a reproduction of the portrait known as *The Only True Likeness of Our Saviour*, referred to by James Burns in his book *The Christ Face in Art* (1907). The image, which Burns regarded as probably a fourth-century forgery, was derived from a portrait carved on the face of an emerald by order of the emperor Tiberius (42 BC–AD 37).[91] The reproduction of this picture was accompanied by a printed extract of the letter by Publius Lentullus of Rome, to which reference is also made in Thomas Henry Thomas's lecture. In it the writer recounts what purported to be first-hand testimonies of Christ's physical appearance. John Thomas photographed the reproduction, perhaps with the intention of printing and distributing the image commercially. It is difficult to know whether there would have been a market for the image among Welsh Nonconformists **(26)**.

Just how true Nonconformists believed supposed likenesses to have been may have depended, perhaps surprisingly, on the theological persuasion of the individual regarding the historical authenticity of the Scriptures. The orthodox position had been challenged by the scholarship of German higher-critical theology since the mid nineteenth century, which suggested that many books of the Old and New Testaments had been written considerably later than traditionally believed.[92] Like the authenticity of the Gospels, the veracity of the 'true likeness' portraits depended on establishing that they had been made either while Christ was on earth or during the first century from the descriptions of those who had seen Him. Heaphy was quick to see the consequences that denying the one would have for the other:

But doubts have been recently disseminated as to there being any foundation for our conceptions respecting the personal resemblance of the Saviour. And when we find these doubts entertained and promulgated especially by a class of writers professedly denying the authenticity of the Gospels, we are forced to

26 'A True Likeness of "Our Saviour"', photograph by John Thomas of a photolithograph (nineteenth century, second half).

conclude that in denying the traditional Likeness, and asserting that it originated in the artistic imagination of the sixth and seventh centuries, they intend thereby to infer a doubt of the truth of other records concerning the person represented.[93]

Thus Heaphy saw a belief in the 'true likeness' as inextricably bound up with a belief in the historical reliability of the Scriptures. This parallels the way in which visions were used to defend orthodox views on theological issues. As was suggested earlier in the chapter, one of the reasons why the visions were readily accepted by many Nonconformists during the revival was because they provided evidence to confute those who did not believe in either the spiritual realities for which the revival stood or the revelatory nature of Christianity in general. By tolerating the portrayal of God the Son through the accounts of visions, and in prints and painting, Nonconformists broke the Reformation's prohibition on the representation of the Deity in accordance with the second commandment. Attitudes to representing Christ were, therefore, at best ambivalent and determined as much by theological expedience as correctness. The visionary portraits of Christ (exemplified by the visions of the old lady before the revival and that at Island Place after) followed the stereotype of the handsome Caucasian, with beard and parted hair, which was perpetuated by the 'true likeness' tradition. The reason for this was not only that their visual concept of Christ was informed by reproductions of the 'true likeness' such as the photogravures of paintings by the great masters in illustrated Bibles, but also possibly because it helped prove the authenticity of the 'true likeness' tradition, and thereby the authenticity of the Gospels. The visions of Christ also followed in the tradition of the 'true likeness' in that they were believed by at least some of the visionaries to be real encounters with the Saviour, and would therefore have been regarded as incontrovertible manifestations of what He looked like.

The equation of the representational with the physical presence of Christ also occurred in the experience of some who viewed paintings around the time of the revival. Jeremy Maas, tracing the international tour of Holman Hunt's third version of *The Light of the World* (1904), which began in 1905, described the mystical reverence with which some people, who had little exposure to painting, beheld the figure – as though they thought it the very presence of Christ Himself.[94] Similarly, an almost sentient faculty was attributed to the then famous painting of *Christus* by Herman Salomon (no known dates), exhibited at the Andrews' Building, Queen Street, Cardiff in July 1905. Like *The Light of the World*, a painting which enjoyed enormous popularity among evangelicals and Nonconformists, it is an example of the phenomenon of single-picture exhibitions that travelled around the country during the nineteenth and early twentieth centuries.[95] A description of the painting appeared in the *South Wales Daily News*:

> This is, to say the least, a remarkable picture. Christ is represented in half-length, full-face, with a golden light behind the head. The strange part of the picture is that the spectator at one moment sees the eyes closed and the next, uplooking. The transition is imperceptible, but the difference is as clear as possible. As one can penetrate behind the picture and prove the absence of any apparent mechanism or contrivance of any kind, the mystery is much enhanced.[96]

Among those who saw it were Nonconformist ministers; many of them, we are told, wrote appreciative letters about the work (presumably to the newspaper) declaring that they did not consider the painting to be irreverent in any way. Thus there was evidence, as Thomas Henry Thomas implied in his lecture, that evangelicals were abandoning their Puritan moorings in condoning the representation of Christ, a shift in outlook which was also demonstrated by Christ-representations in the visions.

The spiritual enigma surrounding a painting like *Christus*, as Burns realized, was attributable wholly to the artist's skill rather than to any consciousness residing in the figure of Christ itself. Speaking of a different example of eye movement he wrote: 'Many of the studies of the face of Christ represent Him as looking out of the canvas at the beholder. The result is that wherever you go, into whatsoever side or corner of the room, His eyes follow, they are ever upon you.'[97] The observation could provide an explanation for the curious phenomenon of Christ's eyes in the Island Place vision which appeared as though 'They watched every movement of the Pastor as he went to and fro, this way and that way on the rostrum'.

The visions also brought Christ out of the pages of biblical history into the present world, making Him a tangible part of everyday life. The visionaries of the revival could be said to be involved in the same endeavour as the advocates of the social gospel insofar as both wished to bring Christ out of the past and to integrate Christianity with the contemporary world (see Chapter 3). In this sense, the visions also correspond to the works of a number of European painters at the end of the nineteenth century who endeavoured to express the convictions of the social gospel pictorially. In *The Christ Face in Art*, Burns championed their cause and forwarded a manifesto of what he believed should be the objectives of modern religious art. The artist was to share in the process of integrating Christianity with the needs of the age. Christ was to be de-ecclesiasticized, taken out of the stained-glass window, as it were, and portrayed walking the streets of the poor and in the hovels of the stricken:

> We need the Gospel re-interpreted to us in terms of the present, and painted for us with such truth to modern needs, that when we think of Christ we shall not think of Him as One who lived in the long ago, and died on Calvary; nor of One who moved pitifully for three short years in distant Palestine with a halo around His head, and purple-clad disciples following in His train, but as One who to-day is near us in our need, living in our midst as actually as He lived in Palestine twenty centuries ago.[98]

Burns's manifesto is exemplified in Léon Lhermitte's (1844–1925) *Christ Visiting the Poor* (1905). Here Christ, dressed in the white robe with which He is associated in traditional biblical illustrations, stands in the centre of a group of French peasants in late-nineteenth-century costume. Paintings like those Burns referred to were often reproduced in chromolithographs and hung in Sunday schoolrooms. An illustration of Christ in the contemporary world that captured the imagination of Calvinistic Methodists in Wales was Harold Copping's

(1863–1932) *The Hope of the World* (*c*.1921), published in various sizes by the London Missionary Society **(Plate 2)**. The title was perhaps an oblique reference to Holman Hunt's painting which, incidentally, represented Christ in a contemporary context too. Copping illustrated Bible stories for children's books with a flair for historical and geographical verisimilitude which appears to have owed much to orientalist painters. The subject of *The Hope of the World* is essentially a contemporary interpretation of the text illustrated by the German painter Fritz von Uhde (1848–1911). In the 1880s Uhde had come under the influence of the modern Dutch school and produced an interpretation of the text 'Suffer little children to come unto me' (Luke 18: 16). Christ sits on a chair in the middle of a contemporary Dutch schoolroom surrounded by peasant children, such as the artist would himself have seen.[99] In Copping's painting Christ sits in a landscape; the children who gather around Him are in contemporary national costume.[100]

'Entombed – Jesus in the Midst' in the Visionary Tradition

Nicholas Evans's painting fulfils Burns's longing for a modern religious art that represented Christ as 'living in our midst as actually as He lived in Palestine twenty centuries ago'. In *Entombed – Jesus in the Midst*, Christ presences Himself with the poor and stricken, as in Lhermitte's painting – miners who deserve that description not only because of the normal rigours of their work and their living conditions, but also on account of the predicament confronting these trapped men. Evans represents Christ not in the white robes in which He appears in traditional Christian iconography and even in paintings where He is depicted in the context of the modern world, but dressed as the miners. (Correspondingly, in first-century Palestine He would have been clad in the same clothes as the Jews.) In this way Christ is fully de-ecclesiasticized.

Entombed could be readily deconstructed as a visualization of the social gospel's ethic. However, I would suggest that the visionary tradition supplies a more appropriate cultural and social context within which to read the image, since Evans's theological allegiance is to the separatist-moderate position of Pentecostalism which embraces the visionary tradition of the revivalists. The face of Christ in *Entombed* follows the stereotype of the 'true likeness'. One could be excused for interpreting it as a concession to the iconography of western religious painting, but it should be borne in mind that this conception of Christ is also informed, and indeed confirmed, by the visionary tradition of revivalism, most notably by the vision at the Island Place Mission Hall.[101] Therefore, if Evans's representation of Christ owes something to the conventions of traditional religious painting, it is by way of the visionary portrayals.

The tradition of visionary encounters with Christ provides a precedent for construing the figure in *Entombed* as a vision, either an imaginal vision seen in the mind of one or more of the miners, or an external vision, in which Christ is apparently as substantial as objects in the material world. An interpretation of the figure as a vision of Christ is encouraged by certain concomitant details. The keys He holds out in His right hand would seem to allude to the apostle John's vision of the Son of Man on Patmos: 'I am he that liveth, and was dead; and, behold, I am alive for evermore, Amen; and have the keys of hell and death' (Revelation 1: 18). The apostle John's description of the glorified form of Christ refers to Christ's head and hair being 'white like wool, and white as snow' (Revelation 1: 14), while he likens Christ's countenance to the sun shining in its strength (Revelation 1: 16). It is arguable whether Evans has adapted these characteristics to his representation of Christ. His hair is streaked with white (as in the Island Place vision) and His face is pale – inherent physical qualities perhaps, or from the illumination of the lamp on His helmet and the one he holds in His left hand. The manner of representation in the painting is not, however, sufficiently insistent for us to conclude that it draws upon the details of Christ's appearance described by John.

The interpretations of the figure of Christ in *Entombed* either as a vision or as a figurative symbol of His 'being near us in our need' (to quote Burns again) do not have to be mutually exclusive. There is a sense in which every vision of Christ is a symbol of His nearness, inasmuch as it is a visual token of His perpetual spiritual presence with the believer. The painting can accommodate both meanings because the composition or title of the work does not delimit its narrative. The simultaneous presence of aspects such as the possible allusions to visionary appearances of Christ in the New Testament, and the painting's resemblance to late-nineteenth-century religious painting makes the work equivocal.

In terms of Evans's experience of artistic inspiration, the visionary content of *Entombed* and his later works is unambiguous. His conception of the way in which he visualizes his paintings prior to their execution corresponds to the way in which visionaries experience their visions. The act of painting too, he believes, is facilitated by divine intervention. In these respects Evans's understanding of creative experience reflects a revivalist and Pentecostal theology of the Holy Spirit and spiritual gifts (*charismata*), of which inspired acts are one manifestation.

5
Images of God: Inspiration and Instrumentality

What artists call inspiration – described by one psychologist as the 'unusual [capacity] to perform without knowledge and education' a creative act – is often a complex psychological process.[1] As Ernst Kris and Albert Rothenberg have shown, the idea of 'inspiration' is ultimately created by personal, cultural, and historical factors. With Nicholas Evans, these factors include the revivalist tradition of Welsh Nonconformity and his Pentecostal mind-set. Evans interprets his creative experience not according to a natural hypothesis but with recourse to the concept of *theopneustia* (divine inspiration); he believes himself to be a channel for the direct enabling of God. He also describes it in terms of a visionary encounter and revelation, and of divine inspiration comparable to that experienced by Pentecostal preachers.

Painting and Preaching

Since antiquity, the term 'inspiration' has designated what Rothenberg defined as 'special conditions of creation' in which creations appear to spring all at once from their creators.[2] It is with this extraordinary mode of creativity that Evans identifies himself. He speaks of the apparent effortlessness with which he conceives his paintings: 'I look at a board four by four feet, and as I look at the board I can see the figures on the board; I can see my pictures complete.'[3] On other occasions Evans has referred to his experiences of visualization as unsummoned, somewhat surprising; they are spontaneous, coming upon the artist all at once. It is, he remarked, like cheating, as though he were painting by numbers.[4] The analogy implies that he has been supplied with a preordained pattern that has only to be followed for the image to be realized. What Evans suggests he 'sees' is a picture projected on to the white ground of the support, perceived with an inner eye. It is a visionary blueprint foretelling and directing the outcome of his labour. Not only do the visualizations or pictorial ideas come without prior consideration and effort but also in great numbers and quick succession.[5]

Evans stands in a visionary tradition that goes back through the history of Welsh Pentecostalism to the 1904–5 revival (see Appendix 4). Evan Roberts considered his visions to be one manifestation of a gift of prophecy, which he believed he had received as a result of baptism of the Spirit on two occasions during 1904.[6] He believed that his own preaching could be thus inspired as a result of this gift. As Awstin (the *Western Mail*'s chief reporter on the revival) reported: 'Roberts, who speaks in Welsh, opens his discourse by saying he does not know what he is going to say, but that when he is in communion with the Holy Spirit the Holy Spirit will speak, and he will be the medium of His wisdom.'[7] The gift was further expressed in the content and purpose of his preaching.[8] The idea of the prophet-preacher like Roberts was often assumed as a model for Pentecostal ministers. Pentecostals, particularly in the early years of the movement, had a somewhat different evaluation of the qualifications for the ministry from mainstream Nonconformist denominations. The latter insisted that a man's calling to the office of minister must be substantiated by, among other things, the possession of the requisite intellectual and oratorical abilities and supplemented by theological training. His sermons were, similarly, to be the product of diligent study and arduous preparation.[9] Pentecostals by contrast regarded the baptism of the Spirit as the sole requirement to preach. Cyril Williams has observed that even today, in some Pentecostal assemblies, pastors enter the pulpit without a prepared sermon, believing that they will be led by a direct and spontaneous 'word from the Lord' given to them as they speak.[10] Evans adopts the idea of the inspired preacher or prophet when he describes the divine enabling:

> I am allowing God . . . to express himself through me, through my fingers. It's a way the preacher has . . . He's in the pulpit . . . and he gives himself over to be controlled, like a musical instrument, now, like a piano being played on by the master musician; and, it's God is playing through him the music [*sic*], the sermon is coming through the preacher to the congregation; he's in touch, he's in tune with the infinite. And I'm the same, I feel God is painting through me . . . through my hands, through my vision, through my appreciation of what I am.[11]

As a preacher himself Evans believes that he speaks 'as he is led', entirely dependent on the Holy Spirit to fill him with words.[12] Preparatory notes, drafts, or a verbatim manuscript are therefore both unnecessary and even a hindrance to the delivery of a sermon. Evans claims that God paints through him in the same way.[13] His paintings are executed spontaneously and directly on to the hardboard support without the intervention of compositional studies or preparatory drawings.[14] Inspiration therefore comes, in painting as in preaching, during the performance rather than in the premeditation of the act. Like Evan Roberts, he regards himself as merely a channel through whom God expresses Himself.[15]

One can recognize in this idea a Christianized version of Plotinism as adapted in the Renaissance, in which the artist becomes the inspired man, a pencil in the hand of God.[16] There is no reason to believe that Evans has consciously adapted his idea of inspiration from these topoi; long and frequent usage has made them commonplace metaphors for the enigma of creativity and the imagination.[17] There is also the alternative tradition of artistic *theopneustia*, which is more immediate to Evans and which enables him to short-circuit the ideas of inspiration in classical antiquity.

Bezaleel and Evans

In an article on Evans which appeared in the Apostolic Church's magazine *Riches of Grace*, the divine inspiration received by the Old Testament artisan Bezaleel was identified as a precedent for Evans's own experience.[18] Kris and Otto Kurz believed that Greek ideas of inspiration were themselves influenced by this biblical model.[19] The baptism or filling of the Holy Spirit which the artisans experienced resulted in a type of artistic inspiration that varies in many important respects from what Evans claims to experience. In the Bible, the filling with the Spirit of God is not for the purpose of artistic creativity alone. In both the Old and New Testaments God often filled individuals with the Holy Spirit to enable them to perform particularly difficult tasks that were beyond the scope of their natural abilities.[20] Most of the references to Bezaleel and Aholiab are found in Exodus chapters 31 to 40, which records the account of the construction of the Tabernacle. The designs for the tent and the several pieces of elaborate furniture and utensils it contained had been conveyed to Moses on Mount Sinai with the attendant command that they be executed exactly as prescribed (Exodus 25).

God marked out, commissioned, and empowered Bezaleel for the task. Presumably Bezaleel was chosen because he was already renowned as a competent craftsman, possibly Israel's finest, and had therefore shown a potential for doing the job well. Indeed, it was a prerequisite for anyone who wished to work on the construction of the Tabernacle that he possess some degree of skill as a craftsman (Exodus 35: 10). God not only called but also equipped and enabled Bezaleel to perform the task, filling him with His Spirit for the purpose of artistic endeavour (Exodus 31: 3–5). Thus Bezaleel possessed a natural talent for craftsmanship, which on ordinary occasions could be utilized without the special divine assistance. The effect of being filled with the Spirit was to heighten rather than to supply the skill *in toto*.

The practical outworking of Bezaleel's filling with the Spirit was the reception of skill, ability, and knowledge or, as the Authorized Version translates it, 'wisdom . . . understanding . . . knowledge' (Exodus 31: 3): 'wisdom', that is an expert knowledge of the techniques of craftsmanship and the ability to employ them; 'understanding', that is an ability to make deductions, to solve any problem that may arise in the course of the work; and 'knowledge', a storehouse of expertise which grows with experience.[21] Bezaleel was thus endowed with an ability far beyond his experience and years. The texts suggest that the special dispensation of the Spirit was given to Bezaleel once, for a specific occasion, and not for all time. As with other instances of filling with the Spirit in the Bible, the empowering lasted only as long was necessary. Evans, conversely, appears to claim a continuous enabling. Nowhere are we given the impression that Bezaleel's hand was guided by God, that he was merely a tool in God's hand. On the contrary, all that followed on from divine infusion was an extraordinary enhancement of his creative faculties. In comparing Evans to Bezaleel, the Apostolic Church has syncretized the Renaissance idea of inspiration with its theology of Old Testament infusion. Like the Plotinic conception, this view of artistic inspiration, as exemplified in Evans, also has its roots in cultic traditions of the Bible, more specifically in the Pentecostal understanding of the New Testament manifestation of the baptism of the Spirit and the gift of speaking in tongues.

Talking Pictures

Common factors between speaking in tongues and artistic inspiration were identified in a lecture on the gift of tongues given by the Welsh Nonconformist minister J. Cynddylan Jones in 1877. Cynddylan Jones argued that the inspiration of the biblical artisans Bezaleel and Aholiab was only one instance in which God spiritually transfigures the abilities of men beyond their native condition:

> The Holy Spirit, it is admitted, ennobles other faculties; then why not the faculty to speak with other tongues? He filled Bezaleel and Aholiab, and made them skilful in all things pertaining to the efficient workmanship of the Tabernacle. And I believe he still endows men with the knowledge necessary to the successful prosecution of Art.[22]

Here tongues is understood as *xenoglossolalia*, the faculty to speak foreign languages fluently 'without undergoing the drudgery of learning them', which was manifested among the disciples on the day of Pentecost (Acts 2: 3).[23] Pentecostals do not concur that the gift represented an ennobling of the faculty to learn foreign languages. On the contrary, they believe that speaking in tongues has nothing to do with education or linguistic ability but is, rather, the evidence of a miraculous spiritual endowment.[24]

The possession of abilities not born of intellect or study is an accepted phenomenon among Pentecostals. It is evident in what W. R. Jones classified as spiritual gifts of illumination and communication. In both kinds of gifts God, it is said, inspires and reveals to the Spirit-baptized believer unlearned supernatural capacities.[25] A parallel between tongues-speaking as a supernaturally endowed, fully matured ability and other manifestations of unlearned creative expression can be seen in relation to T. B. Barratt. He was a notable Pentecostal minister, who as well as being able to speak in tongues, experienced divine inspiration in the form of songs and poetry. Of these gifts he wrote:

> The most beautiful of all was *the singing* – when the inspiration reached its climax I burst out in a wonderful baritone solo. I never heard the tune before, and I did not understand the words but it was a most beautiful language, so smooth and easy to pronounce . . . It seemed to me the rhythm in the verses and chorus, was as perfect as it is possible to be . . . I have recited poem after poem, that were given me instantaneously by the Spirit.[26]

In a similar way, Evans regards his ability to paint as neither learned nor cultivated by practice, but received fully developed. His view of creativity as being aided by a

Plate 1 Nicholas Evans, *Entombed – Jesus in the Midst* (1974), oil on canvas, 137.2 × 91.

Plate 2 Harold Copping, 'The Hope of the World' (*c.*1921), chromo lithograph (London Missionary Society).

Plate 3 'The Broad and the Narrow Way', chromo lithograph by Charles Montague, designed by Charlotte Reihlen, painted by Herr Schacher (London: Morgan & Scott; S. W. Partridge & Co. (nineteenth century, second half)).

Plate 4 'The Gospel Ship' (nineteenth century, second half), chromo lithograph, designed by 'Hy P' (Cardiff: A. M'Lay & Co. Ltd.).

Plate 5 Nicholas Evans, *Pit Closure – Miners Coming Up for the Last Time* (1977), oil on board, 122 × 122.

power outside himself would seem to be further justified by his lack of any formal training in art. His ability has not, according to him, been the product of human tuition or any application in the acquisition of skills. Painting for Evans is not a discipline but a gift that has been given – not as a capacity to be developed over a period of time by arduous labour, but already fully matured.[27]

Pentecostals believe that speaking in tongues, like prophecy, is a

> manifestation of the mind of the Spirit of God employing human speech organs. When man is speaking with tongues, his mind, intellect, understanding are quiescent. It is the faculty of God that is active. Man's will, certainly, is active, and his spirit, and his speech organs; but the mind that is operating is the mind of God through the Holy Spirit.[28]

Here we have a lingual model for human instrumentality analogous to the concept of the artist as the 'stylus of God'. In both cases the recipient is simply a channel through whom God expresses Himself. The illusion of instrumentality is at least partly due to what other commentators have distinguished as the strong sense of compulsion felt by the recipient to practise the gift; it is as though he or she were possessed by, rather than the possessor of, the gift.[29] Cynddylan Jones believed that this 'spiritual impulse' was characteristic of tongues-speaking at Pentecost, and made the disciples incapable of restraining speech (Acts 2: 4).[30] Evans has remarked on several occasions on the intense, almost pathological urge he feels to exercise his gift of painting – the 'divine madness' – which he views in terms of a motivation distinct from himself.[31] The impression he has of being the channel of an external agent is further endorsed by the consummate ease with which he feels able to paint. Similarly, the tongues-speaker's fluency in his or her newly acquired 'language' encourages the belief that it is God and not the individual who structures the content.[32]

A correspondence between the formal characteristics of Evans's paintings and *glossolalia* (the ability to speak in unlearned unknown languages) can also be established. This is with reference to what W. J. Samarin described as the repetition of the same basic sounds recurring in a particular *glossa*.[33] Within the particular tongue or language in which the recipient is assumed to be speaking can be perceived reiterating patterns of intonations, stresses, and, Jim Davidson added, 'the same sounds' or 'group of sounds, like a recurring phrase'.[34] In Evans's work there is a corresponding economy of elements and formal patterns which are repeated throughout the body of his work. Chief among these are their format (in all but a few cases four-foot square), colour (almost invariably black and white), and subject-matter (usually scenes of coal-mining).

Within the common format there is a recurrence of a limited range of compositional devices undergirding the arrangement of the painting. The figures and objects in foreground, middle distance, and background are arranged parallel to the picture surface and hence to one another. There is consequently very little perspective in the works, the elements appearing to recede only by virtue of falling one behind the other and ascending the picture-plane. Many of the compositions are made up of elements – faces or figures – repeated in horizontal or diagonal rows parallel to one another, crowding the surface of the painting, as in, for instance, *Pit Closure – Miners Coming Up for the Last Time* (1977) **(Plate 5)**.

Not only is the colour of the paintings uniform but their general tonality is also consistent in density. This is derived from the constancy of the colour saturation (the pigment applied straight from the tube), and of the fixed ratio between black and white in each work. The manner in which Evans has applied the paint, using only fingers and rags, is also restricted, and the lexicon of mark-making, the vocabulary of gesture, line, and pattern he uses to denote objects, remains essentially static. This means that an object is usually rendered in one painting in essentially the same way as it is in another. The language of representation is thus generally constant or reiterative. The variety of represented objects is limited, owing largely to the narrowly defined subject-matter. For example, the landscape in the background of scenes on the surface of the mine invariably comprises several of the following elements: a patchwork of rolling hills in the far distance, overshadowed by a cushion of dark cloud that traverses the horizon, in front of which are a trio of coal-tips clustered together, together with colliery buildings, the pit-head, and rows of miners' cottages. These occur over and over again in a similar arrangement throughout the body of the work. With so many constants, the considerations and decisions Evans has to make in the creation of each painting are arguably far fewer than those encountered by many other artists. This would facilitate speed of execution and go some way to explaining his prodigious output, just as the repetition of phrases and the phonemic economy of tongues facilitate fluency of speech.

The facility to paint is also enhanced by the absence of certain technical considerations which might otherwise slow down the process of execution or make it more difficult to resolve the image successfully. Traditional single-point or multi-point perspective is omitted, the only exception being some of the colliery buildings, which are represented in oblique projection. In such instances, however, one of the sides of the building is maintained parallel to the picture-plane and at right angles to the horizontal, which means that only one dimension has to be considered in perspective and there is no need to calculate the illusion of the convergence of their parallel lines. By filling the foreground and obscuring the middle distance with figures, Evans has obviated the need to devise a means to effect a successful transition of the foreground, through the middle distance, into the background. Compositional complexity and decision-making have been reduced by crowding the picture-plane with a single repeated element – usually faces – knit together in parallel rows from the top left to the bottom right of the painting. One could say that, by a process of adding successive rows of faces, the composition could extend indefinitely either way, rather like knitting. The cumulative effect of repetition, a fixed formula of representation, and the avoidance of certain technical difficulties would contribute to Evans's sense of his ability coming easily to him, a phenomenon which he, like the tongues-speaker, attributes to divine enabling.

Evans's gift of painting and the Pentecostal gift of tongues are also analogous in their improvisatory nature. Evans begins his paintings by 'doodling', a procedure which is not as absent-minded as the epithet may imply. He manipulates black paint over a white ground, matching the accidental black marks on the surface of the board with salient features of the miners that congregate his imagination.[35] In the same way novices are sometimes initiated into tongues-speaking by being told to play with a word, often 'hallelujah', repeating it over and over. As they gradually increase the speed of utterance the sounds trip over themselves to become a jumble, as it were, of Hebraic-sounding syllables.[36] Out of this improvisation, as in Evans's doodles with paint, come forms suggesting meaning. These constitute, in the case of tongues-speaking, an apparent language, that is, sounds like those of a real language, appearing to have syntax, recurring phrases, and a lexicon, though their meaning may be entirely foreign to the speaker. In the case of Evans's painting, they constitute perceived objects.[37]

Evans has referred to his painting as an act of worship.[38] In private devotion and prayer, tongues-speaking is used as a means of worship. In this respect a further analogy can be drawn with the devotional function of *glossolalia*. Conceivably, the benefit that the practitioner derives from this is the emotional release that arises out of what Walter Hollenweger called this 'non-intellectual form of worship'. This results in a refreshed constitution and closer communion with God.[39] Like tongues, the content of Evans's paintings is not intrinsic to the act of worship. With the former, the practitioner does not understand what is being said, although presumably he or she believes that the *glossa* is conveying praise. In Evans's painting, the subject-matter in all but a few cases is not overtly religious. For this reason his idea of his painting as an alternative to worshipping God through song, as expressed in the title of his radio broadcast 'A Kind of Singing', is unhelpful. In hymns the principal means of worship is the doxological content, together with one's understanding of it. Evans's use of painting as a means of worship does not, however, lie in its intellectual content. Rather, it is in the spirit in which the paintings are executed, following the injunction of Colossians chapter 3, verse 23. In this way painting with an eye to pleasing God with the best of one's ability becomes an act of worship. Worship also consists in offering or giving back to God His gifts to be used and sanctified by Him.[40] A sense of worship is also experienced, as with tongues-speaking, because of the assumed operation of the Holy Spirit in the creation of the work. Through his painting Evans contacts divinity. God is 'speaking' through the medium of pigment and gesture. It is in the realization of being a channel of this divine activity that the sense of reverence may be experienced; painting, like tongues-speaking used in personal prayer, enhances Evans's communion with the Godhead.

Evans's belief in the possibility of art as a directly inspired gift invests the paintings with an intrinsic religious significance. For him they represent images made by the invisible God. By dint of their purportedly supernatural origin and mode of reception they perpetuate and make tangible the Nonconformist visionary tradition. Moreover, in Evans's perception of creativity, work and worship, and the sacred and mundane are fused. These concepts are also associated in the culture and imagery of coal-mining and Nonconformity during the nineteenth and early twentieth centuries (see Chapters 7 and 8). Likewise, the identification of Evans's experience of creativity with that of the Tabernacle's artisans evokes the fusion of contemporary and Old Testament times. This fusion was at the heart of national, Nonconformist, and political consciousness in Wales especially during that period (see Chapter 6).

6
Cymro and Gomero, Pit and Pithom: The Bible in Wales

On the first page of O. M. Edwards's (1858–1920) *Hanes Cymru* (1895), below a watercolour landscape of *Eryri* by the Nonconformist minister S. Maurice Jones (1853–1932), the author placed a biblical text taken from Moses's blessing of the twelve tribes of Israel in Deuteronomy chapter 33. For Edwards, Wales, tokenly represented by the painting, evoked Israel and was thus heir to its spiritual prosperity.[1] This coupling was one expression of a more general identification established between the two peoples which assumed a particular intensity and pervasive influence around the turn of the twentieth century. This was at the height of the so-called Celtic Renaissance and a period of burgeoning national prestige. The association connected the history, land, language, and culture of the Welsh and the Jews, enabling the Celtic race, and Nonconformists in particular, to partake of a lineage stretching back into the annals of the Old Testament. This assumed kinship enabled Wales to lay claim to the special attention of God; this, some asserted, was especially evident in the blessing of recurrent religious revivals. For many, the religious revival of 1904–5, with its visions, prophecies of the end-time, and accompanying outpouring of God's Spirit, clearly represented evidence of divine favour. Wales at the beginning of the twentieth century was considered the context for the consummation of biblical history.

Wales and Israel

In 1901 Ernest Rhys remarked:

> It is not a mere ingenious idea that the Welsh people have felt at times in their history that it had a very strange parallel in the history of the Jews. There is even a spiritual affinity between the two races that lies deeper than we know; and when a Welshman thinks of the Holy Land he is very apt to think of it as another Wales in the East.[2]

A year later J. H. Edwards suggested specific correspondences between the chronicles of the two peoples. The Jews had been defeated in battle, taken captive, exploited, persecuted, and their land occupied; the Welsh had known a comparable subjugation and suppression of national character from the Egyptians, Assyrians, and Babylonians personified in the 'enemy across the border'. The Old Testament Israelites had experienced periods of religious declension and revival. It was a pattern of fortunes analogous to Wales's religious history from the proto-Protestant era of the early Celtic Church, through the years of superstition and idolatry during the Elizabethan period to the Methodist awakening of the eighteenth century. By the end of the nineteenth century, the fire of both the eighteenth-century and 1859 revivals had dissipated to a smouldering ember; in the absence of the restraining influence of spiritual enthusiasm, irreligion and immorality had become a widespread malaise (see Chapter 7). Nevertheless, Edwards believed that the 'nation now stood on the threshold of the promised land' whose milk and honey were spiritual prosperity. (His optimism was uncannily prophetic of the reignition of religious fervour in 1904–5.) The parallelism between the two nations, he considered, made Wales a special repository of God's blessing and had elected the Celt 'to carry on the work of the Hebrew as bearers of a message to the hearts of the people'. In particular, Wales would be an instrument of instruction and rebuke against the excesses of materialism to which England might succumb.[3] The potency of its messengers even warranted the most elevated comparison. As Lucius Morgan remarked: 'probably not since the Hebrew prophets fulminated in Israel has so powerful a ministry been heard in any land as that which the awe-struck mountains of Wales echoed and re-echoed for more than a hundred years'.[4]

Another manifestation of the 'spiritual affinity' between the Celt and the Hebrew was evident, according to Wynne Evans, when one 'remembered how adapted to the Cymro's mind is the Old Testament'. It was not, he considered, 'difficult to believe that the Welshman and Hebrew are brothers in the wilderness'. Further to this:

> There is much again in common between the Welsh and Hebrew languages, and I have it on good authority that our Welsh translation of the Old Testament Scriptures comes nearer to the Hebrew original than almost any other. Welsh hymnology also bears a closer resemblance to the style and spirit of the Book of Psalms than any other known to me.[5]

The origins of the notion of linguistic kinship go back to the eighteenth century. Following a thesis of philological comparability, Theophilus Evans (1694–1767) in his *Drych y Prif Oesoedd* [A View of the Primitive Ages] (1716) posited the genesis of the Welsh language at the time of the destruction of Babel. In the confusion of languages that ensued, Gomer, son of Japheth, son of Noah, received the Welsh tongue and became the progenitor of the Celtic race. As practical proof of this certainty he asserted: 'We might refer to the name by which we are generally known. (*Cymro*,) Which plainly proves our origin; for there is little difference between *Cymro* and *Gomero*, as it is easy to observe.'[6] In support of this proposition, Evans appealed to the work of the seventeenth-century French philologist Paul Pezron (1639–1706). Pezron's investigations had shown, so he thought, that the *Celtae* had arisen in Asia Minor, near the ark on Mount Ararat.[7] Evans and Pezron thus ascribed to the Welsh and their language an impressive pedigree, which gave them reason to believe that, like the Hebrews, they were a singular and elect people. Glanmor Williams concluded that 'These concepts of the Welsh people and their language as the objects of special concern on the part of the Deity were to be more than ordinarily congenial in the intensely religious climate of the nineteenth century'.[8] The linguistic identification of Wales and the biblical world extended beyond putative philological similarities. The persistent exposure of the Welsh congregations to the Bible during the nineteenth century, wrote E. T. Davies, meant that 'the words and phrases of the Bible were so well known as to pass into current speech'.[9] The language of their prayers and preaching was embroidered with the phrases, verb endings, pronouns, and syntax of the Authorized Version of the Bible. This mannerism invested their speech with, at best, a godly style and, at worst, pious cant.

Rhys's conception of the Holy Land as 'another Wales in the East' acquired a visual manifestation in the form of a map published by the Sunday School Union of Great Britain around the beginning of the twentieth century. The map was entitled *Gwlad Canaan; Ar Gynllun Gogledd a Deheudir Cymru i Blant* [Land of Canaan: On a Plan of North and South Wales for Children]. It showed the geographical location of the lands of the twelve tribes of Israel in Old Testament times and the regions into which Palestine was divided in New Testament times, set within the boundary of Wales **(27)**. Together with rivers, seas, and mountain ranges, *Gwlad Canaan* also illustrated the disposition of Israel's lands in relation to the twelve counties that comprised mainland Wales. Each land connected with the name of a county, for example the land of Benjamin was twinned with Flintshire, Judah with Carmarthenshire, and Zebulun with Denbighshire. As far as possible the principal towns and cities of the Holy Land matched those towns and villages of Wales situated in roughly the same position. Thus Jerusalem corresponds to 'Llandilo Fawr', Nazareth to Dolgellau, and Hebron to Swansea. The map would have enabled Welsh children to comprehend better the relative size and relations of the two countries which, as Archdeacon Howell observed, bore 'a striking similarity . . . in their general formation and their dimensions'.[10]

Travellers to the Holy Land further cultivated the geographical identification of Palestine and Wales. Arthur Penrhyn Stanley, for one, described Hebron as follows: 'The hills, except where occupied by vineyards and olive groves are covered with disjointed rocks and grass, such as brought back dim visions of Wales.'[11] This affinity was also evident in topographic engravings of Wales and Palestine from the second half of the nineteenth century. For example, some of those in *Welsh Pictures* (1892), a collection of illustrated essays by historians and Nonconformist ministers on the country's most picturesque scenery, and *Y Bibl Darluniadol* [The Illustrated Bible] (1844). The latter featured a number of engravings of prominent places mentioned in the Bible.[12] The publications' respective illustrations of 'The Pass of Llanberis' and 'Ebal a Garizim' [Ebal and Garizim] (two mountains referred to in Deuteronomy chapter 27) depicted dramatic landscapes which shared features such as imposing craggy mountains and outcrops, and a bleak uninhabited terrain through which

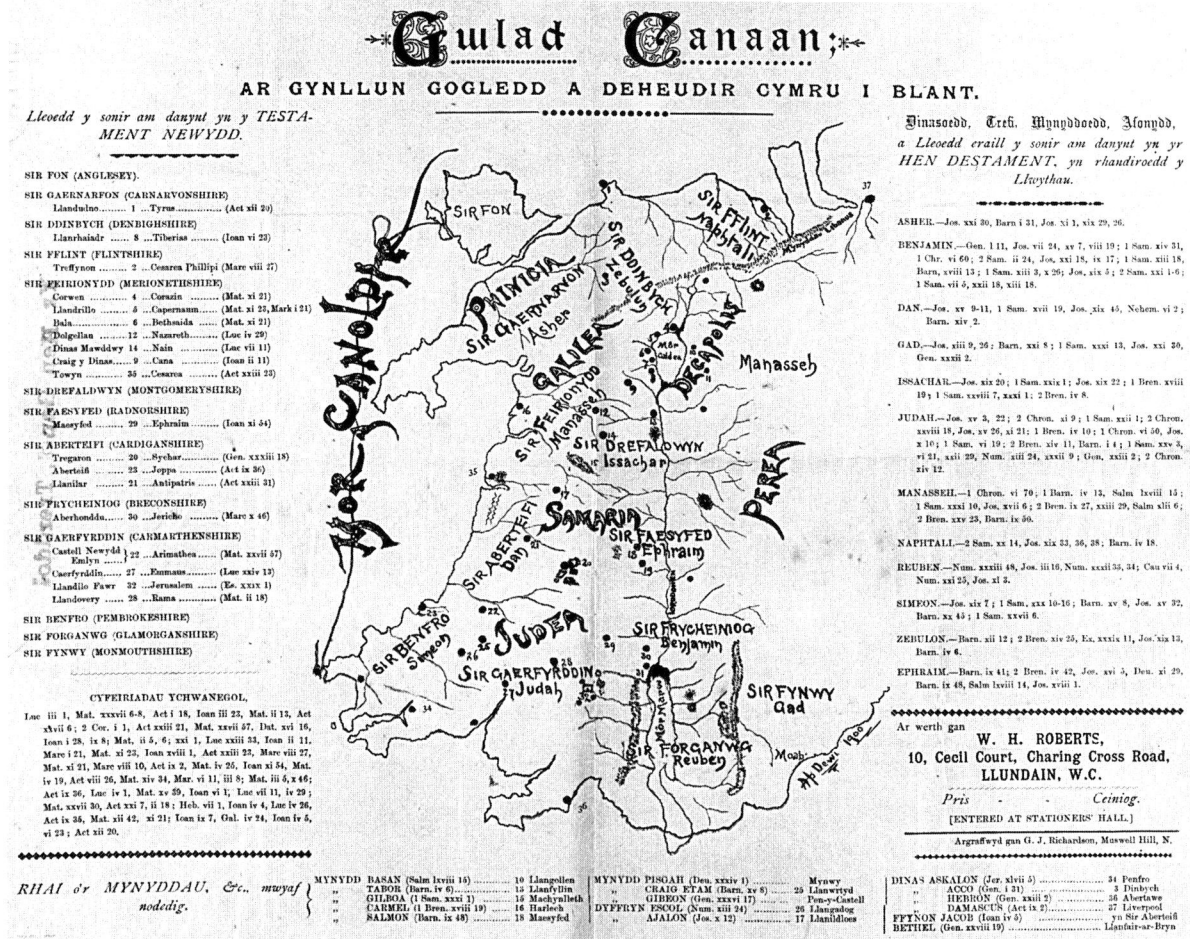

27 *Gwlad Canaan; Ar Gynllun Gogledd a Deheudir Cymru i Blant* (nineteenth century, second half), lithograph, 29.4 × 37.4, Sunday School Union of Great Britain.

travellers journey **(28, 29)**. Another example is an engraving entitled 'Y Nahr Quades yn Mynydd Libanus' [The Nahr Quades in Mount Lebanon] which accompanied a commentary on Psalm 1, and an engraving of 'Pont Aberglaslyn' **(30, 31)**. The former alludes to part of the third verse of the Psalm, 'And he shall be like a tree planted by the rivers of water'. The latter provides an extensive setting surrounding the subject of the image, the bridge. In both pairs, the images' commonality is based on the physical attributes of the countries' geography and the aesthetic idiom into which both had been translated — the picturesque, classical, and topographic traditions of composition and selection.[13] Furthermore, the tendency of the medium to generality, and the absence of architectural and costume details, divest the landscapes of peculiar attributes that might otherwise have distinguished time and

28 'Ebal a Garizim', steelplate engraving, *Y Bibl Darluniadol* (London: Simpkin, Marshall and Co. (1844)).

29 'The Pass of Llanberis', steelplate engraving, *Welsh Pictures* (1892).

30 'Y Nahr Quades Yn Mynydd Libanus', steelplate engraving, *Y Bibl Darluniadol* (London: Simpkin, Marshall and Co.; Caerleon: A. H. Hughes (1844)).

31 'Pont Aberglaslyn', steelplate engraving, *Welsh Pictures* (1892).

place. Deprived of the caption, the illustration of the coast between Tyre and Sidon could pass for a topographical rendering of many a wave-beaten cliff face on the seaboard of Wales. The similarities in the contour and proportion of the mountains Ararat and Snowdon gave rise to a visual analogy for the phonetic assonance between '*Cymro*' and '*Gomero*' **(32, 33)**. In this way, the putative site of the *Celtae*'s origin had a permanent memorial in the Welsh landscape. Likewise, an Egyptian pyramid, as depicted in an illustration accompanying the book of Exodus, had more than a passing resemblance to a south Wales coal-tip **(34)**.

Tabernacle – Temple – Chapel

The map of Wales at the end of the nineteenth century bore a striking resemblance to *Gwlad Canaan; Ar Gynllun Gogledd a Deheudir Cymru i Blant*. Many towns and villages had come to adopt the names of places referred to in the Bible, such as Bethel, Saron, and Nebo. These were taken from the chapels around which the communities had developed. Bethesda, Caernarvonshire, for example, was the biblical name of the

32 'Mynydd Ararat' ['Mount Ararat'], steelplate engraving, *Y Bibl Darluniadol* (London: Simpkin, Marshall and Co.; Caerleon: A. H. Hughes (1844)).

33 John Sell Cotman, *Snowdon* (*c.*1809–10), water-colour, 23.7 × 36.4.

34 'Pyramidiau yr Aipht' ['Pyramids of Egypt'], steelplate engraving, *Y Bibl Darluniadol* (London: Simpkin, Marshall and Co.; Caerleon: A. H. Hughes (1844)).

the Calvinistic Methodist chapel established there in 1820.[14] During the nineteenth century Nonconformists had names derived from one or more biblical characters and places, reviving the practice of their Puritan ancestors. The forenames of religious leaders and principal characters of the Old Testament, such as Ezekiel, Hezekiah, Jeremiah, and Zechariah, were a popular choice, and apposite in the case of those who entered the ministry in later life. Names like Caleb Morris (1800–65), the notable Congregationalist minister, conjoin the distant and historically resonant world of the Old Testament with the present and mundane. Perhaps the most notable example in Wales at the turn of the century was that of the Calvinistic Methodist minister Seth Joshua (1859–1925) whose affiliation with Old Testament worthies was doubly sure. As Patricia Hanks and Flavia Hodges have observed, 'A person's given name is a badge of cultural identity. Cultural identity is closely allied to religious identity.'[15] The use of Hebraic names signified the Nonconformists' desire to establish a continuity between Old Testament culture and their own. The conflation was a particular manifestation of a much more widespread identification between the two cultures which was expressed, among other ways, through the conception and construction of Nonconformity's places of worship.

The biblical names given to many chapels were also a means of conveying cultural and religious identity. The name Ebenezer referred to a memorial stone set up by

Samuel in thanksgiving to God after his defeat of the Philistines (1 Samuel 7: 12). It was commonly adopted by both chapels and Nonconformists. The application of biblical names is coterminous with the evolution of the chapel from domestic building to architectural edifice at the beginning of the nineteenth century.[16] The setting-up of the names of Old and New Testament places, such as Carmel and Calvary, on the façades of classical chapels endowed the buildings with a biblical ethos, and thereby counterbalanced the pagan associations of the architecture.[17] Likewise on Gothic chapels, these place names would have served to underline Nonconformity's independence from the Anglican and Roman Catholic Churches. The latter favoured the names of the Godhead, apostles, evangelists, the Virgin Mary, and the saints of their respective traditions. Nonconformists did not hold to the practice of canonizing saints or venerating them by means of icons, reliquaries, festivals, and dedicated churches. Consequently, very few chapels were named after saints, and then only the most distinguished persons associated with the New Testament, such as St Paul and St James. Moreover, it appears to have been only the Methodist Church which countenanced the practice. This reflected Methodism's historical and cultural antecedents in the Established Church from which it had begun to secede in 1797. Although they had no qualms about naming themselves after Old Testament characters, Nonconformists did not call their chapels by these names, possibly for the same reasons they had refused to adopt the appellation of saints. It was more sensible to associate them with localities, since chapels were places and not people.[18] Thus, the adoption of biblical place names signified not only Nonconformity's bibliocentricity and kinship with the Old Testament Israelites but also its distance from the ecclesiology of its competitors.

Congregations also referred to their chapels affectionately as the 'house of God', 'sanctuary', or 'temple'. While intended as a figurative association with Israel's places of worship, the terms reinforced their Old Testament turn of mind. The inauguration of a new chapel sometimes recalled the language and imagery associated with the dedication of Solomon's Temple and the Temple of Jerusalem (2 Chronicles 5, Ezra 3). The historian of Havelock Street Presbyterian Church, Newport, Monmouthshire, wrote concerning its opening in 1864:

> Pastor and flock went forth rejoicing to take possession of the structure which they had watched patiently rearing its walls on the chosen site. To them, a small band of faith-seeing devoted ones, every stone of the new edifice was as precious as those of the Temple of Jerusalem in days of yore, were to the Jews of the captivity who had returned with Zorababel . . . They were entering their Shiloh and prayerfully desired the Spirit of the Most High to encompass them.[19]

A report of the service appeared in the Calvinistic Methodist journal the *Treasury* for December of that year. The employment of Old Testament imagery, again, identified and invested the occasion with a strongly biblical ethos: 'The services of the opening were indeed precious. The candlestick appeared to have taken its place, its oil

35 Unidentified chapel interior, (nineteenth century, last quarter).

36 Baptist Chapel, Newtown, Powys (1881).

burning freely, and its lamps giving bright and heavenly light. The bright side of the pillar was towards the tribes of Israel, the unction of the Holy One descending with the truth.'[20] The services that accompanied either the founding or dedication of chapels followed the pattern of Old Testament ordinances: God received praise and thanksgiving through congregational singing, accompanied by instrumental music, and oration (2 Chronicles 5: 13; 6: 3–11, Ezra 3: 10–11). In the dedication of the chapel, the cloud that filled the 'house of God' translated into an expectation that the Holy Spirit would anoint the preacher's sermon.

The aggrandizement of the interior and exterior of many chapels during the second half of the nineteenth century cultivated a more literal identification with the conspicuous splendour and craftsmanship of Old Testament places of worship **(35)**. Solomon's Temple was a building of prepared stone, with 'windows of narrow lights', and covered within 'with boards of cedar, both the floor of the house, and the walls of the ceiling' (1 Kings 6: 4–15). The description bore more than a passing resemblance to the stone externals, slender, arched windows, and pine-clad interiors of a Bethel in Wales. Likewise, the temple's cedar interior 'carved with knops and open flowers' was not dissimilar to the richly ornamented Gothic-style pulpits (1 Kings 6: 18).[21] In the design for Ezekiel's Temple, given by God to the prophet in a vision, the building sits on a platform mounted by ten steps (Ezekiel chapters 40 to 43). The more substantial classical chapels deploy variations on this device as means of ascending from street-level to the portico **(36)**. Positioned to the left and right of the Temple's porch were two pillars of brass (named Jachin and Boaz) approximately eight and a half metres high, and surmounted with 'chapiters' (capitals) of lilies and pomegranates (1 Kings 7: 15–21). Scholars argue that they allude to the pillars of fire and cloud that went before the Israelites in the wilderness (Exodus 13: 21). Furthermore, 'the pillar of cloud stood over the door of the Tabernacle' (Exodus 33: 9, Deuteronomy 31: 15); the proximity of the Temple's pillars to the entrance of the portico would have endorsed the association. The pillars of fire and cloud were the visible presence of God; thus, those of the Temple had a divine significance in the Israelite tradition. Tall columns or pilasters often crowned with still-leaf capitals graced the porticoes of many classical chapels. The Nonconformists' biblical disposition would have encouraged a mental connection between the pillars of the chapels and the Old Testament exemplars rather than with their prototypes in Graeco-Roman antiquity.

'The glory of Solomon's Temple', wrote one nineteenth-century antiquarian, 'did not . . . consist in its size, but in its exquisite workmanship and costly materials.'[22] The same is true of many Welsh chapels. Both Solomon's Temple and many nineteenth-century chapels were essentially a rectangular box. The Temple was 60 cubits in length, 20 cubits in breadth, and 30 cubits in height (approximately $26.6 \times 8.8 \times 13.1$ metres) including the porch (20 cubits in length and 10 cubits in breadth) (1 Kings 6: 2–3). It was, as Ernest Renan pointed out, 'a domestic Temple, a chapel of the palace'.[23] The overall measure of the Temple proper was commensurate with that of many medium-sized chapels in Wales. The cella of the

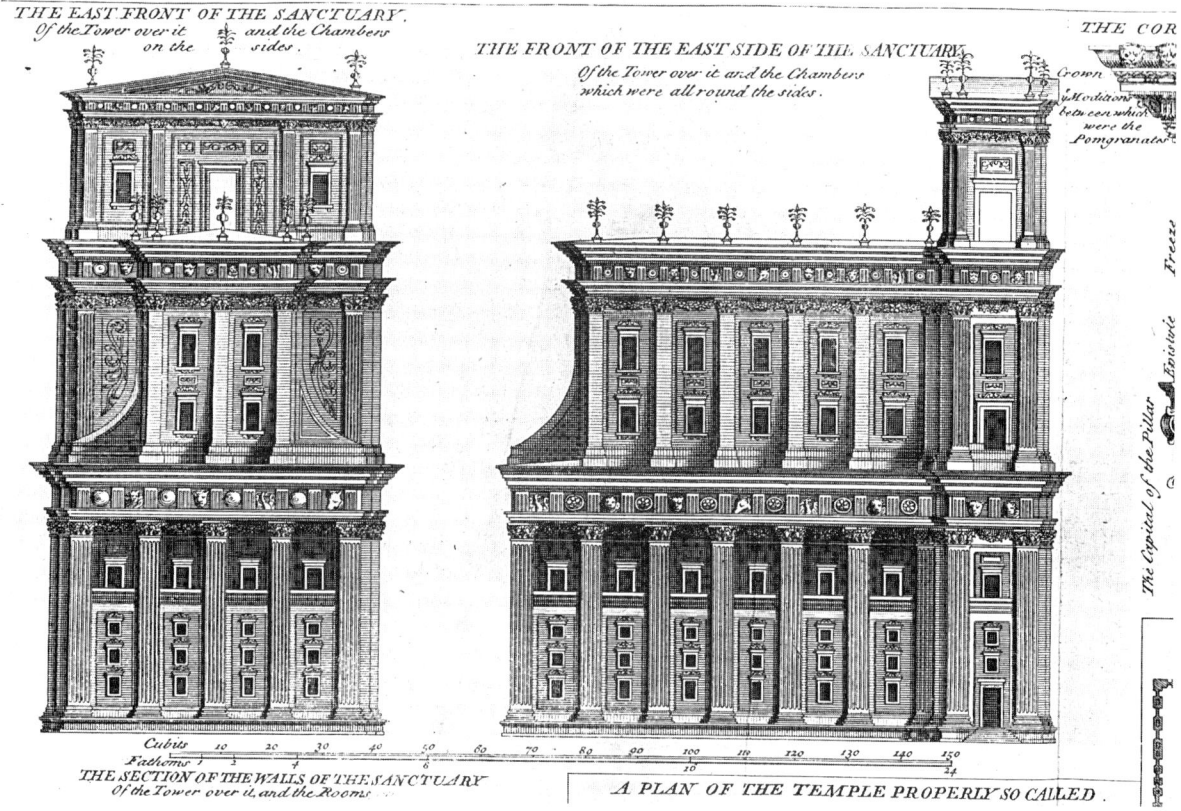

37 Sections and ornamentation of the Temple of Solomon, steelplate engraving, *Dictionary of the Bible* (1732).

Temple (that is, the main body excluding the portico) John Kitto reckoned to be 'about the same length, but not as wide, as St Paul, Covent Garden'.[24] St Paul's church, as Anthony Jones has established, was the model for Peniel, Tremadog (built 1810), the earliest example of the classical-styled chapel in Wales.[25]

During the nineteenth century, the Nonconformists' visual conception of Solomon's Temple would have been at best vague and inconclusive, owing to the unavailability of illustrations, especially reliable ones. Kitto explained:

> There have been many most elaborate treatises on the temple; but the difficulty of the subject – the mistaken reference to classical and ideal models – with a comparative ignorance of the ancient and Oriental architecture, having prevented many a satisfactory result from being obtained. Modern commentators and illustrators of scripture have been so conscious of this that they have generally shrunk away from the subject. Dr Horne says, 'Various attempts have been made to describe the proportions of the temple and several parts of its structure; but as scarcely two writers agree on this subject, a minute description of it is designedly omitted.' Others decline entering into the subject on the grounds that the details would be unintelligible without plates.[26]

38 Bethel Welsh Baptist Church (1880), Aberystwyth.

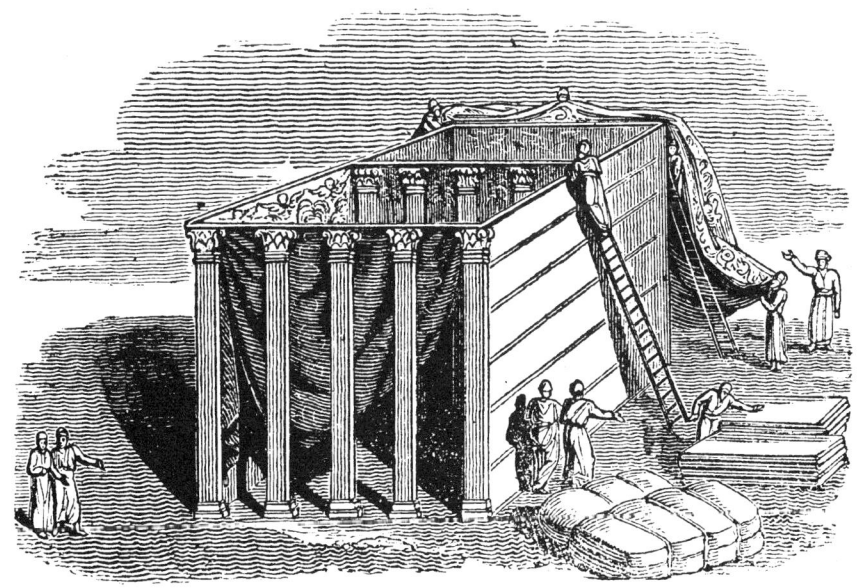

39 'The Tabernacle', *Scripture Antiquities* (1821).

40 'The Ark of the Covenant with the Mercy Seat', *Scripture Antiquities* (1821).

41 Pulpit, Bethel Welsh Baptist Church, Aberystwyth (1880).

The erroneous classical and ideal conception of Israel's places of worship is evident in Bible-reading accompaniments published from the early eighteenth to the late nineteenth centuries. Augustin Calmet's influential *Dictionary of the Bible* (1732) is copiously illustrated with Graeco-Roman interpretations of biblical monuments and principal buildings, such as the Temples of Ezekiel and Solomon and the Tabernacle. They include a set of elaborate designs by the Spanish Jesuit John-Baptist Villalpandus (d. 1608) proffering a putative visualization of the Temple of Solomon replete with pilasters, balustrades, and myriad other architectural details **(37)**. Calmet castigated Villalpandus for venturing where other illustrators had feared to tread:

> He has introduced many embellishments which are not mentioned in the sacred Text, but which ought to have been there according to the Rules of Architecture, which it is supposed *Solomon* could not be ignorant of, as if the same taste must prevail in Architecture among all Nations, as in all Ages. And as if *Solomon*, who lived so long before the first architects of Greece, must needs have followed the same Rules that they found out and gave afterwards.[27]

The visualization of biblical antiquities in the nineteenth century perpetuated the same misapprehension. John Jones's *Scripture Antiquities* (1821) and the anonymous *Scripture Illustrations* (1824) depict the sanctuary of the Tabernacle (the basis for the design of Solomon's Temple) as an oblong box with a façade of fluted pillars crowned with Corinthian capitals **(39)**.[28] The Ark of the Covenant, which was set up in the Tabernacle's most holy place, is visualized in the latter volume, its sides adorned with foliate relief decorations like an antique sarcophagus **(40)**.

The most conspicuous dissimilarity between Israel's places of worship and a classical-type chapel is the latter's gable roof. Illustrations of the Temple and

42 Tabernacle, *Biblical Antiquities* (1888).

Tabernacle show flat roofs, with one exception. In *Biblical Antiquities* (1888), Edwin Bissell conceives of the Tabernacle as having a gable roof:

> while Moses is spoken of as 'erecting' the tabernacle, he is said to have 'spread' the tent, that is, the second covering, over the tabernacle, and to have put the covering of the tent, that is, the tent of rams' skins etc., 'above upon it; as the Lord commanded Moses.' The Hebrew used is peculiar and makes the impression that the covering of skins was of the nature of a roof somewhat elevated above the others.[29]

Bissell's visualization was idiosyncratic and appears to have exerted no influence on subsequent illustrations of the subject **(42)**. Nevertheless, it does prompt a fresh perception of the simple box-shaped, gable-roofed chapels as a kind of stone tent, a connotation that would not have been lost on Nonconformists familiar with the appellation of 'the tabernacle of the tent of the congregation', as the Tabernacle proper (or Holy of Holies) was sometimes referred to (Exodus 39: 32) (see Chapter 7).

The classical conception, or, rather, misconception, of Israel's places of worship would have enabled Nonconformists to identify the architecture of the nineteenth-century classical-type chapel with an Old Testament, rather than pagan, paradigm **(38)**. Classical-styled architecture had already given Nonconformity an appearance of antiquity that belied its comparative recentness as a Christian sect. The association of this style with the origins of the Judaeo-Christian tradition gave Nonconformity a stake in a far more remote and grand history. In this way the classical chapel also provided a visual expression of their claim to ancestry.

Wise to the wild speculations of their seventeenth- and eighteenth-century predecessors, commentators and illustrators during the second half of the nineteenth

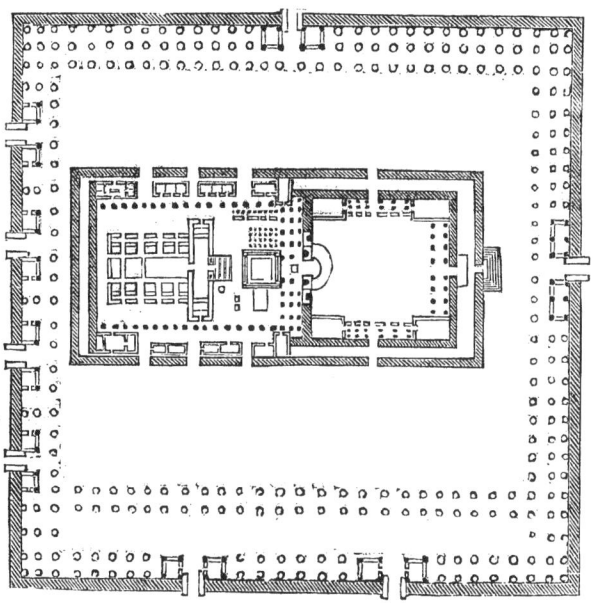

43 Ground-plan of the Temple of Solomon by Prideaux, *Pictorial Bible* (1847).

44 Pulpit and *sêt fawr*, Bethel Welsh Baptist Church, Aberystwyth (1880).

century were reluctant to pronounce on the architectural structure of Solomon's Temple. However, the general appearance of the Temple's ground-plan, which the textual description delineates fairly unambiguously, was undisputed and frequently diagrammatized **(43)**. Illustrators depicted the main hall or Holy Place of the Temple as consisting of three sections: an ante-room (Hebrew *ulâm*), a main room for divine service (Hebrew *hekhâl*), and the Holy of Holies (Hebrew *debïr*). This division roughly corresponds to the three principal sections of a chapel: the vestibule, the 'sanctuary' or main room for meeting, and an enclosure made up of the *sêt fawr* [big seat] and pulpit **(44)**. The *sêt fawr*, bounded by a wooden or a wrought-iron balustrade, accommodated the deacons and elders. In some chapels it extended no more than a few feet in front of the pulpit, enough for chairs and the communion table to occupy, while in others it extended several metres into the chapel. The Holy of Holies was a discrete chamber adjoining the main room of the Temple, while the chapel's enclosure was contained at the centre and front of the main room for meeting. In this respect, the arrangement of the chapel's ground-plan had more in common with that of the Tabernacle, the portable sanctuary inhabited by God during Israel's sojourn in the wilderness (Exodus 33: 7–11). The Tabernacle proper (an oblong open-frame enclosure covered with curtains and skins) is situated in exactly the same position relative to the Tabernacle's courtyard (a rectangular structure of poles bounded by linen curtains) as the enclosure to the main room **(1)**. The structural similarities between chapel and Tabernacle also create a correspondence between the hierarchical organization of the Nonconformist and Israelite congregations. Just as the ordinary member of a chapel sat in the area outside the *sêt fawr*, so the Israelites could enter only into the court of the Tabernacle. The *sêt fawr* was reserved for the officers of the chapel, the deacons and elders; similarly, only the Levitical priesthood could enter the Holy Place. The pulpit, like the Holy of Holies, was the exclusive province of the head of the congregation – the preacher and the high priest respectively.

The ground-plans of the Tabernacle proper and the chapel's enclosure were also analogous; each consisted of two adjoining sections: the Holy Place and Holy of Holies and the *sêt fawr* and pulpit. The Holy Place contained two pieces of furniture: the Altar of Incense and the Table of Shewbread on which lay plates (probably for the bread), dishes, spoons, and flagons and bowls for the drink offerings. Likewise, the *sêt fawr* accommodated the communion table or Lord's table, on which lay plates bearing bread and a goblet or cups of wine during the Lord's Supper.[30] Bissell remarked of the Table of Shewbread, that 'In form it was like an ordinary table'.[31] The illustration of the Table of Shewbread in Kitto's *Pictorial Sunday Book* (1855–6) established a marked resemblance to the simple communion table common in chapels from the mid-nineteenth century onwards **(45, 46)**.[32] Nonconformists, in keeping with Reformation theology, did not believe that the sacrament of communion had any sacrificial implications. The sacrifice of Christ was a historic and unrepeatable event. The bread and wine signified the body and blood of Christ by token rather than by transubstantiation. For this reason the *sêt fawr* did not require a piece of furniture corresponding to the altar in the Holy Place.

45 Table of Shewbread, *Pictorial Sunday Book* (1855–6).

46 Communion table (twentieth century, first half), Alfred Place Baptist Church, Aberystwyth.

The Holy of Holies contained the Ark of the Covenant and the lampstand. The ark was a rectangular wooden box covered with gold, measuring 2.5 × 1.5 × 1.5 cubits (1.2 × 0.7 × 0.7 metres). Judging from illustrations of the Tabernacle in nineteenth-century Nonconformist periodicals, they conceived of the front elevation of the ark as bearing a strong resemblance to the lectern area of some types of pulpit **(41)**. From either side of the lectern extend the front rails of the pulpit: these mimic the horizontal carrying-poles that protruded from the ark. The gas lamps to the left and right of the lectern echo the two cherubim on either side of the ark. The ark contained, among other relics of Israel's history, the two stone tablets given to Moses on Mount Sinai bearing the Ten Commandments. The pulpit too, being the platform for preaching, possesses a powerful association with the Word of God. The materials of the Tabernacle increased in splendour and costliness as they approached the Ark of the Covenant, suggesting a hierarchy of holiness.[33] Like the Holy of Holies, the pulpit is often the most elegantly crafted and expensive piece of furniture in the chapel.

In some cases, the correspondence between chapel and Tabernacle and Temple extended to include other elements of interior design. A veil (Hebrew *paroket*) separated the Holy Place and Holy of Holies.[34] In a number of chapels a curtain was hung behind the pulpit in a moulded archway in the centre of the wall behind the pulpit rising some 5 metres above the pulpit platform, and echoing the shape of the windows. While serving to baffle the preacher's voice, it was also a potential metaphor for the veil of the Tabernacle to which the apostle Paul referred. He regarded the Holy of Holies as a type of heaven into which Christ passed through the veil (Hebrews 9: 23–6). In the context of the chapel, the curtain served as a visual reminder of the heavenly realm that lay before the congregation. The relation between the chapel and the Temple and Tabernacle was, therefore, not only of a general resemblance of division, location, and gradation, but also of fixture and fitting.

The contrast between the mid-nineteenth-century chapel and the meeting-houses and early chapels of the eighteenth century was not only of material splendour. It also signified a movement in the opposite direction to that taken by the New Testament church, towards visible religion. The architectural elaborations, furnishings, and other decorative appurtenances invoked a concept of the sacred building which was at odds with the requirements of New Testament and Calvinistic theology. Nonconformity's adoption of the religious externals was undoubtedly due to a number of factors. Calvin had interpreted the introduction of ornament into the Early Church as symptomatic of a decline in the purity of its doctrine.[35] By the late nineteenth century higher criticism and the new science had undermined the orthodox convictions of many preachers and congregations in Wales. Furthermore, they blunted evangelical fervour (a tendency that was briefly thwarted by the religious revival of 1904–5). (The cold formalism of the neo-classical style was an apt architectural expression of the spirit of rationalism which underpinned the new theology.) In 1898 Kuyper identified the return to symbolism in nineteenth-century Calvinism as indicative of a loss of religious ardour.[36] In other words, the vacuum created by the absence of love for the invisible God was filled with visible signs. Vernacular style also had as great an impact on chapel-building in the nineteenth as it had during the previous century. Whereas in the rural areas of Wales the vernacular consisted in agricultural and domestic buildings, in the industrial towns of south Wales it took the form of a prevailing architectural or building style. The development of more cultivated and wealthier middle-class congregations, and the concomitants of class taste and increased disposable income, facilitated both the desire and the resources for building grander contexts in which to worship. Given their spurious affinity to the Tabernacle and Temple, neo-classical chapels were also an apposite visualization of Wales's identification with Old Testament religious culture. Furthermore, it is not surprising that Nonconformists, as people of the Word, should look to the Bible for architectural precedents and principles, as they did for all the other rules of living.

Miners and Israelites

Nonconformist preachers identified the Old Testament and contemporary worlds, in a more general way, by the use of metaphor in sermon illustration and typological symbolism. For example, Israel's captivity under Pharaoh in Egypt (Exodus chapters 1–13) was seen by a Pentecostal writer as follows: 'Egypt is a type of the World, and Pharaoh is a type of Satan; the Israelites a type of all God's subjects, in bondage to sin and Satan, and in desperate need of Redemption.'[37] Preachers frequently employed this analogy to illustrate the spiritual condition of the unconverted in the sight of God. In south Wales the association of the congregations with the Israelites in Egypt was the more pronounced owing to strong similarities in the hardships and struggles of the Israelites and of the miners who constituted a large proportion of the chapel membership. The Israelite community is first mentioned at the beginning of the book of Exodus, the book of Genesis having dealt only with individuals and families. They were the offspring of the household of Jacob, who had gone down into Egypt and multiplied greatly, so that the land was now full of them (Exodus 1: 7). Because their numbers and strength posed a threat to the Egyptians, they were afflicted and burdened by taskmasters set over them by Pharaoh in order to keep them down. The taskmasters conscripted the Israelites as forced labour to build the cities of Pithom and Raamses (Exodus 1: 11), making them serve with rigour, and 'their lives [were] bitter with hard bondage' (Exodus 1: 13–14). Elsewhere we are told that the Israelites sighed and sorrowed because of their bondage (Exodus 2: 23; 3: 7). Thus the experience of the community at this time was of strenuous, unremitting labour, oppression, and grief.

The language of the Authorized Version of the Bible, as we saw earlier, had passed into the common parlance of the south Wales communities: miners often derived their political language from the Bible, speaking of their struggles in the phrases and images used of the Israelites in captivity. During the south Wales coal strike of 1898, a letter to the *Evening Express* voiced dissatisfaction with William Abraham's ('Mabon') (1842–1922) leadership of the dispute in the following terms: 'Had "Mabon" been at the head of the children of Israel in Egypt they would still be making bricks.'[38] Advocating the need for Welsh miners to be better organized to fight exploitation by the management, Ben Tillet addressed a crowd of miners in Pontypridd in 1893 using the illustration of the Israelites' experience after the exodus: 'I am sorry that the body of Welshmen are a mere rabble . . . If they were the chosen people, they had been 20 years in the wilderness without a Moses or an Aaron.'[39]

In describing the psychological buoyancy of the miners in spite of their appalling social conditions R. J. Barker used an allusion to the Israelites in captivity in Babylon (Psalm 137): 'These men who toil in the depths of the earth have music in their heart; unlike the Hebrews who could not sing in exile, the song in their heart is irrepressible.'[40] The colliers sang of their struggles and exploitation using images of the Old Testament Israelites in bondage to the Egyptians. The following stanzas are from a song entitled 'The Pitman's Complaint':

> Thou heard the Israelites of old,
> And led them to a blessed fold;

> Deliver us from slavery
> And set the Sons of Britain free.
>
> . . .
>
> Arise my brethren from the dust,
> And in the Lord let's put our trust,
> Then all our woes he will confound,
> And in the sea proud Pharaoh drown.[41]

Many other songs, such as 'Clydach Vale Lock-Out', 'The Miner's Life', and 'The Cummer Colliery Explosion', all of which originated in the coalfields of north and south Wales, were likewise suffused with a Christian consciousness (see Appendix 1).[42] As in the songs of the Israelites, captive in Babylon, one of the great themes of the collier's lyric was of the God who hearkens, protects, comforts, and saves. Among the standards of the brass band repertoire were transcriptions of pieces from religious oratorios and Italian opera, such as Rossini's (1792–1868) *Mosè in Egitto* [Moses in Egypt] (1818) – the test piece for the British and National Contest of 1879.[43] In the light of the miners' self-identification with the Old Testament Israelites, selections from this opera would have had particular poignancy for colliery bands and audiences in south Wales.

The identification of miners with Israelites is connoted in Nicholas Evans's paintings, and it contributes to the biblical ethos of the work. By ethos is meant 'the characteristic spirit of community, people, or system' (*OED*). Like the Old Testament, the body of the mining paintings chronicle the history of a community which spans the primitive age of the coal industry in south Wales in the eighteenth century to the deprivations and National Strike of the 1920s, concentrating largely on the suffering of the miners – the conditions of labour, strikes, lock-outs, unemployment, death, and bereavement. Evans has portrayed the rigours of labour as they affect not only the miner but also the women and children, both in the work underground and in the hardship of widowhood and orphanhood following a disaster. The distress of women and children is a frequent theme in the lamentations of the prophets during Israel's captivity and exile. The grieving mothers of Aberfan find a poignant parallel in the New Testament narrative of the women of Jerusalem weeping over the massacre of the innocents (Matthew 2: 16–18).

Nicholas Evans's mining paintings present a community comparable to the people of Israel as described in the Bible. This sense of community has been expressed visually in terms of various groupings: the pressing crowds that congregate around the scene of a disaster; row upon row of colliers huddled together in drams or constrained within the frame of a painting; a work-force compacted in the close confines of a heading; crowds protesting against redundancy and poor wages. Never do we see an individual in isolation, singled out for special attention or made to stand for the class of all colliers, but always in solidarity with another or others.

47 Nicholas Evans, *Strike – Gleaners on Slag Heap* (1978), oil on board, 122 × 122.

48 Nicholas Evans, *All Out – End of Shift* (1978), oil on board, 122 × 122.

The idea of Israel crowding the land of Egypt has a formal analogy in the crowds of faces or figures that often completely fill the picture-plane or most of the landscape of Evans's work. The image of the Israelites serving with rigour aptly describes the scenes of strenuous effort in which the miners are engaged at the coal-face, hewing, drilling, prising, heaving, scraping, and lifting together in close confines, yet so absorbed in their labour as to be apparently oblivious of one another's presence. Evans emphasizes the suffering that results from appalling working and living conditions, exploitation by coal-owners, poverty, industrial disaster, and unemployment. The facial expressions of the figures are, appropriately, consistently dour, browbeaten, or chronically worn, creating an impression of a community in a perpetual state of mourning.

One can also identify a more direct correspondence with the narrative history of the Israelites in Egypt in Evans's *Strike – Gleaners on Slag Heap* (1978) **(47)**. The burden of the Israelites grew when Pharaoh commanded the taskmasters to make them do the same work of building with reduced resources: 'Ye shall no more give the people straw to make brick, as heretofore: let them go and gather straw for themselves' (Exodus 5: 7). In political language miners were identified with the Israelites in relation to this incident, as in the *Evening Express* article cited above. However, one can draw another parallel. Because of Pharaoh's edict the Israelites were scattered over the land to gather stubble with which to make the bricks (Exodus 5: 7–10). During strikes and lock-outs miners and their families suffered a comparable indignity, being forced to scour the land near the pit for fragments of coal to keep themselves warm or to sell. Evans depicts a large number of men, women, and children picking coal, or loading and removing sacks of coal from the tip. It is a communal enterprise, the figures crowding the foreground and middle distance. The account of the Israelites gathering stubble tells of how they were scattered abroad over the land. Evans locates his coal-pickers together. This does not correspond to the biblical text, but the composition does evoke the image of the Israelite community as covering or filling the land. What gives the coal-pickers their connotation of stubble-gatherers is an evocation of the Egyptian landscape by the image of the two coal-tips in the background, faceted like the pyramid illustrated in *Y Bibl Darlundialol* (1844) **(34)**. (The similarity between these forms has also been observed by both the poet Meurig Walters, who wrote of the 'tips now pyramids mock a sterile age', and a fellow artist of the coalfield, Josef Herman (b. 1911).)[44]

The oppression of Israel under Pharaoh ended with the exodus when the Israelites, their cattle, flocks, and herds came out of Egypt on foot (Exodus 10: 11; 12: 37–42). The theme of a mass evacuation of men and animals has its counterpart in *All Out – End of Shift* (1978) **(48)**. Here too labourers, as an army, leave the place of bondage to toil. Prominent in the Exodus account is the image of the doorpost and lintel upon which the blood of the Passover lamb was spread as a sign of protection against the destroyer of the first-born (Exodus 12: 7, 23). A similar motif is suggested in the timber supports that bolster the walls and ceiling of the heading, and feature in paintings such as *All Out – End of Shift* and *Women Coal Carriers* (1978). As the tips evoke pyramids, so the supports evoke doorposts and lintels, when the traditional conflation of the miner-Israelite typology is brought to bear on them.

The evocation of a more primitive community than that denoted by the south Wales miners is aided by the paucity of what Michael Driskel, referring to Édouard Manet's (1832–83) *Jesus Mocked by the Soldiers* (1864–5), called 'historical markers of time and place'.[45] This is a consequence of Evans's simplification of the denoted subjects, his tendency to depict the universal rather than the particular form of objects. (The device, as was observed above, facilitates an association between the landscapes of Wales and Israel in nineteenth-century topographical prints.) For example, in Evans's paintings of the early period of underground mining, the miners' tools, such as picks and shovels, are represented schematically, with a tendency to the emblematic. Thus they are able to transcend the immediate and local association with eighteenth- to early-twentieth-century coal-mining, and to take on symbolic form representing the class of all labourers' tools.[46] The miners working at the coal-face are often depicted naked from the waist up, and for the most part share the same physique, physiognomies, and expression. Their partial nakedness divests them of the signifiers of clothing that would otherwise specify the particular period of industrial history to which they belong.

The depiction of men and women working and living in man-made cavities under the earth contains resonances of prehistoric civilizations whose shelters were holes in the rock and subterranean caverns. The scenes of the miners in company with pit ponies evokes an edenic state where man and animal lived together in harmony; or again, the custom of leading the ponies to drink, shown in *The Water-Hole* (1983), summons up images recorded throughout the Old Testament of shepherds and travellers watering their animals. The evocation of earlier civilizations is strengthened by the connotations of primitiveness in Evans's style of representation. The angular faces of the miners, increasingly in the paintings after 1978, are reminiscent of the Iberian tribal masks and sculptures introduced into the formal vocabulary of European art by Georges Braque (1882–1963) and Pablo Picasso (1881–1973) in the period 1906–8 and more recently seen in Josef Herman's depiction of the miner. The disproportionate and disfigured forms of Evans's miners speak of a world and of modes of realization that preceded the development of aesthetic conventions of the western European figurative tradition.

The absence of historical markers of time and place and the presence of primitive resonances in the formal character of some of Evans's paintings act together in a number of different ways to loose the subjects from their historical moorings. The conflation of Wales and Israel, miner and Israelite, in Nonconformist culture evokes a specific community in the past: within that tradition the mining communities take on the identity of the oppressed work-force at the time of Israel's captivity in Egypt. The biblical mind-set of Evans's generation of Nonconformists, together with the use of biblical imagery in the political discourse of mining in south Wales, indicates that the two subjects could be indivisibly fused in his mind, so that the one automatically alludes to the other. In this way Evans has cast biblical stories in the mould of his own world. The miner as a type of Israelite in Egypt is one of a number of ways in which he became an emblem for religious concepts during the nineteenth and early twentieth centuries. The next two chapters explore the transformation of the miner into a symbol for the contrasting identities of saint and sinner within the cultural conflation of labour and religion and of mining and Nonconformity.

7
Work and Worship, Pit and Piety: Labour Transfigured

The concept of work in the second half of the nineteenth century had strong religious connotations. Work was regarded, variously, as the moral centre and redemptive purpose of life, as the sphere of spiritual service, and as having almost sacramental significance.[1] The association of labour with religion was the theme of several notable paintings of the period. These were seized upon by Nonconformists as ready object-lessons in the integration of secular employment and Christian values, and of the dignity and rights of the common worker (see Chapter 2). The close relationship between mining and Nonconformity in south Wales reflected this association. It was manifest in the conception of the miner as the redeemed sinner – visualized in pictorial representations of him in the popular press during the 1904–5 revival, and subsequently in Nicholas Evans's paintings – and in the structural affinity between colliery and chapel.

Emblems of Labour

Jean François Millet's *The Angelus* was one of the principal progenitors of the image of the pious labourer. From around 1875 onwards the painting became a popular emblem for the ideal of labour **(49)**. *The Angelus* commanded considerable respect among, and was used by, Nonconformists because it visualized a Protestant conception not only of work but also of art. The painting was one of the most celebrated religious pictures of the nineteenth century. The Victorian artist Henry Wallis (1830–1916) considered that 'For expression of devotion equally genuine we must go back to the works of the early Italian masters'.[2] *The Angelus* is one of the most famous examples of a redefinition of religious art which took place in the nineteenth century – what Linda Nochlin refers to as the 'religious genre' category of painting, in which objective descriptions of the religious customs of rustic folk in the provinces replaced the traditional representation of stories and characters of the Bible.[3] Unlike Italian Renaissance painting, it visualized religious concepts without recourse to traditional Roman Catholic imagery and symbolism, which some Nonconformists regarded as often at variance with biblical history and truth. The painting's religious content consisted in a single act of piety – two peasants pronouncing benediction on the day's work. In one of his series of articles published in 1915 entitled 'Picture Talks to Boys and Girls', the Revd Evan Williams spoke of the painting as being

49 Jean François Millet, *The Angelus* (1857–9), oil on canvas, 55.6 × 66.

not like the sacred pictures with which we are familiar. No angels and crosses and saints with haloes round their brows, but just a tiny little church in the distance, and two peasants in a field, a man and a woman, with bent head, closed eyes and clasped hands. They have been working all through the day, and now in the stillness of eventide, the sound of the Angelus bell comes from the distant church. At the sound of the vesper bell the man takes off his cap, the woman clasps her hands together, and with bowed heads they say their prayer.[4]

The juxtaposition of labour and peasant piety also provided ministers with a pliant pictorial text capable of sustaining a variety of sermonic readings.[5] Williams's article identified and expounded the painting's religious significance and lessons that it taught. His approach was derived substantially from an extensive discourse on the painting by James Burns in *Sermons in Art by the Great Masters*. The essence of the work, according to Burns, was its representation of 'those primitive emotions which link us with nature, and with humanity, and with God'.[6] With regard to nature, the painting evoked a sense of man's primal origins, his kinship with the soil, and his mortality, echoing the biblical pronouncement, 'for dust thou art, and unto dust shalt thou return' (Genesis 3: 19).[7] Burns's exposition, in turn, was indebted to Henry Naegely, who, a decade earlier, had also understood the painting to be about the above verses from Genesis chapter 3, which describe man's destiny to struggle with the anathematized and recalcitrant ground:

cursed is the ground for thy sake; in sorrow shalt thou eat of it all the days of thy life; thorns also and thistles shall it bring forth to thee; and thou shalt eat the herb of the field; in the sweat of thy face shalt thou eat bread, till thou return to the ground. (Genesis 3: 17–19)[8]

Burns also made a similar connection between labour and the curse of sin, the allusion probably evoked for these authors by an association of the man and woman with Adam and Eve; the earth on which they stood acquired the connotation of fallenness by a typological relation to the blighted ground after the Fall.[9]

The humanity of *The Angelus*, Burns considered, resided in Millet's reverential treatment of the peasants, in contrast to their derisory representation by previous painters, such as Bruegel. Burns elevated the painting above the level of humanist sentiment and read Millet's depiction of the peasant as an expression of distinctly 'Christian piety'. It also served as a propagandist tract about the 'Christian recognition of the rights and needs of the neglected'.[10] The most obvious religious expression of the work was its denoted subject, the portrayal of the two peasants praying as the angelus bell tolled. For Burns the painting was a visualization of man's religious nature and his dependence on God: the man and woman exemplified a simple and trusting faith.[11] Burns, and Williams especially, read the juxtaposition of labour and piety as signifying the consecration of toil: 'They have turned from their labour to pray with perfect naturalness, without the slightest sense of discord. In their lives these two acts are wedded together. The transition from the one to the other requires no effort.'[12]

The latter reading of *The Angelus* reflected traditionally Protestant and contemporary speculations among Nonconformists on the relationship between a Christian's work and worship, which many considered should ideally be united, religion providing a sanctifying, inspiring influence. 'Religion', wrote one Nonconformist, 'enables a man to perform "secular" work from "sacred" motives . . . And for this reason it is wrong for a man to separate business and religion, toil and worship.'[13] Such sentiments militated against a tendency, prevalent during the latter part of the nineteenth century, to relegate business and religion to discrete, watertight compartments in life. The attitude was denounced by the Revd Hugh Price Hughes (1847–1902), an articulate advocate of the integration of Christian ethics with social issues:

> We can never be said to do the Will of our Father on earth as angels do it in heaven, if we do that Will only at certain times and in certain places. Ruskin is quite right in stating that if our religion is good for anything it is good for everything.[14]

Hughes's conviction derived from the biblical principle of doing all things wholeheartedly 'as unto the Lord' (Colossians 3: 22–4), a disposition which not only enriched satisfying employment but also, as George Herbert (1593–1633) had observed, made 'drudgery divine'.[15] Thus consecrated, wrote the hymnist John Ellerton (1826–93), labour became devotion and was thereby united with it:

50 Ford Madox Brown, *Work* (1852–65), oil on panel, 134.6 × 195.9.

> Work shall be prayer, if all be wrought
> As Thou wouldst have it done;
> And prayer, by Thee inspired and taught,
> Itself with work be one.[16]

The concept of work as spiritual endeavour was closely allied to the Reformation emphasis on the biblical idea of vocation, in the original theological sense of a person's work being a divine calling: 'one man is a schoolmaster "through the will of God", and another a university professor, and another a lecturer on chemistry, and another an architect, and another a painter, and another a poet.'[17] Evan Williams, once a minister in south Wales, applied the lessons of *The Angelus* to the working class, interpreting the conflation of work and worship in terms of a fusion of sacred and mundane, thereby dignifying common people and common toil: 'The man and woman are serving God by digging potatoes as much as the priest who conducts the service in the distant church.'[18] This correspondence between labourer and religious officiant restated Luther's contention against the erroneous medieval distinction

51 Nicholas Evans, *Coalface (2)* (1976), oil on board, 122 × 122.

between clergy and laity: 'A cobbler, a smith, a farmer, each has the work and office of his trade, and yet they are all alike consecrated priests and bishops.'[19]

Thomas Carlyle (1795–1881) advocated the ennoblement of labour and labourers and their identification with holy persons in *Past and Present* (1843). However, Carlyle saw work not in the Protestant sense of purposeful effort sanctified by faith, but rather as an alternative religion, by which a man could purify himself of base desires, fulfil his earthly destiny, and rise to heroic stature and saintliness.[20] This ethic of redemption through labour was visualized by Ford Madox Brown (1821–93) in the celebrated painting *Work* (1852–63) **(50)**. Like *The Angelus*, *Work* was commonly understood as a profoundly religious painting, not by virtue of traditional Christian subject-matter or symbolism but, as John Linton asserted in 1916, because, like many other examples of recent religious painting, it revealed 'the inner spiritual significance of common things and common happenings'.[21] The spiritual significance of *Work* was signified by four biblical texts inscribed on the frame which extolled the virtues as well as the concomitant drudgery of work.[22] In contrast to *The Angelus*, Madox Brown exemplified the virtues of labour not in the form of the humble peasant-type but in the depiction of navvies (navigators), here represented (as in many other Victorian paintings) as muscular and stalwart figures. The navvy was the urban counterpart of the rural peasant to whom Millet had imputed nobility, a figure of dignity raised to a position of social equality with the philosopher and the intellectual, the martyr and the saint.[23] The labourer had become a religious

52 Ainslie, 'A Colliery Explosion: Volunteers to the Rescue',
steelplate engraving by Fromert, *Illustrated London News*
(25 February 1882).

archetype, albeit religion, as Herbert Furst described it, in the 'garb of budding socialism'.[24]

Nonconformist respect for the labourer in the nineteenth century emphasized both his saintly and his heroic aspects. The Independents, whose membership came largely from the ranks of the working class, were chief among the denominations to show esteem. W. R. Lambert observed that they were 'fairly convinced of the value of the worker and his importance in society'. An article in an early number of *Y Gweinwr* [The Common Man] stressed the dignity of every honest calling in life. In 1859 *Y Diwygiwr* [The Revivalist] severely criticized the custom of some middle-class people to despise the workers.[25] In the same spirit, Jay Gee had his fictional hero Collier Jack reprimand a Bible class: 'don't look askance at the miner as he passes by and say, "He's only a collier," for underneath his grim exterior he has a generous heart. He is as brave as the most heroic soldier on the battle field.'[26] Throughout the serial Gee described the miner as risking and laying down his life for his workmates, battling valiantly against the natural elements, and overcoming dangers.

The association of mining and heroism acquired a graphic expression in the representations of coal-mining disasters during the second half of the nineteenth century. In 1882 the *Illustrated London News* published a double-spread engraving which homed in on volunteer rescuers (portrayed as a navigator-type, an image of the miner popular in English illustrated journals at that time) about to descend a pit **(52)**. The illustration depicted a scene of valour such as might have occurred at the two colliery explosions during the previous week, one in Wales killing six men (probably that at Coedcae, Monmouthshire on 11 February).[27] Similar representations also appeared in the popular press in Wales. Staniforth's imagined illustration of the Senghennydd explosion published in the *Western Mail* on 17 October 1913 depicted the courage and fortitude of the rescuer at the heart of the disaster. 'The Welsh Hero' showed the muscular figure of a rescuer striding through the blazing interior of a heading, carrying an unconscious miner slung over his shoulder. Journalists' reports of the disasters frequently described similar acts of valour.

Apart from scenes of fortitude and bravery, the heroic and somewhat idealized representation is rare; more often the miner – at play, on strike, at the pit-top or working underground – is portrayed, like the male peasant in *The Angelus*, cowed, work-worn, and clad in soiled and ill-fitting clothes. Whereas the image of the robust, muscle-bound miner was, following classical theory, an externalization of inner qualities of strength and fortitude, the genre-type portrayal reflected more accurately the consequences of unremitting labour and social deprivation. Thomas Henry Thomas – possibly the first Welsh artist to depict the subterranean aspect of coal-mining – employed this realist approach in a number of small, intense watercolours of the Rhondda and Forest of Dean coalfields painted during the 1880s. The paintings documented miners and pitboys descending the pit, pulling drams, and during mealtimes. In shape and demeanour they were reminiscent of the endearing rustic types common in the early illustrations of coal-mining in Wales nearly a century earlier, by artists like Paul Sandby (1725/6–1809) and Julius Caesar Ibbetson (1759–1817). However, Thomas's miners were not dull, mindless bumpkins rendered with uncomprehending detachment; the studies clearly expressed the artist's respect and affection for the miners, and, in turn, his subjects' keen interest and pride in their labour.

Miners Redeemed

Like Millet, Thomas also depicted the religious customs of the labourers. He later translated a study of miners listening intently to a preacher in the confines of an underground road into a woodblock illustration for David Davies's book of Welsh reminiscences, *Echoes from the Welsh Hills* (1883) **(53)**. The image is a pictorial

53 T. H. Thomas, underground service, woodblock engraving, *Echoes from the Welsh Hills* (1883).

precedent for a number of newspaper illustrations of religious services held in the pit during the revival of 1904–5. Visual representations of the devotional habits and practical godliness of the miner reflected a significant shift in public perception of his character during the period of the revival. In the half-century prior to 1904, Nonconformist literature and sermon illustrations had portrayed the miner as an emblem of the typical sinner, a representative of the most hardened reprobate on the broad road that leads to destruction (see Chapter 1).

Henry Hughes described the morality of the miners in *Y Genedl Gymreig* [The Welsh Nation] on 28 March 1905:

Rhaid i bawb addef, oedd wedi sylwi ychydig ar agwedd y wlad, fod golwg dorcalonus iawn arni cyn dechreu y Diwygiad presenol: yr oedd fel pe buasai wedi cael ei rhoddi i fyny i'r diafol: yr oedd anffyddiaeth ac anghrediniaeth yn uchel ei ben: yr oedd rhyw farweidd-dra barnol ar yr eglwysi: yr oedd y dosbarth gweithiol wedi myned i ryw galedwch a bryntni arswydus: yr oedd y wlad wedi suddo i ryw ddyfnder o lygredigaeth: yr oedd glythineb, a meddwdod, ac ofer-gampau, yn llenwi'r tir: bydolrwydd oedd yn meddianu braidd bob dyn.[28]

54 J. M. Staniforth, 'A Changed Home. An Improvement', pen, ink, and wash, *Evening Express*, revival edition (9 January 1905).

[Everybody who has taken a little trouble to observe the condition of the country must agree that there was a heartrending sight to be seen before the commencement of the present revival. Most people seemed to have given themselves up to the devil. Agnosticism had raised its ugly head very high. There was a terrible apathy inside the chapels and churches. The workers had fallen into a state of frightful callousness, and the whole country had descended into the pit of corruption. Lust and drunkenness, worldliness and worthless things had possessed the minds of all people.]

Many people hoped that the religious revival would be a divine visitation to the miners in particular, to rescue them from their moral degeneration. In the opinion of one reporter, there was ground for optimism; of all Welsh people, the miners were, by dint of their precarious livelihood, most predisposed to having their religious affections rekindled: 'Coming in contact daily with the mysterious forces of nature, reminded so often of the uncertainty of life, the religious traits of the Welsh temperament are intensified in the Welsh collier, who is responding with intense earnestness to the spiritual influences of the revival.'[29] This earnestness was evident in an enthusiasm for worship, increased productivity and reduced absenteeism at the colliery, sobriety, good citizenship, moderation of temper, and a spirit of penitence.[30]

55 'Revival Service in a Coal Mine', pen and ink, *South Wales Daily News* (22 December 1904).

As a result of the awakening, the popular image of the miner changed from sinner to a man who had a deep-seated love of religion.

The reformation of the collier in the revival was the subject of its most famous illustration, Staniforth's 'An Improvement', first published in the *Western Mail* on 26 December 1904, and in a modified version in the *Evening Express* of 9 January 1905 under the title 'A Changed Home. An Improvement' **(54)**. It shows a collier and his family at the dining-table on Christmas Day. In the caption Father Christmas, addressing the collier, remarks on the contrast in his circumstances from the previous Christmas.[31] The implication is that on that occasion the collier was inebriated in the public house rather than in his right mind and with his family. Percy Hicks observed that prior to the revival 'Wales at Christmastide has generally been a land of somewhat excessive revelry on account of the numerous drunken orgies among certain classes of the people. But at the festive season of 1904 it was a land of universal prayer.'[32] Staniforth's unpublished cartoon 'A Result of the Revival. Then and Now' (c.1904–5) encapsulated the effects of the contrast for pitmen, publicans, and police alike (see Chapter 3 **(17)**).

In the weeks leading up to Christmas 1904, a number of illustrations accompanying newspaper reports of the revival were dedicated to the prodigal miner's return. On 23 December the *South Wales Daily News* published a composite illustration entitled 'Revival

Scenes' drawn by one of the newspaper's artists, Chag. W. Nicholls. In the central section, miners are shown in attitudes of contrition or ecstasy, holding a prayer meeting in a railway carriage on their way to or from work; to the left of this vignette, in a drawing subtitled 'A Sketch at Mid Day near Hirwain', one miner clasps his hands in the act of saying grace before his meal underground, while to the right, another sings hymns on his way from the colliery to the chapel; at the bottom of the illustration were scenes showing a converted collier persuading another collier to refrain from entering a public house and to come to a revival service, where he too is subsequently converted.

The descriptions of many underground services held in the south Wales coalfields during the revival emphasize the redemption of the miner. A drawing of one underground meeting, entitled 'Revival Service in a Coal Mine', appeared in the *South Wales Daily News* on 22 December 1904 **(55)**. It illustrates an incident recorded by the newspaper's correspondent in which one of the miners asked:

> 'Now, boys, those of you who love Christ up with your lamps.' In a second scores of glimmering lights flicker in the air . . . Only two or three have refrained from raising their lamps, and they are not allowed to go unnoticed. A kindly arm steals round their neck, prayers are silently offered on their behalf, and, when a prodigal sends a lurid glare across the 'top' by raising his lamp aloft his fellow-workmen burst into a wild shout of joy.[33]

The artist has focused on the repentance and consolation of one of the miners referred to in the report.

Staniforth's image of an underground service (which appeared in the *Western Mail* on 3 December 1904) accompanies a report of an underground service held at the Nantymelyn Colliery, Cwmdâr, Glamorgan on 1 December 1904 **(56)**:

> Seventy yards from the bottom of the shaft, in the stables, we came to the prayer meeting. One of the workmen was reading the 6th chapter of St. Matthew to about eighty comrades. He stood erect amongst the group, reading in a dim, fantastic light that danced with the swinging lamps and vanished softly into the surrounding darkness. A number of lamps were attached to a heavy post closely wedged to support the roof, and around the impressive figure the colliers grouped themselves. Some were in the characteristic stooping posture, others half-reclined against the side of the road, with their lamps fastened to their pockets; others, again, stood in the middle of the passage. Earnest men, all of them; faces that bore the scars of the underground toiler; downcast eyes that seemed to be 'the homes of silent prayer'; strong frames that quivered with a new emotion.[34]

While the artist of 'Revival Service in a Coal Mine' represented the miners responding to a call for repentance by an outward demonstration of faith, Staniforth showed them in attitudes of prayerful penitence and submission under the preaching of the Bible. In this sense Staniforth's image was indebted to Thomas's original

56 J. M. Staniforth, 'The Religious Revival' (1904), pen and ink, 12 × 16.5.

57 Rembrandt, 'Christ Preaching the Remission of Sins' (c.1652), etching, 15.3 × 20.5.

representation of such a scene; the figures of both the miner in the former and preacher in the latter stand before an open Bible with one hand raised in a gesture of exhortation.

'The Religious Revival' also resembles *The Angelus*, and may be considered a transposition of the latter into the mining genre. Millet's painting portrays peasants thought to be pronouncing a benediction on the day's work they have performed; Staniforth's illustration shows miners gathered together before the commencement of the night shift, when, as Awstin observed, many prayers were offered asking God's blessing 'for the honest and proper execution of the work'.[35] Staniforth followed Awstin's description of the prayerful disposition of these miners, depicting them in various postures of worship. The figure standing against the wall on the extreme left of the illustration echoes the attitude of the man in *The Angelus*. Millet placed a hoe next to the man, symbolizing the labour from which the peasants had retired, while Staniforth placed a pick next to one of the miners, symbolizing the labour upon which they were shortly to embark.

The religious content of Staniforth's drawing consists not only in the denoted scene of miners expressing piety but also in the connotation of biblical imagery through association with religious art. The composition of the scene is reminiscent of Rembrandt's (1606–69) etching 'Christ Preaching the Remission of Sins' (*c.*1652) **(57)**. Both scenes are set in an enclosed space, the figure of the miner and Christ occupying the same position at the centre of the scene, surrounded by the other figures, their hands raised in a similar gesture of supplication. The identification of the miner with the preaching Christ is further established by the correspondence of the portion of Scripture being read by the miner (Matthew chapter 6, which records part of Christ's Sermon on the Mount) to its original context in Rembrandt's etching. Within the context of this association, the miners surrounding the central figure became transpositions into the contemporary world of the disciples and hearers present at Christ's sermon. This association, moreover, represents a specific, if unintentional, exemplification of the conflation of Wales and the biblical world (see Chapter 6).

Colliery and Chapel

The images of miners labouring at prayer and praying at labour represents just one manifestation of a fusion between work and worship. From the mid nineteenth century to the beginning of the twentieth century, work and worship were also united in the relationship between the colliery and the chapel. As has been shown, there was a two-way traffic between colliery and chapel; ministers descended the mine to lead the underground services, while miners ascended the pulpit to become preachers, adapting the harsh realities of coal-mining to sermon illustrations (see Chapter 2). D. Ben Rees has suggested three further links: first, between the management of the mining industry and Nonconformity, where the miner's advancement

58 John Thomas, Capel Mair, St Clears, Carmarthenshire [n.d.], photograph.

underground led to a corresponding promotion in his status in the chapel, which resulted inevitably in the rise of that 'influential figure in industrial Nonconformity – the Colliery-Manager Chapel-Deacon or Elder'; secondly, the emotional and fervent manner in which some miners' leaders addressed Federation meetings reflected the 'enthusiasm or hywl of impassioned preaching'; and thirdly, structural similarities in the way work at the colliery was organized and chapels administered.[36]

Structural correspondences between them were expressed architecturally by what John Hilling considered 'a strong similarity between the less pretentious chapels and some of the colliery buildings which were built during the same period, probably by the same craftsmen'.[37] This is most evident when one compares chapels and the colliery engine-house and fan-house from the late Georgian period to the mid nineteenth century **(58, 59)**. Externally, this similarity is evident in the box-shaped construction in brickwork or dressed stone with pitched roof and gable ends, together with the tall round-arched windows on the façade and along the sides. Engine-houses in the second half of the nineteenth century kept pace with the architectural developments of the chapels, sporting brickwork versions of Palladian semi-circular windows, architraves, quoining, pilasters, pediments, and simple entablatures. In some cases, it was only the absence of stucco rendering or a plaque bearing a biblical name that distinguished these buildings from their religious counterparts.

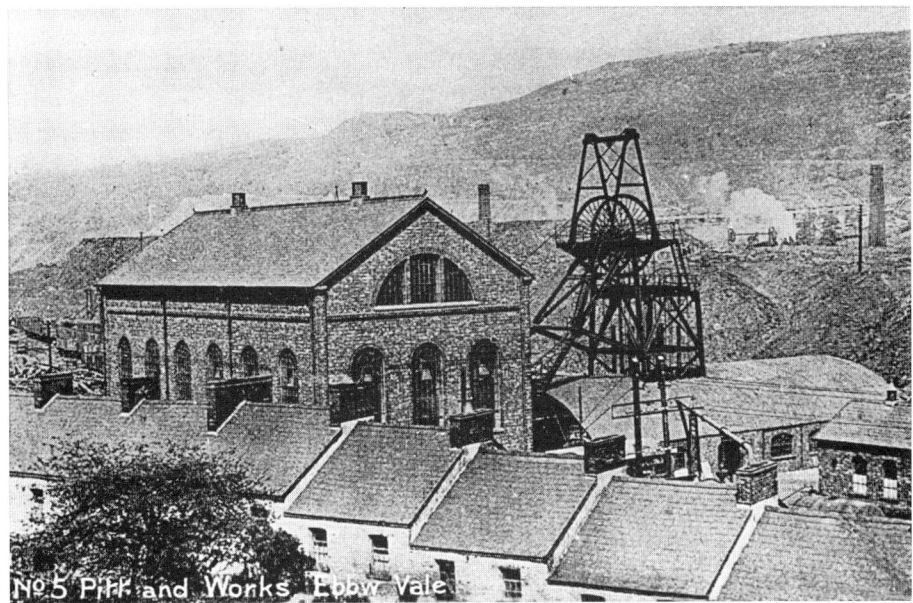

59 Engine-house no.5, The Prince of Wales Pit, Ebbw Vale, Monmouthshire, (twentieth century, first quarter) postcard.

In spite of increasing ornamentation, the external aspect of the engine-house maintained a closer link with the functional and austere chapels of the late eighteenth and early nineteenth centuries than with the eclectic edifices erected during the last quarter of the nineteenth century. However, internally some engine-houses exhibited features that would not have been out of place in a lavish Victorian chapel. The walls of the engine-house of Bargoed Colliery, Monmouthshire were finished in painted stucco, and ranked with a series of moulded architraves that surrounded the windows and spanned pilasters capped by Corinthian entablatures. Glazed tiles incorporating ornamental motifs faced the dado, while the gas engine was further dignified by a decorative wrought-iron rail, not unlike that enclosing the *sêt fawr*, and a floor made up of encaustic tiles, such as was commonly used in chapel vestries **(60)**. In the latter part of the nineteenth century, Nonconformists affectionately called the chapel 'the powerhouse of prayer'. The architectural correspondences between God's house and the colliery's engine-house bestowed on the metaphor an unusual poignancy. The interior of the engine-house at Bargoed Colliery reflected an age when art and industry, beauty and technology, despite being considered incompatible by William Morris (1834–96) and the Arts and Crafts Movement, performed in unison. Classical motifs and ornamentation graced the most functional of mechanical apparatus, lavishing the splendours of high culture on the machinery of utility. The vertical steam winding engine at Glyn Pits, Pontypool is a fine example. Enclosed by cast-iron Roman Doric columns supporting a Tuscan stone entablature, the engine became a veritable shrine to efficiency and production. Such

60 Gas engine, Bargoed Colliery, Monmouthshire (*c*.1913), photograph, *Coal Mining and the Coal Miner* (1920).

embellishments ennobled the concept and context of labour. By this means classical form gave the machine a heroic aspect and a conspicuous dignity, as it had done for the labourer in Madox Brown's *Work*.

The architectural relationship between colliery and chapel extended below the surface of the pit. W. Gerwyn Thomas related how in 1866, at the Mynydd Newydd Colliery, Forest Fach, near Swansea, miners constructed a chapel underground. This was occasioned by an awakened awareness of God and of their own mortality in response to an explosion at the colliery which had killed three fellow miners:

> A chamber was hewn out of the solid coal and supported by timber along the sides and in rows across. The roof and sides were whitewashed and rough plank seats placed between the rows of timber. There, every Monday at 6 a.m. for the next sixty years, until the colliery closed in 1932, a service was held before the men proceeded to their working places.[38]

An illustration of the colliery chapel appeared in the *Sunday Magazine* in 1899 (61).[39] It was the only chapel ever built without an exterior aspect, in other words whose external walls were the whole earth. While above ground chapel buildings were assuming mid-century vernacular styles and gathering ever more architectural and decorative accretions, this coal-house of God returned to the roots and fundamentals of Dissenting 'architecture'. Like the barn-type chapels of the early eighteenth century, the underground chapel was constructed using the skills, tools, and materials of the workmen who worshipped there. In its plainness and practical austerity the underground chapel echoed the spartan interiors of whitewashed walls, columns and crude furniture of timber, and, in some instances, the bare compressed earth floor of its predecessors.[40] In this way the architecture of anthracite revived a context of religious worship unadorned, beyond necessity, by the artifice of man – one which made seeing subservient to listening, where the only ornament was the rhetoric of preaching, singing, and prayer. For the miner, daily facing the peril of death, a vision of God's grandeur during the underground services would have been of greater practical comfort than a sight of architectural splendour. One aspect of the interior decoration of chapels above ground did descend into the pit. During the 1904–5 revival, the painted biblical texts which silently preached from the chapel walls became solemn declarations to 'get right with God' chalked on drams. At Cwmaman Colliery texts discouraging blasphemy, issuing biblical warnings, and commending God's love and commandments were daubed on the underground doors of the chambers and roads of the pit, a literary parallel to the stucco images painted on the walls of the early Christian catacombs.[41]

The colliery chapel was situated on the border of the perilous chambers and roads of the pit which, because of its associations with darkness and devastation, preachers and miners likened to Hades in the homiletic tradition. Against the background of that tradition, this underground 'sanctuary of the Most High' connoted a sort of limbo, more specifically *Limbus Patrum* – the underworld abode of the saints which was located somewhere between, and which combined aspects of, heaven and hell. Accordingly, the preacher's journey down the mine to minister at the chapel's services took on a typological correspondence to Christ's descent into limbo to deliver the souls of the saints imprisoned there. Likewise, the saintly miners, incarcerated in the pit and awaiting liberation by Christ the rescuer-redeemer, can be interpreted as a type of captive spirits.

Work and Worship in the Later Paintings of Nicholas Evans

Entombed – Jesus in the Midst stands as an emblem of the religious revival of 1904–5. The image is a visual echo of H. Elvet Lewis's portrait of the revival, *With Christ among the Miners*, published in 1906, whose title suggests a view of the awakening as a divine mission to the south Wales miner in particular, as mentioned above. The fusion of religion and mining occurs covertly in a number of Evans's later works. Evans's *Standing a Post* (1976) connotes the themes of the saintly labourer and the consecration or sanctity of work in Staniforth's drawing – for which *The Angelus* became an emblem in the homiletic tradition **(63)**. The painting does not depict a scene of mining during the revival or indeed an overt act of piety but evokes the ethos of the revivalist and religious-genre traditions. It does this by embodying these themes in its portrayal of two miners working together to stand a beam of wood between the floor and roof of the heading. The religious element is not therefore in

61 Mynydd Newydd Colliery, Forest Fach, Swansea, *Sunday Magazine* (1899).

the denoted subject of the painting, but consists rather in the connotations of certain compositional and iconographic signifiers which create a religious ethos that pervades the work.[42]

The two miners are on either side of the post in a static pose which is strangely out of keeping with what one imagines to be the rigorous physical effort involved in the work of erecting the post. Both are in semi-profile and have the same physique and very similar physiognomies: the resulting symmetry imparts a heraldic or emblematic character to the composition. Both men kneel as they position the post securely against the low ceiling of the stall. The attitude of prayerfulness that this position connotes is further emphasized by the closing of their eyes, a feature which also endows their faces with a mystic serenity. Their arrangement on either side of the upright timber evokes a formal correspondence with the kneeling figures of the votaries at the foot of the crucifixion as in, for example, Raphael's (1483–1520) *Christ on the Cross with the Virgin, John, Jerome and Mary Magdalene* (*c.*1503). If one brings to the work a further aesthetic knowledge of traditional Christian iconography, the radiance encircling the candles on their caps connotes haloes – like the light on Christ's cap in *Entombed* – thereby signifying the saintliness of the two miners. Together with their physical composure and posture, this feature adds to the aura of sanctity that envelops an otherwise mundane job. In a secondary and connotative sense the miners are shown canonized, high priests of the liturgy of labour. Furthermore, in *Standing a Post* the labourers' worship does not follow their work, as in *The Angelus*, or precede their work as in 'The Religious Revival', but occurs

62 Nicholas Evans, *Underground Chapel during 1904 Revival* (1977), oil on board, 122 × 122.

63 Nicholas Evans, *Standing a Post* (1976), oil on board, 122 × 122.

simultaneously with work: work is worship. The two are inextricably fused; labour is sanctified in the doing of it.

Evans has publicly decried the social stigmatization of the miner in the nineteenth and early twentieth centuries and has endeavoured through his work to make his public appreciate the appalling circumstances which these men and women endured to finance the civic development of Wales. In contrast to the contempt with which miners were commonly regarded by the upper class during the nineteenth century, he insisted, 'the miner, he's a man . . . the navvy digging a hole, he's a man'.[43] Evans has expressed his esteem for the miner by transforming his physical aspect, following, to some extent, the classical aesthetic of conveying the inward nobility of saints, prophets, apostles, and martyrs through the idealization of their outward appearance, thus making external form consistent with greatness.[44]

Evans depicts the nobility of the labourer not only in his gigantic physique but also through the performance of acts of almost Herculean strength. In *Miners Approaching Workplace* (1978) they appear like lumbering, bullish giants, walking two abreast and almost filling the width and height of the road. *Early Mining* (1976) shows two miners arranged in profile and, as in *Standing a Post*, almost symmetrical on either side of the vertical centre of the format. The powerful diagonal dynamics of the square pass through their shoulders, conferring gravity to the curling-box being lifted by the miner on the left and to the downward pull of the miner on the right wielding a pick. The rippling musculature of their chest and arms, overdeveloped by the rigours of labour, gives these underground excavators a monolithic presence. *The Dignity of Labour* (1983), which title clearly reflects Evans's affirmation of the stature of the miner's calling, shows eight colliers in close proximity, hewing as though to cut a space for themselves to breathe (Evans entitled an almost identical composition, painted in the same year, *Claustrophobia*). It is an image of communal labour, a team of men engaged in a common effort, their mighty strength connoted pictorially by a compositional dynamic which erupts from the base of the picture like water thrust from a geyser.

The muscularity of Evans's miner follows in the nineteenth-century tradition of the heroic worker, exemplified in *Work*. However, Evans's figures depart from this tradition in many important respects, conveying a view of the labourer at variance with the traditional ideal. Compare the figure of the navvy with a spade standing in the hole in *Work* with that of the miner shovelling coal in *Coalface (2)* (1976) **(51)**. The navvy stands upright, his legs straight and astride, with the resolute expression and arrogant strength of Michelangelo's *David* (1501–4). Like *David*, Madox Brown's navvy is also an ideal conception of manliness, perfect in surface and proportion, his skin and clothes unsullied by the earth and grime of his occupation. The overshirt he wears shines brightly in the sunlight like the white robes of the redeemed (in the Carlylean theology of work this is precisely what labourers were). The posture of Evans's miner expresses neither determination nor physical might. He stoops forward, his body and legs buckling under in the effort to lift the weight of coal with the spade. He looks down at the floor of the heading with a wide-eyed stare of resignation at the prospect of relentless toil. Skin and clothes are soiled by both coal-dust and the black water that seeps through the roof of the heading; prominent is an ugly coal-stain as a result of the custom of miners infrequently washing their backs.[45] Thus dignity and nobility are not accorded a fully idealized form but rendered defiled by the conditions of labour which threaten to undermine these values altogether. The representation of the miners in a mixture of classical and genre styles is also evident in Evans's *Underground Chapel during 1904 Revival* (1977) **(62)**. The heroic form is substantially deformed: the miners are large but cumbersome, almost pathetic figures in worn, ill-fitting clothes, with nothing in their form or demeanour to commend them. In this respect they echo Staniforth's representation of the miners in 'The Religious Revival'. Here the artist shows them not with their shoulders thrust back but stooped, their heads bowed in an attitude befitting men who have been humbled by the admonitions of the Sermon on the Mount.

Thus, while in Evans's paintings the image of the miner connotes saintliness and nobility by means of the classical aesthetic, these attributes are mitigated by aspects of outward appearance, which evoke contrary readings. The tension between the polarities of dignity and humility, strength and weakness, represented by the synthesis of the aesthetics of classical and genre, are rooted in Evans's theology of man. According to the traditional Protestant confession, work – whether physical or moral endeavour – is not a means of redemption but the fruit of it.[46] What redeems a person is the grace of God alone through salvation, while what dignifies the labourer is the idea of work as a divinely appointed task. Contrary to Carlyle, Evans does not believe that labour is a means by which man may perfect himself. Only at the resurrection will the ideal state be realized.[47] In this world man bears the marks of his fall in Adam together with the vestiges of nobility derived from having been made in the image of God. The aesthetic synthesis is, in this way, a formal connotation or metaphor for that spiritual duality. The final chapter explores this idea more fully.

8
'The Shadow of Death': Mining and Mortality in the Paintings of Nicholas Evans

> Pit. A simple word
> With black connotations.
> A Bible word between covers
> That are always dark.
> Robert Morgan, 'Word'[1]

For most of his life Nicholas Evans has been a member of the Apostolic Church, an arm of the Pentecostal movement which grew out of the 1904–5 revival. Many of the Church's early members had been converted in the revival and perpetuated its spirit of radical separatism. This required the renunciation of cultural and material interests in favour of exclusively spiritual pursuits (see Chapter 3). While Pentecostals resisted many forms of popular culture during more than eighty years of their existence, a more moderate position regarding the media, learning, and the externals of religion has since evolved.[2] Apostolics now acknowledge that they have some limited benefit for the believer as long as they do not usurp his or her spiritual priorities. Spiritual utility and expedience would appear to be still an important criterion for involvement in cultural pursuits, and painting has entered the life of the Apostolic Church on this basis.[3] Evans is a rare, possibly unique, example of a Pentecostal who has achieved an international reputation as an artist. More usually, Pentecostals who possess a natural capacity for, and interest in, art either give up or relegate their ambitions to their leisure time after conversion.[4] Some who enter the ministry bring their gift of art into their services of worship as a means of illustrating the sermons they preach.[5] These attitudes suggest that while Pentecostals do not repudiate art it is, nevertheless, subordinate to the higher priorities of the culture of the soul and the Christian's mission in this world, which art is sometimes called to serve. For Evans too art has a spiritual utility; he has spiritualized the act of painting by conferring on it the status of a private liturgy: it is for him a means of communion with God, a hymn of praise and adoration. He also describes it in terms of visionary encounter and revelation, and of divine inspiration comparable to that experienced by Pentecostal preachers (see Chapter 5).

Apostolics recognize a further expression of spiritual utility in the relationship between Evans's painting and preaching.[6] The correspondence, according to the writer of an editorial in *Riches of Grace*, lies not in the particular subject-matter of the pictures but in their universal themes. He compares the representations of coal-

64 Nicholas Evans, *'Ashes to Ashes, Dust to Dust'* (1978), oil on board, 122 × 122.

65 Nicholas Evans, *'The Trumpet Shall Sound'* – *Resurrection!* (1978), oil on board, 122 × 122.

mining to preaching, both of which address the great issues of life and the realities of the human condition – suffering, fear, courage, death, bitterness, helplessness, heroism, fortitude, and disappointment. The paintings have a specifically religious content too, communicated through their ability to evoke 'thoughts about . . . the terror of inevitable judgement; and the inexplicable confidence arising from the all-pervading presence of a God who became a Working Man and Who still drinks the cup of human pain and suffering with us'.[7]

Entombed – Jesus in the Midst denotes explicitly the theme of Christ's incarnation and identification with the working class. *'Ashes to Ashes, Dust to Dust'* and *'The Trumpet Shall Sound' – Resurrection!* illustrate clearly the themes of death and judgement. The former shows the coffins of miners killed in a pit disaster being interred in a common grave, wreathed with mourners, with the clergyman pronouncing the committal prayers (as the title suggests) **(64)**. *Resurrection* depicts a cemetery at the day of resurrection, with the resurrected bodies of those who died believing in Christ rising to meet Him in the air **(65)**. In a number of Evans's other paintings of mining there are two iconic messages in operating simultaneously: what Barthes observed to be the 'perspective' or 'denoted' message, and the 'cultural', 'symbolic', or 'connoted' message of an image. The connoted meaning can be read only by bringing to the image a certain 'practical, national, cultural, aesthetic' knowledge.[8] For example, it was demonstrated in Chapters 6 and 7 that biblical concepts permeate Evans's works which appear to be historical documents of mining only. If we bring to the paintings a knowledge of national and cultural ideas about Israel and

Wales, some of theses images also evoke a correspondence between the community of the Old Testament Israelites under the yoke of the Egyptians and that of the south Wales miners. By bringing to the paintings an aesthetic knowledge of western religious painting, we may consider several of them to be religious according to a nineteenth-century definition of religious art as paintings that deal not with the representation of biblical stories but with the religious customs of the peasant class. Evans's work follows in the tradition of paintings such as *The Angelus* and the representations of miners engaged in devotions underground, drawn during the religious revival of 1904–5.

Evans's representation of the saintly labourer is in many ways very different from the noble classic form given to the labourer in Victorian painting, as exemplified in *Work*, in that his figures appear defiled and deformed. This portrayal of the miner reflects the Protestant view of man's fallenness and subjection to death and judgement. Evans's paintings fulfil the condition for modern religious art proposed by the liberal theologian Paul Tillich (1896–1965), who looked for an art that could express a Protestant understanding of man and his spiritual condition, one that could emphasize man's distance from God, his 'finitude, his subjection to death, but above all, his estrangement from his true being and his bondage to demonic forces – forces of self-destruction'. Tillich considered Picasso's *Guernica* (1937) to be 'a great Protestant painting': if the painting was considered 'as an example – perhaps *the* outstanding one – of an artistic expression of the human predicament in our period, its negative-Protestant character is obvious. The question of man in a world of guilt, anxiety, and despair is put before us with tremendous power.' However, it was not the subject-matter of the work that gave it a Protestant character for Tillich – 'the willful and brutal destruction of a small town by Fascist airplanes' – but rather its style, or more particularly the expressive element of that style, which he defined as the 'radical transformation of the ordinarily encountered reality by using elements of it in a way which does not exist in the ordinarily encountered reality'. Tillich's interpretation of *Guernica* embodied two important ideas: first, the possibility of art having religious significance without recourse to the traditional store of Christian iconography, and secondly, the potential for the language of painting itself to become a vehicle for religious expression.[9]

Any attempt to draw parallels between Tillich's theory of religious art and the Protestant significance in Evans's work requires careful qualification. Evans's theological convictions, rooted in the theology of conservative fundamentalism, are in many respects far removed from Tillich's liberalism.[10] The doctrines of these two schools of thought regarding the nature of Christ, the Church, redemption, the doctrine of man, and the Bible are, at many points, opposed to one another. Evans's view of religion is not principally one of an attitude of seriousness or 'ultimate concern', or of an existential encounter with 'the ground of being'. For him religion is the expression of a practical and obedient response to the principles embodied in the Bible: the Bible is the focus and content of religion. Consequently, any attempt to discuss religious expression in relation to Evans's painting must take into account this biblical basis. The religious expression of Evans's work will not therefore be considered in Tillich's sense, of the artist laying bare his own religious essence, and that of reality, through colour, gesture, and line. The 'negative-Protestant' message resides in not only the stylistic form of Evans's painting – the 'radical transformation of encountered reality', as Tillich put it, but also the paintings' titles and composition in some cases – resulting from their intersection with the traditions of western European art, and the Nonconformists' visualization of religious and biblical concepts. The theme of man and his spiritual predicament (his sinful condition and consequent mortality) is connoted when a cultural knowledge of the tradition of homiletic illustration in particular is brought to bear on them (see Chapter 2).

Titles and Texts

None of Evans's mining paintings displays biblical imagery and symbolism, or yields a homiletic narrative, as readily as *Entombed*. Nevertheless, as with *Entombed*, some of Evans's later works intimate the theme of mortality in conjunction with their titles or texts. Henry More had advised that biblical texts be appended to religious paintings in the form of 'proper *Inscriptions*' (see Chapter 1). These add a literary gloss to the visual image, one intended to interpret the biblical meaning of the pictures, to elevate them above the merely sensual, and to direct the looker towards the true source of spiritual edification. Evans's titles serve a similar function. As with the phrase 'in the midst', they allude if not to biblical texts then to biblical concepts, elevating the works' significance above that of the denoted subject, and addressing the looker to more universal themes.

For the most part the relation of title to image in Evans's paintings follows nineteenth-century categorizations. Gombrich identified three classes: anecdotal, descriptive, and referential.[11] Arguably, the titles *A Place of Refuge*, *The Broken Rope*, and *The Last Bond*, for example, transcend the class of the anecdotal to become referential, what Gombrich also called generalizing, portentous, and mood-setting titles, which create a quasi-religious ethos, and allude to the precariousness of human existence. *A Place of Refuge* describes a manhole set in the side of the main road where miners could go for safety to avoid the train of drams that could suddenly hurtle down the tracks. Several miners are squeezed tightly into its confines, keeping their distance from the lash of the drams' tail rope which is still vibrating from the force of the descent. The title is contained in the following verse from Isaiah as a figurative description of God as protector and shelter for His people in danger and extremity: 'And there shall be a tabernacle for a shadow in the daytime from the heat, and for a place of refuge, and for a covert from storm and from rain' (Isaiah 4: 6). The language of the Old Testament, Edwyn Bevan wrote, 'suggests a world more primitive than ours'. If we possess the requisite cultural knowledge of the biblical text, the title casts what Bevan describes as reflections of the biblical world upon the subject of the painting.[12] The idea of the refuge occurs most frequently in the

66 Nicholas Evans, *The Broken Rope* (1979), oil on board, 122 × 122.

Psalms where this shelter of God is likened to that of a rock (Psalms 91: 9; 94: 22). Toplady adapted this metaphor in the opening lines of his hymn: 'Rock of Ages, cleft for me, / Let me hide myself in Thee.' Quarles represented the concept with the image of the child-figure hiding in the cave from the vengeful Cupid (see Chapter 1 **(10)**).[13] It is through the mediation of both Toplady's image and Quarles's engraving that the biblical metaphor is evoked in Evans's painting of the miners hiding in the depression cut in the side of the road to avoid death. The image in relation to these references is an illustration in mining terms of God sheltering His people. The Welsh translation of a 'place of refuge', *noddfa*, was also often used to name a chapel. It emphasized the concept of the building as a sanctuary or tabernacle (see Isaiah 6: 4 above), terms which Nonconformists frequently and affectionately substituted for 'chapel' when referring to their place of worship. Therefore within the culture of Nonconformity the title had inescapable religious connotations.

The title of *The Broken Rope* belongs to three paintings each depicting the carnage and destruction following the severance of the rope used to pull and lower the drams from the coal-face to the surface of the colliery. The drams have hurtled down the track and crashed into the miners and ponies working below **(66)**. Since all the major mining disasters in Wales have resulted from explosions, it is curious that Evans should choose to attribute the death and destruction in all three paintings to a comparatively mundane cause; stranger still, since – with a different title – the 1979 version could just as well illustrate a catastrophic scene underground after an explosion or a pit-fall. The title can be read not only descriptively, but also – like the title of *Entombed – Jesus in the Midst* – as a text. It is ambiguous, interpretable not only as indicating the cause of the disaster, but also as a euphemism for death, derived from the commonplace metaphor of life as a thread. The metaphor is implied in Hezekiah's contemplation of his impending death: 'I have cut off like a weaver my life' (Isaiah 38: 12). In referring to the disasters by the title of *The Broken Rope*, Evans transcends the contemplation of a local and particular instance of human mortality to evoke a universal application. Within the homiletic tradition's use of disasters, the predicament of the miners can stand for the lot of all sinners. The sentiment expressed may be as follows: just as their rope was severed, so the rope of every man's life will one day be cut.

The title of *The Last Bond* also suggests a *double entendre*. In mining terminology the term 'bond', in its strictly technical sense, is a synonym for the cage which confines the miners and carries them down the pit-shaft.[14] However, the meanings one normally associates with the word include imprisonment, slavery, and binding together (*OED*). These emotive overtones invest the title, and the image in turn, with other nuances of meaning in a way that the title *Pit Closure – Miners Coming Up for the Last Time*, given to an almost identical painting, does not. On one level both paintings depict the same subject, that of the last cage of miners to ascend the pit-shaft before the colliery is finally closed. In the former painting, however, 'bond' evokes the additional sense of the common humanity, circumstance, and outlook that unites these miners, a solidarity endorsed by the uniformity with which Evans has portrayed their facial expressions. In this way the image transcends the mere description of an aspect of mining history. The prefix 'last' indicates the approaching termination of this association. But since the subject of the painting is not explicit, we are free to speculate as to what will bring the solidarity of these miners to an end, be it redundancy or an impending colliery disaster. These connotations are corroborated by the compositonal allusions and stylistic form of a number of the paintings.

'Iconnotation': Evocations of Judgement, Hell, and Death

The denoted subjects of some works connote concepts associated with mortality and judgement by their resemblance to compositional motifs in western religious painting. Compositional affinities and allusions have already been observed between the graphic representation of mining art and of biblical scenes in Staniforth's 'The Religious Revival' and Rembrandt's 'Christ Preaching Remission of Sins' (see Chapter 7) **(56, 57)**. *Entombed* manifests an affinity with Piero della Francesca's (*c*.1410/20–1492) *Resurrection of Christ* (1474). The formal parallels are considerable. In both, Christ stands with His head at the apex of a classical-pyramidal composition, with four figures at the base of the triangle, their bodies directed inwards and their feet meeting at a common centre. The soldier at the front left of

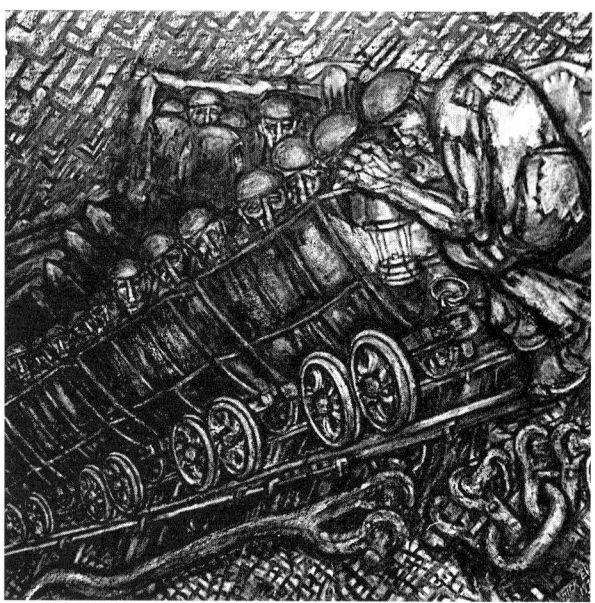

67 Nicholas Evans, *Transport to the Far End* (1976), oil on board, 122 × 122.

68 Nicholas Evans, *Journey to the Far End* (1979), oil on board, 122 × 122.

the picture is crouched sleeping, with his face buried in his hand, like the collier at the rear right of *Entombed*. In the *Resurrection of Christ*, Christ holds the long-shafted flag emblematic of His victory over death. Evans substitutes the biblical symbol of the lamp, and portrays Him holding the keys of death and hell instead of clasping His robes (as in della Francesca). The theological content of Evans's work is richer, Christ being depicted symbolically both as victor over the grave and as the God of comfort and judgement. The trees on either side of Christ in della Francesca correspond to the position of the upright timbers in *Entombed*, and the classical sarcophagus, symbolic of Christ's tomb, out of which Christ emerges, is in Evans's painting the cavernous interior of the sealed pit. In both cases the biblical idea of Christ's place of burial has been exchanged for an equivalent concept of a tomb contemporary to the artist's milieu. *Entombed* is not, however, the *Resurrection of Christ* in a modern setting. The former stresses the imprisonment of men while the latter depicts the release of Christ.

Another compositional analogy occurs in two works dealing with the same subject which are themselves compositionally alike, *Transport to the Far End* (1976) **(67)** and *Journey to the Far End* (1979) **(68)**. Both depict colliers travelling in drams to their place of work under the charge of the rider who stands on the wire rope outside the last dram.[15] In the bottom right-hand corner of the *Last Judgement* (1536–41), Michelangelo has represented the classical myth of Charon, the official boatman of the Underworld, ferrying the souls of the damned across the river Acheron towards the infernal regions. This myth is evoked pictorially in Evans's picture by the correspondence of the rider at the rear end of the dram to Charon, who is usually

69 Nicholas Evans, *The Last Bond* (1983), oil on board, 103 × 122.

70 *The Last Judgement* (detail), (*c.*1000), ivory, 15.5 × 21.5.

depicted standing or sitting at the rear of the boat, and of the forlorn cargo of miners compacted into the transport to the despairing damned facing their ultimate journey. In the iconography of Charon, often only the stern of the boat is represented; Evans depicts the rear end of the train of drams, the forward section having already disappeared into the tunnel (68).[16] Metaphorically, both journeys have the same destination, the pit being likened to Hades or hell in the homiletic tradition.[17]

Three other works by Evans show affinities with paintings illustrating concepts in Christian mythology, that is, beliefs adhered to by some sections of the Church which are not explicitly taught in the canonical writings of Scripture. *Pit Closure – Miners Coming Up for the Last Time* (1977), *The Last Bond* (1979), and *The Last Bond* (1983) all depict a group of colliers in the cage or bond for the last time, perhaps prior to the closure of the colliery. In this sense the paintings, like the theme of Charon, depict an ultimate journey. The image of the bond in the 1983 version

71 John Petts, *The Cage* (1949), cellulose enamel on board, 51 × 76.

appears like a door-frame behind which the colliers are barred. This ambiguity is due to there being only three sides of the cage visible, two verticals and a horizontal. As such, it is reminiscent of scenes depicting the myth of the harrowing of hell, which is derived from an interpretation, largely rejected by Protestants, of New Testament texts in which Christ is said to have descended into hell to release the righteous of pre-Christian times.[18] Certain Italian early Renaissance paintings show prisoners crowded around the threshold of a doorway from which Christ has removed the gates (the gates of hell). In *The Last Bond* (1983) the colliers press against the bond's gate, the lateral bars evoking the bars of a prison. The gate of the bond is also, metaphorically, the entrance to the pit of hell **(69)**.

A similar formal arrangement of heads and bodies as that in *Pit Closure* **(Plate 5)** and *The Last Bond*, together with their skull-like physiognomy, can be found in a relief panel of the *Last Judgement* (*c*.1000) **(70)**. In the bottom right-hand corner is a square section bisected vertically, the right-hand part being divided again horizontally. In the upper square of this section are eight skulls, and in the bottom section eight heads, both sets arranged in a 2–3–3 formation. The conscious patterning of these elements confined within a square is the essence of Evans's painting. In the vertical section to the left of the two squares are three rows of standing figures pressed in on all sides by the enclosure of a rectangle, as the miners were similarly constrained by the frame of the bond. To the left of them are two figures, who according to eschatological theology are the resurrected in Christ emerging from the tomb to the sound of an angel's trumpet (1 Corinthians 15: 51–2). The standing figures –

confined within a frame like the miners in the cage in *The Last Bond* (1983) – are thus either believers or sinners awaiting their turn to emerge from the grave. The harrowing of hell is a thematic precursor of Evans's *Entombed*. Christ comes to those imprisoned in the pit of hell bearing the keys of death and hell, signifying His ability to release those bound in their sins.

Miners in a bond or cage are also the subject of John Petts's (b. 1914) *The Cage* (1949), but its treatment is quite different from Evans's **(71)**. The miners' heads are arranged informally, the use of perspective being the more conventional one of overlapping heads as opposed to the 'inverted perspective' of the two versions of *Pit Closure* and *The Last Bond*. The expressions of the faces are varied and animated, conveying different emotions, whereas the uniform emotion in the miners' faces in Evans's work suggests the expressionless stare of skulls arranged row upon row in ossuaries. Petts's work, by virtue of its more documentary approach to the depiction of miners, does not possess the secondary allusions to death of Evans's paintings.

Memento Mori: Death and the Miner

Even though the denoted subjects are not all mining disasters, the covert references or allusions to mortality and judgement give Evans's paintings the status of *memento mori*. Again, this is most clearly exemplified by *Entombed*. Against the background of the homiletic tradition, this scene of disaster and impending death may also be read as an evangelistic tract. Its sentiment is in sympathy with the injunction of the sermon to those at the funeral of the victims of the Cwmtillery Colliery explosion – 'how important it is to be ready to meet the Son of Man!' Evans's representation of miners meeting Christ face to face can be read as a metaphor for the inevitable confrontation into which death will propel them. While the miners live, the figure of Christ is only a presage of their impending audience, and therefore they still have time to make ready. In many of the later works this reminder of death is conveyed not in a narrative as in *Entombed*, but metaphorically, incorporated into the representations of the miners themselves. In the same way as Holman Hunt presaged the death of Christ by the shadow of the cross cast on the wall by His outstretched arms, so Evans has symbolized the presence of death by natural means.

In *Coalface – Tight Squeeze* (1980) the miners' bodies are, at first sight, barely differentiated from the rock they hew, being unified by colour and variegations of tone and pattern **(72)**. Their appearance is like the petrified bodies of the Pompeians who were frozen in the act of labour by the stream of lava which moulded itself upon their bodies like a death-mask. Gradually the almond shapes of their caps, the bone of an arm, the corrugations of fingers and ribcage, and the protrusions of vertebrae become distinguishable from their surroundings. Once identified, we then mentally fit them together, piece to piece, like the bones in the valley of Ezekiel's prophecy, to form complete men. It is as though we were confronted with an aerial view of decomposing corpses partially unearthed from a common grave.[19]

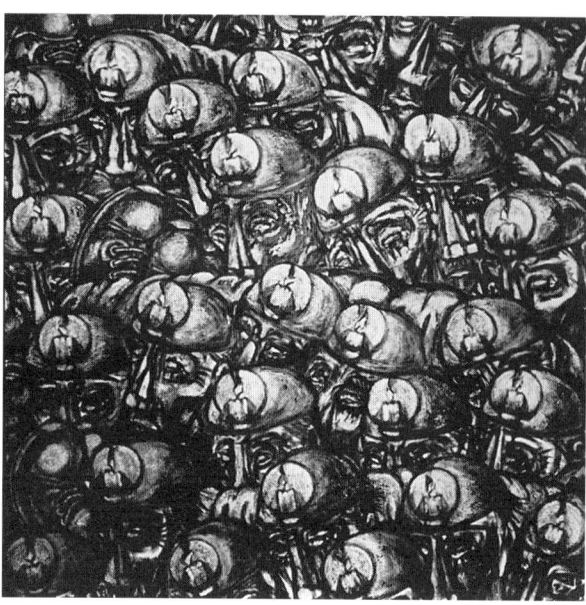

72 Nicholas Evans, *Coalface – Tight Squeeze* (1980), oil on board, 122 × 122.

73 Nicholas Evans, *Candle-Men Carrying Out Dead* (1979), oil on board, 122 × 122.

In *Candle-Men Carrying Out Dead* (1979) the shadow of death is cast across the painting in two ways **(73)**. First, two shrouded corpses are seen being carried from the scene of an underground accident over what Philip Vann aptly described as 'a sea of miners' lamps'.[20] But it is on the faces of the bearers that death is most forcibly represented. They are like skulls: eyes are sunken and closed, and the contours of the bone structure sharply defined by an exaggerated chiaroscuro created by the dark shadows of coal-dust on their faces. This image is not confined to the portrayal of miners in the paintings of disasters alone. Death is written across the faces of miners descending the pit in the cage and at mealtime, and of pitgirls at work. In paintings such as *Coalface* (1978), *Coalface – Tight Squeeze* (1980), and *Coalface 1920s* (1980), the hands and bare torsos of the labouring colliers are skeletal, the shape of their vertebrae, shoulder blades, ribs, and digits being clearly visible, strung with taut muscles. This image of the collier is, in one sense, an objective representation. In 1841, a leading physician described the physique of the young adult collier as 'generally spare, the muscles and sinews being well developed, and well marked in their outlines'.[21] The exaggerated emphasis Evans gives to these characteristics, combined with the appearance of putrescence evoked by the black patches of coal-dust smeared on their flesh, turns the colliers into a kind of half-living, half-dead humanity, evoking images of medieval *transi*.[22]

The allusion to death is amplified in *Pit Closure* and in both versions of *The Last Bond*. The row upon row of colliers' skull-like heads boxed into the confines of the cage resemble arrangements of skulls found in ossuaries or charnel houses. The analogy between the pit and the ossuary was made in the *Mining Journal* in 1846. One writer predicted that if more care was not taken in coal-mining, disasters would become a frequent occurrence and 'South Wales would undoubtedly become a huge charnel-house, before which Northumberland and Durham will sink into insignificance'.[23] Philippe Ariès described how around the fourteenth century it became common procedure to dig up more or less dried-out bones in the older graves in order to make room for new ones and to pile them in the attics of galleries or above the arches of the charnels.[24] *Pit Closure* presents an analogous arrangement of the heads. Evans has conflated the image of the skeleton, the traditional symbol for a *vanitas*, with the representation of the miners: they bear the image and reminder of their own mortality in themselves.

The skull-like faces of the miners represent one aspect of Evans's 'radical transformation' of the human figure. The evocations of mortality and corruption are strengthened when an aesthetic knowledge of classical figure representation is addressed to Evans's miners. They connote a view of man at variance with the humanist ideal. This interpretation is based on the conversion of a formal characteristic of the works into a theological analogy. The approach has been applied to the study of Rembrandt's portrayal of the human figure and pictorial composition in comparison with their counterparts during the High Renaissance. In both, the formal language of the artist is regarded as conveying a philosophical or theological meaning. The classical aesthetic was intimately bound to the world-view of the Renaissance. The Herculean figures – perfectly proportioned, finely contoured, and evenly surfaced – were the visual analogue for the concept of an ideal humanity. With the Reformation, this humanistic confidence was challenged by a view of man which emphasized his innate moral and spiritual depravity, inherited from his forefather Adam. Commenting on Paul's assertions to this effect in Romans chapter 5, verse 12, Calvin wrote:

> Yet Paul affirmeth plainly, that sin hath entered into all which suffer the punishment of sin. And that he urgeth more strictly, when, a little after, he setteth down the reason why all the posterity of Adam is subject to the power of death, namely, (quothe he,) because we have all sinned. Furthermore, this same *to sin*, is to be corrupt and faulty. For that natural pravity which we bring out of our mother's womb, although it do not so soon show forth his fruits, yet, nevertheless it is sin before the Lord, and deserveth his vengeance: And this is that sin they call original. For as Adam, by his first creation, as well received for himself as for his posterity the gifts of God's grace; so he, falling from the Lord, corrupted, vitiated, defiled, and destroyed our nature in himself.[25]

Within the Protestant theological system the realization of the ideal state of man is not possible on earth or in a Platonic realm of pre-existent ideas, but rather belongs to heaven, at least for those who have been redeemed by faith in the saving merit of Christ. This view does not permit an exalted notion of man's glory and achievement.

This radically different evaluation of humanity could not be expressed in the aesthetic of the Renaissance. Rembrandt is credited with having evolved a vision and a representation of man informed by the Reformation experience and conveying the Protestant message. William Halewood commented briefly on the contrast between the illustration of the parable of the prodigal son in prints by Maerten van Heemskerck (1498–1574) and Rembrandt. In van Heemskerck's woodcut and engraving, the penitent son is given the monumentality of a Greek god. In Rembrandt's etching 'The Return of the Prodigal Son' (1636), however, the physical frame of the prodigal is withered, the musculature limp, and the skeletal structure protrudent, imparting an uneven contour to the torso and limbs. Rembrandt presents a visual metaphor for the effects of the degradation of sin and a reflection on man's fallenness.[26]

The prodigal, according to the interpretation of Nonconformist preachers, represented the sinner, while the son's condition of 'riot and ramble . . . represents to us a sinful state, that miserable state into which man has fallen'.[27] The prodigal and his condition were the biblical equivalent for the miner and his lot in the homiletic tradition. Evans's half-naked miners working underground are far more disfigured and defiled than Rembrandt's penitent son. As they wield picks and shovels or push drams, their muscles become taut and pronounced, yet these significations of strength or might are countered by their overriding debilitation; they appear awkward, inelegant, cowed by their cramped conditions of work; their facial expressions are tired and sullen; their heads are sometimes sunk in between their shoulders, or their chins into their chests so that their faces cannot be seen. The anatomy of these broken and anonymous hewing automatons is deformed and out of joint: limbs are disproportionately large, as are hands, which are prominent in the works not only because of their inordinate size but also from the intensity of their realization – they are gnarled, grotesque, and filthy. The surface of their flesh is coarse and lustreless, formed of the same parched black pigment that is dragged and punished in other parts of the canvas to denote coal. The miners, like Adam, are thus formed out of the same stuff as the ground men till by the sweat of their brow (Genesis 3: 19, 23). In terms of the classical aesthetic these men are not endowed with nobility, greatness, grace, or elegance, but instead are shown in a condition of weakness and vulnerability. The stylistic deformation of their bodies may be thought of not primarily as an expression of the artist's inner necessity, impulses, and experiences but as an externalization of the miners' (metaphorically, humanity's) spiritual condition. Their emaciated and defiled appearance is a visual metaphor for the harrowing effects of sin on the individual, a materialization of man fallen from grace or, as Calvin put it, man 'corrupted, vitiated, defiled, and destroyed'.

Black as Sin

Evans's portrayal of miners evokes the apostle Paul's metaphor of 'the body of this death' (Romans 7: 24). The biblical text provided the legend for Book 5, Emblem 8

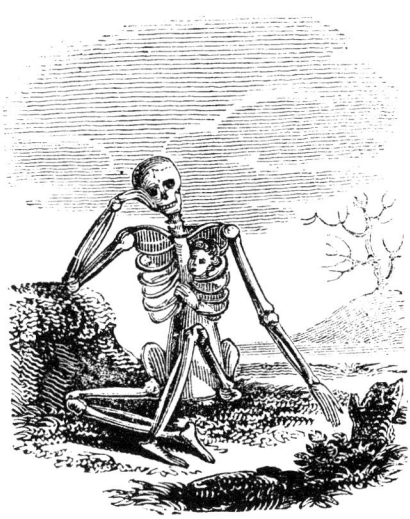

74 Book 5, Emblem 8, steelplate engraving, *Emblems, Divine and Moral* (1818).

of Quarles **(74)**. The engraving shows a *transi* within whose carcass the child-figure (symbolizing the soul) is imprisoned. A literary antecedent for the image is found in Ignatius Loyola's (1491–1556) advice: 'If you want to meditate on something invisible like sin, look with the eye of imagination how your soul is incarcerated in this corrupt body.'[28] As a visual metaphor for the concept of sin in general, Quarles's emblem is unique. Christian iconography has symbols for particular vices only, codified under the heading of the seven deadly sins — avarice, gluttony, sloth, etc. In the iconography of the homiletic tradition, however, sin had several emblems. It was likened to black damp, the noxious gas found in underground workings of the coal-mine, and to the pit itself (see Chapter 2).[29] In a revival meeting of 1905, after prayers had been requested for God's blessing on services at the collieries, the revivalist Sydney Evans asked the congregation whether they believed Christ could wash them whiter than snow, using a biblical metaphor for the forgiveness of sin (Isaiah 1: 18).[30] The immediate context of this enquiry suggests that the congregation and, more particularly, the miners present might have pictured the idea of defilement and cleansing in terms of the ritual washing-off of coal-dust at the end of each day's work. The figurative identification of the pit with hell would endorse coal's connotation of sin. Both had associations with the deepest darkness of the nether world; the effect of sin in the spiritual realm was like that of coal-dust in the physical, that is, it contaminated, debilitated, and produced death.

The association of sin and coal derived from the blackness of the latter and the biblical correlation of blackness or darkness with wickedness. (In both Old and New Testaments, the concepts of 'black' and 'dark' are in some contexts synonymous.)

Similarly, in the Greek of the New Testament, *zophos* the word for 'blackness' (for example, in Jude 13) is, in the apostle Peter's reference to the same subject, also the word for darkness: 'God spared not the angels that sinned, but cast them down to hell, and delivered them into chains of darkness' (2 Peter 2: 4). In this instance blackness and darkness may be considered as attributes of one another. Black operates not as a precise adjective of colour but as a description of the general tone of an object, denoting the absence or obscuration of light and connoting a sorrowful spiritual condition, and as an awesome sign implying the expression and effect of God's judgement of sin.

In the idiolect of a society deeply immersed in biblical culture, black carried with it at the very least echoes of its referents in Scripture, which constitute an unconscious seam of connotations still vital and vivid for the south Walian in the early twentieth century. In the visions of the 1904–5 revival, the devil was often described as black in appearance; Evan Roberts believed that in his vision of the sun the elongated black balls rolling out from it symbolized the kingdom of darkness; and in his vision of two horses, both were wrapped in darkness, which, it would appear, signified the terror of God to Roberts.[31] Nonconformity perpetuated the idea of black as the symbolic antithesis of the biblical connotations of light: spiritual illumination, Christ's kingdom, goodness, and righteousness. In the Nonconformist mind these meanings would be inseparable from the colour. Thus the Calvinistic Methodist R. Williams, in a sermonic article for children entitled 'The Gospel of Colours', posited that black 'is the colour of sin'.[32] In the Bible, black is used as a metaphor for the physical manifestation of the curse of God (Exodus 10: 15 (New International Version); Job 30: 30) and for a characteristic of hell (Jude 13). Hence Williams could concur that black is also the colour of 'sorrow, which in a general way, is the result of sin'.[33] The prophet Jeremiah, for instance, in his lamentation over the consequences of Israel's sin, contrasted the former appearance of her Nazarites, who were 'whiter than milk', with their present condition, in which 'Their visage is blacker than a coal' (Lamentations 4: 8).[34] Likewise, one might speak of the countenance of the miners in Evans's work expressing a blackness that transcends the denotation of coal – the stain of fallenness and corruption. Some miners imputed to the blackness underground the terrors of death and the grave, with the faint echo of the darkness of the bottomless pit in the book of Revelation. Clearly, blackness is frequently used as a spiritual metaphor to connote the fearful unknown, despair, the absence of life, and the foreboding presence of danger and evil. More specifically, blackness symbolized 'the shadow of death', an allusion to the dark valley of Psalm 23 – in the words of one miner, 'the shadows of death ... more terrible than the shadows of night'.[35]

Black is the most immediate and thoroughly pervasive attribute of Evans's painting subsequent to *Entombed* (one of the very few examples of Evans's work painted in polychrome).[36] In *Entombed* the biblical significance of the painting is denoted by the presence of Christ. Thereafter this significance is subsumed into the titles, composition, and style of certain mining paintings, and released when a cultural knowledge of the conflation and homiletic traditions and an aesthetic knowledge of western religious art were brought to it. The paintings after *Entombed* jettisoned not only traditional religious imagery but also variety of colour. In the absence of traditional religious imagery, black too has become a carrier of biblical significance.

The association of black with concepts of sin (and consequent death) is evident when the colour is considered in proportion to, and as the antithesis of, the light in the paintings. What illumination there is does not appear to be cast on the scenes from a single direction or source (except when candles or lamps are prominent in the paintings) but to emanate uniformly from somewhere beneath the surface of things. Fred Licht wrote of how in baroque painting light was thought of as the light of God; in Caravaggio it is the light of heaven shining like a beacon upon the world, while in Rembrandt it is the light of 'God in man shining forth through the dark coils of mortality'.[37] In Evans's painting the light that penetrates the 'dark coils' of the miners' mortality is reduced to a faint glimmer: corroborating the concept of the 'body of death'. In Evans's work the principle of antithesis in equilibrium seen in the opposition of darkness and light in baroque chiaroscuro, is abandoned, the darkness dominating. If the connotation were to be extended, we might interpret Evans as presenting us with a view of man in whom not only death reigns but the image of God (symbolized by light) has also been almost extinguished. Where Rembrandt's use of illumination emphasizes man's glory in spite of the Fall, Evans expresses a 'negative-Protestant' message, stressing the extent of man's depravity even though he still retains something of the divine likeness (see Chapter 1). The gulf that sin has created between man on earth and God in heaven, which Protestants understand to be unbridgeable without the provision of divine faith, may be thought of as further symbolized by the constricting format of the painting. Rudolf Arnheim believed that the square, an emblem for the earth in traditional symbolism, gives psychological expression to the idea of terrestrial captivity, prohibiting the subject of the picture to rise above the gravity of the human condition.[38]

'The Valley of the Shadow'

The blackness of Evans's painting spreads beyond the physiognomy and physique of the miner to the surface of the pit and the landscape beyond, into the hills, trees, and the clouds above. Life above ground, in most instances, is represented as darkly as the underground scenes. The inordinate darkness casts the scenes into what seems like perpetual night. The tonality conveys the connotation of the landscape powdered with coal-dust. This image of the contaminated landscape was reiterated throughout mining poetry of another miner-turned-artist, Robert Morgan (b. 1921). In 'The Donors' he describes the 'bitter soil / Slagblack and bare' and

> the black river . . .
> Its banks littered
> With rags of industry,

and again, in 'Years Ago', 'a river black and banked with mossy slag where grass / And fern were choked or burned or dead'.[39] For Morgan blackness represented the landscape in ruin, pits in a state of dereliction and decay, and the darkened interiors of abandoned chapels. It was a symbol of both the ravages of mining and the death of an era in which mining and Nonconformity were intrinsic to life in the valleys. Evans depicts a period when, historically, labour and religion, colliery and chapel, thrived together. Furthermore, he has never made an issue of the environmental effects of the coal industry; therefore, there appears to be no reason to adduce that this is the primary or principal meaning that the blackened landscapes are meant to convey. The profundity of this blackness is best shown up by a comparison with the landscapes of two other expressionist painters of the mining valleys – Josef Herman and Cyril Ifold (1922–86). In their paintings the black hue that permeates the pigment, while darkening the colours, does not vanquish their sonority and riches. Burgundy, golden yellow, and sun-baked green glow through the veil with an inner light, suggesting that, in spite of the filth, nature still shines through. Evans's landscapes are, by contrast, a wilderness of black, devoid of sensuality and any quality of life.

The inordinate blackness of Evans's landscape is attributable in part to the dark clouds which, either in cumulus form or as an even blanket, are a ubiquitous presence in the pictures. They fill the sky, hug the hills, obliterate the sun, and drastically diminish natural light. They also appear as a dense curtain which separates earth and sky or as an artificial ceiling which turns the world below into a dark and claustrophobic enclosure analogous to the subterranean world of the miner. It was precisely this correspondence between the pit and the world that formed the basis for the homiletic illustration of mining, in which the collier underground was compared to man in his unbelief (see Chapter 6). The concept of the pit as a microcosm of the world provides one explanation for the unnatural darkness with which the surface of the colliery and its surrounding landscape is rendered.

The image of dark clouds in the Old Testament is used as a visual symbol for the judgements and terrors of God (Deuteronomy 4: 11; Hebrews 12: 18). These associations were very much alive in the Nonconformist mind-set at the beginning of the twentieth century. In the 1904–5 revival one collier spoke of the dark clouds of the day of judgement which he felt were hanging over him, creating a visual corollary for his sense of conviction of sin.[40] Evan Roberts repeatedly used the motif of dark clouds as a symbol for divine judgement in his public addresses.[41] Pit tragedies such as that represented in *Ashes to Ashes* were solemn reminders not only of the uncertainty of life but also of the eternal consequences of death – the prospect of judgement and its fearful outcome for those ill prepared for their appointment with Christ. The presence of the dark clouds in this painting evokes the ambiguous resonance of human sorrow and the threatening judgements of God to whom the dead must give account.

The Bible provides one instance of a landscape of extreme darkness – the adumbration of the land of Israel which accompanied the crucifixion: 'And it was

75 Nicholas Evans, *Ecce Homo* (1983), oil on board, 122 × 156

about the sixth hour, and there was a darkness over all the earth until the ninth hour. And the sun was darkened, and the veil of the temple was rent in the midst' (Luke 23: 44–5). Evans has illustrated the event in *Ecce Homo* (1983) **(75)**. The painting's blackness is to an extent denotative, representing the phenomenon of extreme physical darkness described in the biblical account. However, it can also accommodate connotative significations derived from the symbolic meaning of the darkness in the crucifixion narrative. Commentators are generally agreed that there is no single or precise meaning to the phenomenon, which is variously interpreted as an objectification of Christ's dark night of the soul, the mourning of the creation at the death of its creator, a symbol for the mysterious period of three hours in which the atonement was transacted and God's wrath vented and propitiated; a miraculous sign to the unbelieving world to compel it to consider the gravity of the God-man's death, or of the judgement of God on man's sin borne by Christ, as following the principle that 'darkness in Scripture is very often a symbol of judgement'.[42] The same dark clouds that overshadow Jerusalem in *Ecce Homo* hug the mountain tops of Aberdare. Christ and the miner almost two thousand years later are made to occupy the same dismal world. The concept echoes both the sentiments of *Entombed* and the tradition of conflation in which certain features of the landscape of Palestine were attributed to the landscape of Wales. The spiritual connotations of the adumbration – curse, sin, and judgement – are imputed to the darkness enveloping the mining villages in Evans's painting. The attribution of divine anathema to a wasted landscape has a precedent in art. Ruskin, in his critical appreciation of Holman Hunt's *The Scapegoat* (1854), spoke of the Dead Sea on whose shores stood the dying goat as a typological symbol of the curse upon nature as a result of the Fall.[43] The interpretation reflected the idea in Pauline theology that the whole of creation is groaning as a consequence of Adam's sin and waiting for its redemption at the consummation (Romans 8: 22). The blackened landscape, like the blackened faces and bodies of the miners, connotes in a more general sense the result of the Fall.

Painting and Preaching

Black amalgamates with the powerful connotations of sin, death, and corruption summoned by the paintings' titles, composition, and stylistic transformation of the miners to mobilize and strengthen the 'negative-Protestant' message. Like the quasi-Jacobean language and phraseology of Nonconformist prayer, it suffuses the works with a biblical ethos or emotion. In the context of Evans's paintings black acquires a significance antithetical to that of white in meeting-house and early chapel interiors. However, in their use of a single colour, buildings and paintings share an aesthetic of rigorous simplicity, directness, and economy of means which is fundamental to the Protestant plain style, as it is sometimes called. The translation of reality and religious vision to black and white only, moreover, reflects the Protestants' denial of art's sensuous aspect, a conviction which informed both their rejection of icons and the style of emblematic pictures. The binary is also a visual analogy for the moral absolutism of Nonconformist preaching, while the consistent and reiterative use of black throughout Evans's *œuvre*, corresponds to the emphasis on the doctrine of man's inherent sinfulness.[44] The relation of the paintings to preaching is, however, best understood in terms of the visualization of sermon imagery used by ministers preaching in the coal-mining districts of south Wales. Evans's paintings constitute a pictorial parallel for the sermonic metaphors from mining, evoking the typology of the miner as sinner and giving concrete form to invisible concepts such as the uncertainty of life and immanence of death, the spiritual condition of man without God, and the terror of hell. Like Protestant emblems, which yielded their religious significance only when they were read in conjunction with scriptural and pious texts, the biblical content of Evans's paintings is evident only in the context of the homiletic tradition.

In visualizing the homiletic themes of mortality, Evans has revived the spiritual, evangelistic, and meditative character of Quarles's emblems (which was largely abandoned in the late nineteenth century in favour of an emblemature dedicated to morality and extolling exemplary social habits (see Chapter 1)). In this way, Evans has fulfilled the principal requirement of Iona Williams's manifesto for a truly Welsh art, that it would serve religion, reflect the spirituality of the Welsh, and express the 'imaginative power, as often manifested in the discourses of our preachers' (see Chapter 3). The tradition of sermonic interpretations of paintings – which constituted the closest realization of Williams's aspiration for Welsh art – produced a religious art. But it did this by taking English and Italian paintings, often with a non-religious subject-matter, and deconstructing their denoted content to yield a religious or ethical reading. Evans, on the other hand, while maintaining the tradition of investing secular imagery with sacred meaning, has created a religious art from imagery indigenous to the south Wales mining communities. Unlike the sermonic paintings, Evans's synthesis of preaching and painting has produced a religious art which is not overtly didactic or prescriptive in intent.

The advocates of Christian involvement in culture attempted to make Christianity permeate everyday life by reconstructing society along ethical lines. In art this meant reinterpreting the evident meaning of a work by appending to it an often elaborate moral or religious discourse which exceeded the bounds of the painting's subject. At its worst it was a tortuous and highly self-conscious attempt to force two realms to come together. Evans has succeeded in creating an apparently unconscious integration of art and religion, indeed of life and religion, by drawing upon traditions of religious visualization that are native to the community and history of industrial south Wales and the revivalist tradition. In so doing he represents the revival and apotheosis of a failed agenda for art and Nonconformity which was propounded at the beginning of the twentieth century.

Conclusion

God's Word gave Nonconformists not only spiritual and moral teaching but also a cultural, social, political, and visual identity, as well as a biblical ancestry. The Scriptures inhabited their minds and their minds inhabited the Scriptures. Thus inextricably bound together, Nonconformists developed thought-forms and a material expression that were moulded by and resonant with the Word. This is evident in meeting-houses and chapels, the imagery of creative piety (sermons, hymns, prayers, and devotional literature), along with intangible demonstrations of visualization, such as visions. Together these reflect not only the Nonconformists' belief in the invisible spiritual realm but also the need to give visible shape to religious belief and to promote their identity as God's people. This material expression also marks a gradual but significant change, over a period of two hundred years, from a conceptual to a figural approach to religion. By end of the nineteenth century Nonconformists had achieved a dialectic synthesis of Old and New Testament theologies of visualization. Moreover, they had acquired a visual presence which exceeded even that of their Old Testament predecessors. Almost every town and village in Wales had at least one 'Tabernacle' or 'Temple'.

Like the Word made flesh, the Nonconformists' visualization of religion was by nature incarnational. In Christ the spiritual and invisible God clothed Himself in the corporeal; Nonconformists, for their part, embodied biblical concepts in symbols, metaphors, and images based on everyday experiences. Similarly, as He united divinity and humanity, so they fused the eternal and the everyday worlds. By grounding the transcendent in this way, Nonconformists expressed the principle, derived from Christ's parables, of adapting familiar objects, persons, and events as types, allegories, and similes of invisible realities. By this means, Nonconformists related God to man, the heavenly to the earthly, and interpreted the ultimate in terms of common life.

Christ's parables also provided a paradigm for representing God and spiritual concepts without recourse to similitude. The Reformers predicated their emblematic approach to visualizing religion on this example. They conceded that, while the Word prohibited any attempt to make a likeness of God or spiritual entities, it was permissible to convey religious and biblical concepts allusively, in such a way as to identify and dissociate the reality and the image simultaneously. The principle spawned an extensive emblematization of coal-mining in south Wales. This was based on the association between religion and mining and between biblical and contemporary concepts of the pit. Nicholas Evans's *Entombed – Jesus in the Midst* is the pictorial corollary of this tradition. The painting unites labour with devotion, spiritual utility with homiletic imagery, visions and visionary inspiration, and biblical times and places with scenes from Welsh industrial history. As such, Evans's vision is deeply rooted in the Nonconformist culture of south Wales, from which he has derived, like preachers before him, a religious iconography. Evans has transposed the miners and their experiences of working underground into visual emblems for a variety of religious concepts. They include sinner, saint, redemption, judgement, and consolation, and the profound realities of life, sin, death, and eternity. This tradition is expressed in a number of Evans's other paintings. In these works he alludes to themes such as the uncertainty of life and imminence of death, the terror of hell, a general ethos of the Bible in the paintings; Bible stories in terms of coal-mining; biblical characters and types in the figures of the miners; biblical themes and preoccupations in the subject of the works; and biblical symbols. Thus we can speak of Evans's paintings as not only a religious art but also, more specifically, a Nonconformist religious art. Since the mining industry has almost disappeared from the south Wales Valleys, and chapel culture is no longer a vital force in its communities, he is the remnant of the fusion of these two cultures. Through his work, Evans perpetuates the tradition of Nonconformist visualization. Where once that tradition was oral, literary, conceptual, and architectural, it now has pictorial form in his paintings.

Appendices

Appendix 1

Poems and ballads were sometimes composed to commemorate mining disasters and to honour the dead. The following examples drew on the theme of *memento mori* and the identification of miners and sinners:

In Memory of the Miners Who Lost Their Lives in the Terrible Pit Disaster at the Universal Colliery, Senghennydd, South Wales, October, 1913

> In health and strength they left their homes,
> Not thinking death so near;
> It pleased the Lord to bid them come
> And in his sight appear.
>
> Death to them short warning gave,
> Therefore be careful how you live,
> Prepare in time, make no delay,
> For who may know their dying day.
>
> In prime of life they were cut down,
> No longer could they stay;
> Because it was their Saviour's will
> To call them hence away.
>
> They have gone – the grave has received them,
> 'Twas Jesus that called them away;
> They have gone to the Lord who redeemed them
> From night to the splendour of day.

The second piece was composed on the occasion of the explosion at Gresford Colliery, near Wrexham on 22 September 1934:

> You've heard of the Gresford disaster,
> The terrible price that was paid;
> Two hundred and forty-two colliers were lost,
> And three of the rescue brigade.

Down there in the dark they are lying;
They died for nine shilling a day;
They have worked out their shift, and now they must lie
In darkness until Judgement day.

Farewell, our dear wives and our children,
Farewell, our dear comrades as well;
Don't send your sons down the dark, dreary pit,
They'll be damned like sinners in hell.[1]

Appendix 2

The suggestion that drama should also be employed as a handmaid to religion provoked one of the most contentious debates within the Free Churches at the turn of the century. Nonconformists were unanimous in their view that the abstract conception of drama did not in itself contravene the clear precepts and principles of the Bible, and that as a means of recreation and education drama was a very admirable one. However, both from experience and from the history of drama in society, they felt that in practice it was a force for evil rather than good. The content of plays during the late nineteenth century was, in their view, irreverent, irreligious, and vulgar in the portrayal of the serious issues of life. Moreover, the context of play-going and the sensationalism of a performance easily swayed large crowds in their emotions. Acting, they also believed, affected the moral standards of the performers. The disorientation believed to result from impersonating different characters regularly was 'one of the most serious arguments why Christians should not patronize the drama'; that many performers had dubious moral reputations was cited as proof of this.[1] Nonconformist leaders generally acknowledged the propensity of the theatre to foster impure morals in the audience rather than teach goodness and beauty. Judged according to the second and third criteria for acceptability (see Chapter 3), drama was out of bounds for the Christian, as participant and as spectator. Its inclination to stimulate an appetite for itself also condemned it at the bar of the fourth criterion, along with alcohol, for encouraging excess.

However, there were some Nonconformists who maintained that the stage was worth reforming to serve the Church as a religious and moral educator. The Congregationalist minister H. Elwyn Thomas was an articulate advocate of this position. He contended that drama, in its power to govern the affections of men and women, was pre-eminent over the printed word and the picture. This was because its appeal was not to the mind, the eye, or the reason but to the passions and emotions. That potential harnessed by the Church, he argued, would reinvest drama with the moral and religious purpose it had had in the Middle Ages. Thomas envisaged drama as furnishing biblical narrative with 'vivid, life-like description like that of the novelist', for, he contended:

> when one thinks of the success with which [drama] has performed its functions, the realistic manner in which it has presented great and far reaching truths, the way in which it has made dead history and dead persons to live and act again . . . and ambiguous facts alive and real, one cannot but think of the splendid results which would follow were such a power wielded exclusively, or even mainly, on the side of morality and religion.[2]

The idea of religious drama illustrating morals and scenes from the Bible did nothing to stem the criticism of theatre's antagonists. Commenting on Wilson

Barrett's play *The Sign of the Cross*, performed at the Theatre Royal, Cardiff in 1896, the *Baptist Record* praised Nonconformist ministers who had stayed away and castigated the clergy who had attended the performance for their erroneous view of true religion. The theatre did not have the moral integrity to preach the gospel: 'We can only say if the Church goes into the Theatre, and sits at the feet of mere actors, who travesty holy things, there is little hope of sinners coming into the Church.'[3] Nonconformists deemed drama an inappropriate medium of religious instruction also because of the absence of sincerity and reality – which was at the heart of true religion – in the plays. This was evident in the excessive flaunting of stage tricks, and in the sensual indulgence of the audience in its glamour, which detracted from the message conveyed.

However, if the Church could not go to the theatre, perhaps the theatre could come to the Church. Elwyn Thomas could envisage drama making a useful contribution to the social outreach of the chapel of the future. So he proposed: 'Religious drama, to be performed by Christian actors and actresses. Subjects always aiming to reveal the character and record of the great trinity of evils, viz., gambling, social vice, and drunkenness.'[4] He advocated Christian performers, no doubt because they were more likely to portray the subject sympathetically and reverently, and because their morals and life-style would be above reproach. The young people's societies and women's guilds of many chapels during the first half of the twentieth century staged religious dramas depicting scenes from the Old Testament and Church history on platforms erected in front of the pulpit.[5]

Appendix 3

Some years before the religious awakening of 1904–5 Joseph Parry (1841–1903) had foretold that 'the next revival would be a singing revival'.[1] The observation was based on his knowledge of the fifty years preceding the 1859 revival, during which time song had firmly established itself in the Welsh national character. The situation had come about with a revival in congregational singing, which was fostered by the development of *gymanfa ganu*, the introduction of the tonic sol-fa system, and the publication of a book on the grammar of music in 1859 by John Mills (1812–73) and a collection of congregational hymns by his brother Richard Mills (1809–44).[2] The emphasis on singing in the revival of 1904–5 grew in the early days when Evan Roberts dispensed with the opening address at the meetings. His decision was based on the unorthodox conviction that prayer was the primary means for converting sinners.[3] From that time on the meetings were conducted largely by the congregation, and a recognizable pattern developed: hymns were 'given out' by individuals or arose apparently spontaneously from the congregation *en masse* when it was felt that the impromptu prayers – spoken by members of the congregation, often with several praying at once – did not adequately express the sentiments of the moment. The little speaking Roberts did during the services was also frequently subject to these interruptions, which he suffered gladly because he believed that they had been prompted by the Holy Spirit. The use of music in this way supplemented what had in the earlier revivals been one of the functions of preaching – the incitement of emotion.[4] The stirring cadences of the *hwyl* were now replaced by the sway of a pathetic and enthusiastic rendering of popular hymns.

> A hymn-verse is repeated and repeated in triumph, and the genius of the people seems to give newness even to the seventieth repetition. Of the solos, inspired by the wildest emotions and often sung with frenzied gesticulations in appeal to the Almighty – but always well sung – we need not speak.[5]

The congregation's emotions were further regulated by a group of female singing evangelists who accompanied Roberts at nearly every meeting. Either at his direction or following their own 'inner promptings', they would perform impassioned solos and duets to accompany his preaching or lead the congregation in the singing of hymns expressive of the sufferings of Christ, the urgent need for sinners to be reached, and the conversion of the recalcitrant child of a departed Christian mother.

The displacement of preaching by music meant that congregational worship was no longer led by one man – the preacher – but by the body of believers, under the presidency of the Holy Spirit, or so they believed. Consequently, the congregation had more opportunity than ever before to contribute to the content, form, and ethos of a meeting. This democratization of public worship meant that the point of departure for worship shifted from the pulpit to the believer's consciousness, being externalized by means of song, prayer, and public testimony. In this way the apprehension of Scripture became subordinate to the conveyance of inner experience; in other words there was a change in emphasis from religious impression to religious expression. The importance ascribed to inward sensations and compulsions opened the way to sanctioning almost any phenomenon experienced in the believer's consciousness. Consequently not only felt but also perceived spiritual experiences, in the form of visions, were taken seriously and invested with significance.

Appendix 4

The Apostolic Church is fundamentally allied to conservative, Protestant evangelicalism.[1] Its distinguishing tenet, as of the other Pentecostal groups, is a belief in the continuation of the extraordinary manifestations of the Holy Spirit experienced by believers in the New Testament Church.[2] This comprises a powerful and supernatural work of the Holy Spirit in the post-conversion experience of the believer which is called the baptism of the Holy Spirit or the filling of the Spirit, and the practice of spiritual gifts such as prophecy, healing, wisdom, knowledge, faith, miracles, speaking in and interpreting tongues, dreams, and visions. The reception of one or more of these gifts is coincidental with or subsequent to a person receiving the baptism of the Holy Spirit.[3]

In Wales this particular understanding of the doctrine of the baptism of the Spirit is rooted in the theology of revivalism, although Pentecostals trace its line of ancestry to the era inaugurated by the coming of the Holy Spirit upon the disciples on the day of Pentecost (from which they derive their name). However, this blessing, together with its accompanying spiritual gifts recorded in 1 Corinthians chapters 12 to 14, has not always been the constant experience of the Church. Pentecostals believe that the operation of these gifts diminished as the purity of the Church declined, and that it is likely they were withdrawn altogether by the third century. Their restoration, according to Turnbull, a historian of the Apostolic Church in Wales, began many centuries afterwards when, during the Reformation,

> Many truths that had been hidden for centuries were now gradually revealed again, including the pentecostal experience of the Baptism of the Holy Spirit. In France and Germany in the fourteenth and fifteenth centuries there were groups of people who had this blessing and who also had prophets among them. In the sixteenth and seventeenth centuries there were other groups who had this experience, with prophets speaking among them as they were moved by the Holy Spirit. The early Methodists and Moravians also had this same blessed experience.[4]

Bruner attributes the propagation and nurture of the doctrine of the baptism of the Holy Spirit in the nineteenth century to Wesleyan Methodism and American revivalism, the former giving theological definition to the Pentecostal understanding of the doctrine, the latter – chiefly at the hands of Charles Finney – allying it to the methodology of revivalism which stressed the necessity of the baptism of the Holy Spirit for spiritual usefulness, power in preaching, and the promotion of revival.[5] The doctrine in its refined form was brought to England from America by the Holiness Movement, a group which had withdrawn from the Methodist Church, which they believed to have slipped from its Wesleyan moorings, and whose teaching was disseminated through the Keswick Convention held annually from 1875.[6] In 1903, under the direction of Jessie Pen Lewis, a Welsh Keswick Convention was established along the same lines.[7] The teaching of Keswick was further promulgated in

Wales through the American 'Holiness' evangelist R. A. Torrey, who held a mission in Cardiff in 1904, a month before the revival came to public attention.[8] Like Finney, Evan Roberts believed the experience of the baptism of the Spirit to be the essence of revival, the cause 'of not only the Revival in Wales in 1904–5, but of all other Revivals in the history of the world'.[9] Thus revival was seen as a neo-Pentecost, a simultaneous outpouring of the Holy Spirit on many believers like that experienced by the disciples gathered together at Pentecost (Acts 2: 1–4). Apart from the visions that Joel had prophesied would accompany the outpouring of the Holy Spirit, the other Pentecostal signs or extraordinary gifts were isolated rather than usual phenomena of the 1904–5 revival.[10] There were, however, sufficient manifestations of the power of the Spirit comparable to those experienced in the apostolic era to convince later Pentecostals that 1904 had initiated a revival not only of the Church's spiritual earnestness but also of its charismatic endowment. The Pentecostal movement came to be regarded by its leaders as both the progeny of the revival and the repository of the supernatural manifestations of the Holy Spirit after the revival.[11]

Notes

Introduction

1 Edward Morgan, *John Elias: Life, Letters and Essays*, first published as *Memoir of John Elias* (1844) and *Letters, Essays and Other Papers* (1847) (Edinburgh: Banner of Truth Trust, 1973), 340.

2 F. Buchholz, *Protestantismus und Kunst* (Paris: 1928), quoted in: William H. Halewood, *Six Subjects of Reformation Art: A Preface to Rembrandt* (Toronto, Buffalo, and London: University of Toronto Press, 1982), 137.

3 Nicholas Evans, a talk on his life and work, Aberystwyth Arts Centre (1 July 1983).

4 Lawrence Gowing established an approach to discussing Evans's work which has provided the pattern for most of the articles since. He interpreted the subject of Evans's paintings as the portrayal of the working community, and their themes to be nobility and heroism. Barbara Wright largely reconstitutes Gowing's article but advances a secondary reading of Evans's work, suggesting that the paintings not only document the mining community but also evoke the imagery of mythological, ancient, and biblical civilizations. The allusion to another time, place, and people Philip George sees in terms of a 'biblical life' that informs the archetypes and composition of the paintings, and as an expression of Evans's religious convictions. John Russell Taylor suggests, in more general terms, that the paintings reflect imagery which Evans readily employs in his lay preaching, and establishes an analogy between Evans's understanding of his creativity and God's primal act of creation. Philip Vann and Hywel Harries endorse the sense of the paintings' transcendence of locality and history: Harries supports his position by quoting Wright's reading of the paintings and by establishing causal links between Evans's religious background and pictorial expression. However, in *Symphonies in Black*, Rhoda Evans ignores the discourse on the religious allusions in the paintings, and returns to Gowing's view of them solely as historical genre and pictorial documents of the social conditions and dignity of the miners' lives. (*Sunday Times Magazine* (17 September 1978), 103; Barbara Wright, 'Nicholas Evans', *Arts Review*, 30, no. 18 (September 1978), 490; Phillip George, 'Dreamer from Black Eden', *Arcade*, no. 7 (6 February 1981), 18–19; John Russell Taylor, 'Nicholas Evans: Magic and Mystery', *Art and Artists*, 16, no. 186 (March 1982), 23–4; Philip Vann, 'Out of the Darkness', *Artist*, 100, no. 11 (November 1985), 8–11; Hywel Harries, *Cymru'r Cynfas/Wales on Canvas*, 1983, new bilingual edition (Talybont: Y Lolfa, 1988), 26–31; and Nicholas Evans and Rhoda Evans, *Symphonies in Black* (Talybont: Y Lolfa, 1987).)

5 In exploring evocation by this means I will apply a current semiotic theory of visual

connotation (connotation being a special form of evocation). The definition of connotation and denotation is adopted from Roland Barthes who, following the Hjelmslevian tradition, defined connotation as 'a secondary meaning, whose signifier is itself constituted by a sign or system of primary signification, which is denotation'. Accordingly, the biblical evocation of Evans's work should be thought of not as something independent of the images of mining (the level of denotation), as an invisible spirit in the works, but as the flesh upon the bones, to a large extent shaped by the denoted subject. The secondary or connotative level of meaning of an image is mobilized when certain types of knowledge are brought to the image. Barthes gave the illustration of the *Panzani* advertisement, which shows a net shopping bag in and around which were arranged packets and tins of food, vegetables, and fruit. The picture had several connotations for him, 'the composition of the image evoking the memory of innumerable alimentary [still-life] paintings'. This connotation, while being built upon the denoted image, is activated only when Barthes brought to the image an aesthetic knowledge of a genre in western European painting. The image also had a religious connotation for Barthes, the net bag acting as a connotative sign for 'the miraculous draught of fishes'. Thus images have a typological dimension, that is to say, they are signs pointing to realities (significations) beyond themselves. The typological interpretation of an image depends upon what Barthes referred to as the 'lexicon of a person's idiolect' – the store of cultural, aesthetic knowledge which a person brings to the image.

The idea of reading images within an interpretative tradition was inherent in Renaissance religious painting. Norman Bryson believes that the denoted subjects or 'manifest content' of the paintings is identified by reference to a code of interpretation, being the tradition of iconography: 'The denotation of painting consists in its intersection with all the schemata of recognition (Nativity, Betrayal, Madonna Enthroned) codified in iconology: denotation results from those procedures of recognition which are governed by the iconographic codes.' Iconology, which he describes as a 'consensual', socially sanctioned criterion, operated as a social code through which recognition took place (Roland Barthes, *S/Z*, translated by Richard Miller (London: Jonathan Cape, 1975), 6–7. Roland Barthes, *Image – Music – Text*, translated by Stephen Heath, Fontana Paperbacks (Glasgow: Collins, 1977), 35, 46–7; Norman Bryson, *Vision and Painting* (London: Macmillan Press, 1983), 61–2).

Chapter 1

1 John B. Hilling, *The Historic Architecture of Wales: An Introduction* (Cardiff: University of Wales Press, 1976); Anthony Jones, *Welsh Chapels* (1984) (Cardiff and Stroud: National Museum of Wales and Alun Sutton Publishing, 1996).

2 Charles Hodge, *Systematic Theology* (1871–3), 3 vols. (Grand Rapids: William Eerdmans, I, 1986), 378–9.

3 [Westminster Assembly], *Westminster Confession of Faith* (1646) (Glasgow: Free Presbyterian Publications, 1976), 193–7.

4 Thomas Watson, *The Ten Commandments*, revised edition, first published as part of *A Body of Practical Divinity* (1692) (Edinburgh: Banner of Truth Trust, 1965), 60.

5 Matthew Henry, *An Exposition of the Old and New Testaments*, 3 vols. (London: Thomas Parkhurst, I, 1704), 182.

6 [Westminster Assembly], *Confession*, 194.

7 A theophany can be either material or visionary, human or non-human, or angelic. (See Exodus chapter 24, verses 9 to 11 above.)

8 John Owen, *The Works of John Owen*, edited by William H. Goold, 16 vols. (Edinburgh: T. and T. Clarke, XIV, 1862), 125–6.

9 Edwyn Bevan, *Holy Images: An Inquiry into Idolatry and Image Worship in Ancient Paganism and in Christianity* (London: George, Allen, and Unwin, 1940), 87.

10 Henry, *Exposition*, I, 184.

11 Owen, *Works*, XIV, 125–6. Owen's writings and ministry exerted a considerable influence on Welsh Puritanism. His grandfather was Griffith Owen of Talhenbont, Llanegryn, Merioneth. However, there is no proof that John Owen had any contact with his Welsh relations (Honourable Society of Cymmrodorion, *The Dictionary of Welsh Biography down to 1940* (London: B. H. Blackwell, 1959), 711.

12 Thomas Charles Edwards, *The Epistle to the Hebrews* (London: Hodder and Stoughton, 1888), 153.

13 Arthur Penrhyn Stanley, *Lectures on the History of the Jewish Church*, second edition, 2 vols., (London: John Murray, II, 1863), 225. Christ anticipated this development in His dialogue with the woman of Samaria. He spoke to her of a coming time when 'worship of the Father' would not be bound to a physical site but spiritual in nature, localized in a person rather than a place (John 4: 24).

14 Here 'church' (Greek: *ekklesia*) refers to the 'gathering' or 'congregation' of God's people not the building for public Christian worship. The term encompasses the so-called 'Church invisible', the commonwealth of heaven and the 'Church visible', being the body of believers who worship on earth (Owen, *Works*, VIII, 559).

15 Abraham Woodhead, *Concerning Images and Idolatry* (Oxford, 1698), 9.

16 Quoted in: John Phillips, *The Reformation of Images: Destruction of Art in England 1535–1660* (Berkeley, Los Angeles, and London: University of California Press, 1973), 164.

17 Watson, *Ten Commandments*, 62.

18 John Calvin, *Institutes of the Christian Religion*, translated by Henry Beveridge, 3 vols. (Edinburgh: Calvin Translation Society, I, 1845), 128.

19 Christologically, Reformers such as Calvin, Ulrich Zwingli (1484–1531) and Martin Bucer (1491–1551) understood the Johannine use of 'Word' as expressing the idea of Christ, the wisdom of God. More recent Reformed theologians interpret it in terms of a revelation or reflection of the mind of God (J. C. Ryle, *Expository Thoughts on John* (1869) 2 vols. (Edinburgh: Banner of Truth Trust, I, 1987), 7; William Hendriksen, *The Gospel of John* (1959) New Testament Commentary (Edinburgh: Banner of Truth Trust, 1987), 70).

20 Owen, *Works*, VIII, 552–4.

21 William Cowper, 'Jesus, where'er thy people meet', in *Olney Hymns*, new edition, (London: J. Johnson, 1797), no. XLIV, 185.

22 Isaac Watts, *The Holiness of Times, Places, and People under the Jewish and Christian Dispensations* (London: Hett and Brackstone, 1738), 119–20.

23 Owen, *Works*, IX, 59.

24 J. S. Whale, 'Calvin', in *Christian Worship: Studies in its History and Meaning*, edited by Nathaniel Micklem (Oxford: Clarendon Press, 1936), 154–65 (165).

25 Calvin, *Institutes*, I, 136.

26 Ibid.

27 Isaac Watts, *A Guide to Prayer: or, A Free and Rationale Account of the Gift, Grace and Spirit of Prayer* (1715), fifth edition (London: Emmanuel Matthews, 1730), 66.

28 The concept of white walls would also have had a different association for the congregation. The apostle Paul applied the description 'whited wall' as a term of abuse to denounce the high priest Ananias's offence (Acts 23: 3). It was a metaphor for hypocrisy denoting, Henry interpreted, 'a mud wall, trash and dirt, and rubbish underneath, but plastered over, or whitewashed . . . They that daubed with untempered mortar failed not to daub themselves over with something that made them look not only clean, but gay' (Henry, *Exposition*, III, 641). As such the eighteenth-century meeting-house interior was no less a reminder of the heart's dissimulation than would be S. Curnow Vosper's (1866–1942) *Salem* (1908) for congregations in the twentieth century.

29 Huston Diehl, 'Graven Images: Protestant Emblem Books in England', *Renaissance Quarterly*, 39, no. 1 (Spring 1986), 49–66 (54–5).

30 The picture of 'a very grave person' in the first room Christian is shown, Sharrock observes, bears 'a superficial resemblance to Quarles's frontispiece to the first edition of the *Emblemes*' (Roger Sharrock, 'Bunyan and the English Emblem Writers', *Review of English Studies*, 21, no. 82 (April 1945), 105–16 (107)).

31 Karl Josef Höltgen, *Aspects of the Emblem: Studies in the English Emblem Tradition and the European Context*, Problemata Semiotica 2, (Kassel: Edition Reichenberger, 1986), 42.

32 Francis Quarles, *Emblems, Divine and Moral*, new edition (London: John Bennett, 1834), 7.

33 Diehl, 'Graven Images', 56.

34 In the post-apostolic period, however, Christian typology often exceeded the exegetical bounds of the Bible. Divines and preachers deduced correspondences and moral lessons from a variety of Old Testament subjects in a free-style manner. For example, in his commentary on Exodus chapters 25 and 26, Henry forwarded a typological interpretation of the Tabernacle's furnishings and fabric as emblems for spiritual instruction. The Ark of the Covenant, which contained the tablets of the law and was placed in the Holy of Holies, was given

> to teach us to make much of the Word of God and to hide it in our hearts . . . That provision was made for the carrying of this ark about with them in all their removes . . . intimates to us, that wherever we go, we should take our religion along with us.

Likewise, the ten embroidered curtains coupled together to form the Holy of Holies spoke of 'the churches of Christ and the saints, [which] though they are many, yet are they one' (Henry, *Exposition*, I, 184, 186).

35 Henry More, *The Theological Works of the Most Pious and Learned Henry More* (London: Joseph Downing, 1708), 328.
36 Calvin, *Institutes*, I, 127.
37 M. Bath, *Speaking Pictures: English Emblem Books and Renaissance Culture*, Longman Medieval and Renaissance Library (London and New York: Longman, 1994), 264.
38 E. H. Gombrich, 'A Classic *Rake's Progress*', *Journal of the Warburg and Courtauld Institutes*, 15, nos. 3–4 (July–December 1952), 254–6 (255).
39 Priscilla Jane Owens, 'Will your anchor hold in the storms of life', *Christian Hymns* (Bridgend: Evangelical Movement of Wales, 1977), no. 489.
40 Mario Praz, *Studies in Seventeenth Century Imagery* (Rome: Edizioni di Storia e Letteratura, 1964), 228.
41 Alan Wallach, 'The *Voyage of Life* as Popular Art', *Art Bulletin*, 59 (June 1977), 234–41 (235–56).
42 Quarles, *Emblems*, iii.
43 Bath, *Speaking Pictures*, 264–5.
44 Charles Haddon Spurgeon, *John Ploughman's Pictures: More of his Talks* (London: Passmore and Alabaster, 1890), [iii].

Chapter 2

1 Quarles, *Emblems*, 7.
2 W. B. Sprague, *Lectures on Revivals of Religion*, second edition (Glasgow: Collins, 1833), 219.
3 Ibid., 219; Charles G. Finney, *Lectures on Revivals of Religion* (London: Thomas Tegg, 1838), 177.
4 Ibid., 179.
5 [Anon.], 'Williams of Wern', *The Pulpit of Wales*, no. 21 (September 1901), 2–5 (3).
6 Daniel Rowland, *Eight Sermons upon Practical Subjects* (London: Thomas Davies, 1774), [iv]; Christmas Evans, *Sermons, on Various Subjects*, translated by J. Davies (Beaver: William Henry, 1837), [3].
7 Edwin Paxton Hood, *Christmas Evans: The Preacher of Wild Wales* (London: Hodder and Stoughton, 1881), 22.
8 James Buchanan, *Analogy Considered as a Guide to Truth, and Applied as an Aid to Faith* (Edinburgh: Johnstone, Hunter and Co., 1864), 141.
9 Preachers also created new and familiar illustrations by adapting objects and events from outside the Bible. For example, the internal workings of a clock struck Rowland as an appropriate simile for the mystery of Providence:

> In a clock there are several wheels, which run counter to one another; some move slowly, and others whirl about with great velocity: yet all unite in keeping the clock in motion, and contribute their share to make it a true index of the flight of time. So is every event, however opposite it may seem, disposed by the secret, impelling hand of God, to promote his glory, and to further the salvation of his chosen.

Illustrations such as this opened up the possibility for the world of everyday objects to become profound similes of spiritual significance. The most mundane things could, if allied to biblical doctrine, become vehicles for devotional contemplation, a treasury of religious images made out of the fabric of everyday life (Rowland, *Eight Sermons*, 212).

10 [Calvinistic Methodist Church], 'The Lighthouse', *Children's Treasury*, 1, no. 11 (November 1904), 154.
11 Christmas Evans, *The Allegories of Christmas Evans*, translated by R. E. Williams (Aberdare: G. M. Evans, 1899), 89–90.
12 J. Gynoro Davies, *Flashes from the Welsh Pulpit* (London: Hodder and Stoughton, 1889), 62, 89, and 163.
13 Quarles, *Emblems*, 178.
14 William Rees, *Industry before the Industrial Revolution*, 2 vols. (Cardiff: University of Wales Press, I, 1968), 34–6.
15 Ness Edwards, *The Industrial Revolution in South Wales* (London: Labour Publishing Co., 1924), 13–7; Rees, *Industry*, 70–107.
16 Rees, *Industry*, 133.
17 Rowland, *Eight Sermons*, 17.
18 J. Malcolm Maclaren, 'The Occurrence of Gold in Great Britain', *Transactions of the Institution of Mining Engineers*, 25 (1902–3), 435–508 (442–3).
19 Elias employed the metaphor similarly: 'the Bible is a precious mine, full of the most valuable treasures, much better than fine gold' (Morgan, *John Elias*, 340).
20 Evans, *The Allegories of Christmas Evans*, 63.
21 Evans, *Sermons, on Various Subjects*, 348.
22 Ibid., 348–9.
23 The method of raising and lowering coal, to which Christmas Evans referred in his allegory, is similar to that described by William Fairley:

> the modus operandi being as follows: Beneath the platform of the 'carriage' or 'cage' on which the tram is placed, there is an open-topped vessel, so large that, when filled with water, it will, together with the empty tram, bring up the full one on the other end of the rope, which passes over a large pulley on the top of the pit. The vessel beneath the tram is filled from a reservoir or cistern placed near the top of the pit, kept supplied for this purpose. On the cage reaching the bottom of the shaft, the water is let out. (William Fairley, *Glossary of Terms Used in the Coal-Mining-Districts of (First) South Wales, (Second) Bristol and Somersetshire* (London: Colliery Guardian, 1868), 3.)

24 Evans, *Sermons, on Various Subjects*, 150.
25 Ibid., 277.
26 A. H. John, *The Industrial Development of South Wales* (Cardiff: University of Wales Press, 1950), 148.
27 Ibid., 137.
28 Louis L. Simonin, *Mines and Miners; or, Underground Life*, translated by H. W. Bristow (London: William Mackenzie, 1868), 164.

29 G. M. Holmes, 'The South Wales Coal Industry 1850–1914', *Transactions of the Honourable Society of Cymmrodorion* (1976), 162–207 (163).
30 Gwynfor Evans and Ioan Rhys, 'Wales', in *Celtic Nationalism*, edited by Owen Dudley Edwards, Gwynfor Evans, Ioan Rhys, and Hugh MacDiarmid (London: Routledge and Kegan Paul, 1968), 211–98 (239).
31 Ieuan Gwynedd Jones, 'The South Wales Collier in Mid-Nineteenth Century', in *Victorian South Wales – Architecture, Industry and Society*, Seventh Conference Report (London: Victorian Society, 1971), 34–51 (44); Cyril Gwyther records that in the Rhondda at the beginning of this century a large proportion of the congregations was made up of miners and their families (Cyril E. Gwyther, 'Sidelights on Religion and Politics in the Rhondda Valley, 1906–26', *Llafur*, 3, no. 1 (Spring 1980) 30–43 (32)).
32 Robin Page Arnot, *South Wales Miners* (London: George Allen and Unwin, 1967), 26.
33 D. M. Phillips, *Evan Roberts a'i Waith* (Dolgellau: E. W. Evans, 1912), 215.
34 J. D. Douglas et al. (editors), *The Illustrated Bible Dictionary*, 3 vols. (Leicester: Inter-Varsity Press, III, 1980), 1, 234.
35 Jay Gee, 'Down a Coal Mine with His Sunday School Class', *Children's Treasury*, 10, no. 2 (February 1913), 23–4 (23).
36 Jay Gee, '"Collier Jack." V. – The Old-Fashioned Class Meeting – (Continued)', *Children's Treasury*, 10, no. 9 (September 1913), 136–7 (137).
37 T.J.P., 'The Colliery Explosion in Monmouthshire', *Treasury*, 14, no. 160 (April 1877), 73–5 (73).
38 Ibid., 75.
39 Even in recent times mining disasters have had strong biblical associations and served to heighten a sense of eternal issues. One writer describes the disaster at Aberfan, Glamorgan in 1966 as a modern slaughter of the innocents, referring to Herod's systematic extermination of all the baby boys in Bethlehem after Christ's birth (Matthew 2: 1–18). A sermon delivered on the Sunday after the disaster took as its text: 'God is our refuge and strength, a very present help in trouble. Therefore will not we fear, though the earth be removed, and though the mountains be carried into the midst of the sea' (Psalm 46: 1–2). The psalmist's image of the moving mountains would have been transposed in the minds of the congregation into the tip which engulfed the school. Another writer, a minister, compares the Aberfan disaster to the fall of the tower of Siloam during Christ's ministry which killed eighteen people (Luke 13: 3–5). The lesson Christ drew from that catastrophe, the minister said, was applicable to the one at Aberfan: 'It is a call to repentance, to a renewal of obedience and service, to a return to the God who fashioned us to show forth His love.' Christ's use of the catastrophe to speak to the souls of his hearers about their mortality gave Nonconformists a precedent to do the same in the face of mining disasters (*Western Mail* (25 October 1966), 6, (26 October 1966), 8; Edward England, *The Mountain that Moved* (London: Hodder and Stoughton, 1967), 46).
40 Jay Gee, '"Collier Jack." Jack's Sermon – (Continued)', *Children's Treasury*, 11, no. 3 (March 1914), 41–2 (42).
41 *South Wales Daily News* (13 December 1904), 6.
42 John Henry Newman, 'Lead, kindly Light', *Union Hymnal* (London: E. Marlsborough and Co., 1881), no. 493.

43 *Evening Express* (30 January 1905), 2.
44 T. Gasquoine, *Our Evening Hymns* (London: Arthur H. Stockwell, [1904]), 30.
45 R. D. Edwards, 'The Collier's Lamp', *Treasury*, 2, no. 1 (January 1914), 9.
46 *South Wales Daily News* (26 November 1904), 6.
47 James Burns, *Sermons in Art by the Great Masters* (London: Duckworth and Co., 1908), facing 40.
48 Barthes, *Image – Music – Text*, 39.
49 Henry, *Exposition*, III, 104.
50 Vladimir Gurewich traces the abandonment of the left side and the development of a right-side tradition of the wound, together with the subsequent returns to the left made by both Catholic and Protestant artists. Meditation on the Sacred Heart of Jesus was one reason for a reversion to the left-side tradition by Catholic artists. By placing the wound near the heart they thought that Christ's heart, which bore the 'wounds of love', could be more easily reached through devotion. Matthew Henry followed the left-side tradition in his commentary on the account of Christ's piercing (John 19: 34). The sentiments he attached to its significance echo those associated with Catholic devotion to the Sacred Heart: 'Through this window opened in Christ's side you may look into his heart, and see love flaming there, love strong as death.' Many contemporary evangelical commentators have also proposed that, in all likelihood, it was the left side of Christ that was pierced. Nicholas Evans would be acquainted with the evangelical preference for the left side through reading commentaries in preparation for preaching (Vladimir Gurewich, 'Observations on the Iconography of the Wound in Christ's Side, with Special Reference to Its Position', *Journal of the Warburg and Courtauld Institutes*, 20 (July 1957), 358–62 (360); Henry, *Exposition*, III, 503; William Hendriksen, *The Gospel of John*, New Testament Commentary (Edinburgh: The Banner of Truth Trust (1959), 436–9).
51 Jay Gee, '"Collier Jack." The Rescue Party', *Children's Treasury*, 11, no. 9 (September 1914), 139–40 (139).
52 The principle derives from the apostle Paul's prescription that preaching be conducted by 'comparing spiritual things with spiritual' (1 Corinthians 2: 13), or as Henry put it, 'one part of revelation with another. Spiritual things, when brought together will help illustrate one another.' For instance, Henry relates his commentary on the resurrection appearance of Christ in John chapter 20, verse 19 to the promise of Christ's attendance among the fellowship of believers recorded in Matthew chapter 18, verse 20. The former is presented here as an exemplification of the latter (Henry, *Exposition*, III, 743).
53 Eli Ginzberg, *Grass on the Slag Heaps* (New York and London: Harper and Brothers, 1942), 5–6.
54 The abandonment of the traditional representation of the man of Nazareth for one who is identified with a particular section of society also occurs in illustrations for children's religious books. In the centre section of Margaret Tarrant's (1888–1959) illustration of Cecil Frances Alexander's (1818–95) hymn 'All things bright and beautiful', Christ stands in a glade surrounded by the things He has made. He is a blond, cherub-faced child looking down at another child, one of three children in contemporary dress arranged around His feet. While she forsook the traditional iconography of Christ's face, Tarrant retained the

white robes in which He is usually depicted. In *Entombed* this is reversed: Evans holds on to the traditional likeness of Christ's face but sacrifices His traditional vesture.

55 Gynoro Davies, *Flashes from the Welsh Pulpit*, 30–1.

56 Charles Wesley, 'And can it be', *A Collection of Hymns for the Use of People Called Methodists*, third edition (London: J. Paramore, 1782), no. 193.

57 W. K. Wimsatt, *The Verbal Icon: Studies in the Meaning of Poetry* (Lexington: The University Press of Kentucky, 1954).

Chapter 3

1 God anointed Bezaleel and Aholiab with the Holy Spirit and thereby equipped them to be the principal workmen in the construction of the Tabernacle (Exodus 31: 1–6). In his note on these verses, Matthew Henry considered the anointing to have had a broader significance: 'Skill in common arts and employments is a gift of God; from him are derived both the faculty and the improvement of the faculty.' In this he restated Calvin's position that art is a divine dispensation given for the benefit of mankind and for the praise of God. God's metaphorical self-identification with the artisan in the Old Testament further dignifies the concept of art (Genesis 1–2, Psalm 8: 3; 19: 1). Henry compares the work of God in creation to that of an artist who intricately and exquisitely fashioned the heavens: 'He made them with very great curiosity and fineness, like a nice piece of work which the artist makes with his fingers.' The metaphor also had a theological and an evangelistic utility. In his gloss on Romans chapter 1, verse 20 Henry saw the creation as workmanship – or, more specifically, as a work of art – of which the

> variety, multitude, order, beauty, harmony, different nature, and excellent contrivance of the things that are made, the direction of them to certain ends, and the concurrence of all the parts to the good and beauty of the whole, do abundantly prove a Creator, and his eternal power and godhead. (Henry, *Exposition*, I, 115; III, 679; Calvin, *Institutes*, I, 133)

2 Abraham Kuyper, *Calvinism*, new edition (London: Sovereign Grace Union, 1932), 216–17.

3 Furthermore, it was believed that this indifference contributed to the widespread apathy to religion among the working class by frustrating their natural instinct for pleasure and recreation. This, in turn, led to the massive decline in chapel attendance in the latter part of the nineteenth century (Cynddylan Jones (editor), *The Welsh Pulpit Today* (London: Hodder and Stoughton, 1885), 202–4).

4 To this end, prayer, the reading of Scripture, the study of theology and church history, meditation on the works of God in creation, observance of the ordinances, and acts of charity and service were encouraged (E., 'Theology and Culture', *Monthly Treasury*, 6, no. 70, (October 1899), 228–9; [Calvinistic Methodist Church], 'Christian Culture – Private and Public', *Monthly Treasury*, 5, no. 59 (November 1898), 253–4 (254)).

5 Gynoro Davies, *Flashes from the Welsh Pulpit*, 119.
6 Mental cultivation was considered necessary for the successful study of theology and, in the sphere of vocation, a redress to the tendency towards increasing specialization and training in craft and trade. This resulted in the neglect of the broader interests and health of the whole mind – its spiritual aspect in particular.
7 Robert P. Downes, *Pure Pleasures* (London: Charles H. Kelly, 1895), 131.
8 [Calvinistic Methodist Church], 'Christian Culture – Private and Public', 253.
9 Archibald Alexander, *Christianity and Ethics* (London: Duckworth and Company, 1914), 107.
10 Daniel Hughes, in *Sermons by Young Welsh Ministers*, edited by M. E. Jones, Yspryd yr Oes (Zeitgeist) Series no. 1 (Mold: 'Yspryd yr Oes' Co., 1905), 35.
11 Kuyper, *Calvinism*, 218.
12 *Popular Encyclopaedia*, new edition, 7 vols. (London, Glasgow, Edinburgh: Blackie & Son, 1877–79), 342.
13 J. Cynddylan Jones, *The Welsh Pulpit Today* (London: Hodder & Stoughton, 1885), 223.
14 Gwynfryn Jones, in *Sermons by Young Ministers*, 127.
15 T. M. Jones, 'Betting and Gambling', *Monthly Treasury*, 4, no. 3 (March 1903), 49–50 (49).
16 [Calvinistic Methodist Church], 'Card Parties', *Monthly Treasury*, 9, no. 1 (January 1908), 2.
17 L.R., 'Athletics and Christianity', *Congregational Magazine*, 4, no. 12 (December 1921), 150–2 (152).
18 Ernest V. Tidman, 'Monthly Letter to Young People', *Baptist Record*, 1, no. 2 (February 1913), 12–3 (13).
19 The Nonconformists' judgement on the theatre according to these criteria produced much contention and wildly divergent conclusions, so as to merit the observation that the subject of the Church and the stage was 'one of the greatest and the gravest which can be dealt with in the modern pulpit, and it needs all the grace, tact, discretion, and broad-minded charity one can command to deal with it wisely and profitably' (H. Elwyn Thomas, *Pulpit Talks to Young People* (London: H. R. Allenson, 1900), 61).
20 [Congregational Church], *Congregational Year Book* (London: Congregational Union of England and Wales, Unwin Brothers, 1900), 52.
21 Gwynfryn Jones, *Sermons by Young Ministers*, 136; Elwyn Thomas, *Pulpit Talks*, 66. What Nonconformists considered indecent photographs, postcards, magazine illustrations, billposters, and, later, cinematic images were also condemned. Not only blatant nudity but also provocative images of women wearing corsets in advertisements and bathing belles in pictures sold at seaside resorts or viewed through a mutoscope (H. D. Rawnsley, 'The Danger of the Pernicious Picture', in *The Church and Life of Today* (London: Hodder and Stoughton, 1910), 77–90).
22 Elwyn Thomas, *Pulpit Talks*, 62; A. C. Dixon, *Present Day Life and Religion* (London: S. W. Partridge and Co., [n.d.]), 155.
23 Elwyn Thomas, *Pulpit Talks*, 62.
24 W. S. Jones, 'Religion and Business', *Monthly Treasury*, 2, no. 5 (May 1901), 110–111 (111).
25 During the last decades of the nineteenth century the subject of Christianity and the needs and issues of modern life received considerable discussion. For example: R. W.

Dale, *Laws of Christ for Common Life* (London: Hodder and Stoughton, 1884); Hugh Price Hughes, *Ethical Christianity* (London: Sampson Low, Marston and Co., 1892); Hugh Price Hughes, *Social Christianity* (London: Hodder and Stoughton, 1890); H. Clay Trumbull, *Border Lines in the Field of Doubtful Practices* (London: Hodder and Stoughton, 1899).

26 Higher criticism was an anti-dogmatic and anti-fundamentalist theology which attempted to rationalize away the supernatural aspect of the Bible and reconstruct Christianity along humanitarian lines. The Bible was no longer thought of as a divinely inspired book possessing continuity and authority, but as a disparate patchwork of writings by men whose insights were necessarily limited by their own historical perspectives. It reduced the concept of Christ from the God-man of orthodox theology to being only a man who was supremely God-conscious. Sin was de-emphasized and reinterpreted as a synonym for ignorance or, as Campbell defined it, selfishness, rather than as a heinous transgression of God's moral code which resulted in death and eternal damnation for the unrepentant and which required propitiation. Consequently, Christ's death came to be regarded not in terms of substitutionary atonement for sin but only as the highest example of self-sacrifice (Alexander Stewart, 'Higher Critical Theses', *Modern Puritan*, no. 11 (January 1909), 321–4; R. J. Campbell, *The New Theology* (London: Chapman and Hall, 1907), 128).

27 Campbell, *The New Theology*, 142;

> Salvation is a thing which always pushes itself out and out and includes more and more till it has lifted up and leavened the whole of society. So, as compared with the view of Salvation entertained by the old Evangelicals, which was personal, limited and final, now it is social[,] unlimited and with no finality about it. (John Williamson, 'Theological Changes over the Past Fifty Years', *Congregational Magazine*, 6, no. 4 (April 1924), [i—ix] ([vi]))

28 Williamson, 'Theological Changes', [v].
29 The most significant controversy surrounding hymn singing pertained to the introduction of large pipe-organs and small orchestras into the chapels. For some church members these innovations savoured of worldliness, while others regarded them as a God-honouring means of raising the standard of congregational singing. Music – expressed through hymns sung a cappella or accompanied on a small pipe-organ or harmonium – had always been an important feature of Nonconformist worship. Its position in the hierarchy of the public means of worship was, however, below those of preaching, the reading of the Bible, and prayer. The enthusiasm for choral singing spawned numerous chapel choirs whose members, according to T. M. Bassett, tended to sit apart from the rest of the congregation in the front seats. The change in the design of the pulpit from a narrow box to a stage or platform from the latter part of the nineteenth century onwards gave the choirs an elevated position from which to sing. Some chapels constructed rows of seats behind the pulpit for this purpose, while in others there was 'a pipe organ filling up that space . . . symbolic of the change in the status of the music. One might venture another suggestion that, just as the new organ dwarfed the pulpit beneath it, so the singing tended to claim more attention than the sermon.' This innovation, at least symbolically, reflected a parity between the

aesthetic and intellectual elements of Nonconformist worship. Indeed in 1926, in an article reviewing the recent history of trends in worship, the Moderator of the Cardiff and District Congregational Board expressed fears that the aesthetic and emotional aspect of worship represented by music and architecture were in danger of usurping the place of preaching altogether, and proposed that the 'intellectual' element of the service, supplied by the sermon, be re-emphasized. Chapel orchestras along with pipe-organs, were a controversial subject and not readily accepted by some congregations. An argument in favour of their use appeared in 1914. H. W. Jones appealed to the need of the Church to keep pace with the present 'age of progress and improvement', and to attain a standard of music comparable with that of the Roman Catholic churches (T. M. Bassett, *The Welsh Baptists* (Swansea: Ilston House, 1977), 224, 268; David Walters, 'Moderator's Corner', *Congregational Magazine*, 8, no. 11 (November 1926), [i]–[iii] ([ii]); H. W. Jones, 'Chapel Orchestras (Second Article)', *Children's Treasury*, 11, no. 4 (April 1914), 61; H. W. Jones, 'Chapel Orchestras', *Children's Treasury*, 11, no. 3 (March 1914), 46).

30 Bath, *Speaking Pictures*, 246.
31 Höltgen, *Aspects of the Emblem*, 141–3.
32 Davies's book derives from sermons originally delivered to his congregation at Regent's Park Chapel, London. Most discourses on art were not preached but written for a cultured Christian readership. (Sermons as literature, as opposed to published transcripts of preaching, became an increasingly popular genre in the early part of the twentieth century.) Preaching became a fine art full of well-wrought simile and metaphor, intent on stirring the aesthetic and intellectual senses of the readers as much as their spirit (Davies, *Sacred Themes and Famous Paintings*, vi).
33 Burns, *Sermons in Art*, 94.
34 Some Nonconformists considered Holman Hunt, whose religious convictions were far from orthodox, to be a 'prophet on canvas', an appellation given to him in an adulatory obituary which appeared in the *Monthly Treasury*. For many, Holman Hunt was the ideal Protestant artist, a type of Moses who had led religious art out of the wilderness of aberrant Roman Catholic doctrines and legends and an unhealthy preoccupation with the Virgin Mary and saints. His paintings were, by contrast, full of the historicity of the Bible and made much of Christ. A meticulous observation of nature, so the writer of the article believed, had enabled Holman Hunt to fulfil his ambition 'to serve as high priest and expounder of the excellence of the works of the Creator' (Pictor Parvus, 'Holman Hunt', *Monthly Treasury*, 11, no. 10 (October 1910), 196–7 (196); Davies, *Sacred Themes and Famous Paintings*, 41).
35 Burns, *Sermons in Art*, 85–8.
36 W. P. Frith, *My Autobiography and Reminiscences*, 3 vols. (London: Bently, II, 1887–8), 121.
37 [Calvinistic Methodist Church], 'How a Painter Can Preach', *Monthly Treasury*, 4, no. 2 (February 1903), 126.
38 Evan Williams, 'Picture Talks to Boys and Girls. "Hope," by G. F. Watts', *Baptist Record*, 3, no. 28 (April 1915), 15. Like several other ministers, Williams also looked to the world of art for anecdotes to exemplify Christian virtues. The story was related of Murillo who, being too poor to buy canvas, was forced to paint on a common table napkin and thereby

produced his famous *Madonna of the Napkin*. The several lessons extracted included: 'Good work makes the poorest material of infinite worth'; the commonplace in life should not be regarded as an obstacle for doing good, but can be made special by putting one's best efforts into it; and, poor circumstances do not necessarily hinder a person from achieving greatness (Evan Williams, 'Talks to Boys and Girls. Beautifying the Commonplace', *Baptist Record*, 7, no. 77 (May 1919), 7; 'Talks to Boys and Girls. "Madonna of the Napkin", by Murillo', *Baptist Record*, 3, no. 26 (February 1915), 15).

39 Charles T. Bateman, *G. F. Watts, R. A.* (London: George Bell, 1901), 36.

40 During the First World War, the concept of the 'world's hope' would have expressed the longing for peace as much in the terrestrial sphere as in the spiritual.

41 [Baptists], 'The Lacuna of Life', *Baptist Record*, 14, no. 8 (March 1928), 18.

42 Burns, *Sermons in Art*, 5.

43 Downes, *Pure Pleasures*, 139.

44 Burns, *Sermons in Art*, 105.

45 Frederic Leighton, *Addresses Delivered to the Students of the Royal Academy* (London: Kegan Paul, Trench, Trübner and Co., 1896), 39–40.

46 D. Burford Hooke, 'A Word upon Grown-Up People's Pleasures', *Evangelical Magazine*, no. 64 (April 1887), 145–8 (147).

47 W. Jenkins, 'The Welsh Renaissance. II', *Wales*, 2 (1885), 444–8 (448).

48 Hubert Brooke, 'Thoughts for the Day of Days', *The Sunday at Home* (1902–3), 51–4 (51).

49 *South Wales Press* (3 November 1904), 8.

50 R. E. D. Sketchley, *Watts*, Little Books on Art (London: Methuen and Co., 1904), 7; P. T. Forsyth, *Religion in Recent Art* (London: Hodder and Stoughton, 1901), 100–1.

51 Iona Williams, 'Welsh Art', *The Welsh Review*, 1, no. 4 (June 1906), 97–8 (98).

52 In 1895, one Welsh minister wrote of his hope that the University of Wales would produce Wales's own Ruskin, one who would 'open our eyes to the true appreciation of beautiful art, which will teach us ideals through the medium of pictures, and recultivate the true aesthetic feeling' (D. Cunllo Davies, 'Art in Welsh Homes', *Wales*, 2, no. 13 (May 1895), 223–4 (224)). Nonconformists also looked to Ruskin to endorse their convictions regarding a variety of social vices and the moral virtues of work ([Baptist Church], *Baptist Sunday School Record*, 10, no. 17 (December 1906), 199; *Baptist Record and Baptist Sunday School Record*, 1, no. 5 (May 1913), 15).

53 Surprisingly, the writer of an obituary of Ruskin in the *Christian Pictorial* regarded this 'unconversion' as a very light thing, as though the tenets of evangelicalism could outlive their usefulness for such a genius:

> When the boy had grown to be a man he burst forth in the splendour of ethical manhood, which is the fruit of Biblical doctrine. Having applied the teachings of his mother's Bible to his day and generation, he could afford to, and he did, put aside some of the doctrinal wrappings wherewith she had invested it.

Among the wrappings Ruskin discarded was the fundamental doctrine of the divine inspiration of the Bible, dear to the hearts of the old evangelicals. Possibly his habit of ending his lectures about the Bible with a biblical quotation (even though he denied the divine inspiration behind it) and his firm belief in God's other book – nature – made up for his deficient views on the Bible and contributed to evangelicalism's acceptance of Ruskin's unorthodoxy (([Anon.], 'Mr Ruskin', *Christian Pictorial*, 14, no. 361 (25 January 1900), 270; R. H. Wilenski, *John Ruskin* (London: Faber and Faber, 1933), 101, 118).

54 John Ruskin, *The Works of John Ruskin*, edited by E. T. Cooke and Alexander Wedderburn, Library Edition (London: George Allen, IV, 1903–5), 42.

55 Ruskin, *Works*, XVI, 197.

56 Watts's religious instincts did not, however, restrict themselves to the credal confines of the denominations, which he personified as wavering children of a disconsolate ideal in *The Spirit of Christianity* (1875). The essence of religion was for him, rather, ethical determination, a militant hatred of immorality in all its forms, and a desire to do right. This definition does not concur with the Nonconformist ideal of piety; nevertheless it would seem that an art whose motive was moral reform would have appeared useful to the denominations' endeavour to resuscitate the spiritual life of Wales at the beginning of the century (H. W. Shrewsbury, *The Visions of an Artist* (London: Charles H. Kelly, 1918), 25).

57 Roger Fry, 'An Essay in Aesthetics', in *Vision and Design*, 1920, edited by J. B. Bullen (Oxford: Oxford University Press, 1981), 12–27 (20).

58 Clive Bell, *Art*, The Phoenix Library (London: Chatto and Windus, 1914), 81.

59 Fred A. Farrell, 'The Nation and Art – 1', *Welsh Outlook*, 19, no. 3 (March 1932), 68–9 (69).

60 [Anon.], 'Art and National Life', *Welsh Outlook*, no. 1 (January 1914), 25–7 (26).

61 Ifan Kyrle Fletcher, 'The Appreciation of Art in Wales', *Welsh Outlook*, 14, no. 10, (October 1927), 264–5 (264).

62 Ruskin believed that his mission, and that of art, was to mediate that knowledge to man. In 1919, H. R. Thomas, a Baptist, stated Ruskin's theory thus: 'The function of Art is not necessarily to create, but to see and apprehend the hidden loveliness. It is to interpret Nature, God . . . Each one of us then, may become a prophet – a "Forth-Teller" of the "Beauty of Holiness," and the Holiness of Beauty'. The sanctification of natural beauty and its representation in art was the subject of several lectures presented at denominational meetings in 1919 and 1920. For example, F. C. White, Sunday school superintendent at Glyn, Ynysddu, presented a lecture at Swansea on 'Nature, Art, and Religion' in July 1919, and another on art and religion twelve months later (H. R. Thomas, *Art: Viewed from a Moral and Spiritual Aspect* (Llanelli: Guardian Offices, 1919), 8–9; [Baptist Church], 'Cardiff Joint Meetings', *Baptist Record*, 7, no. 79 (July 1919), 3–4 (3); [Baptist Church], *Baptist Record and Baptist Sunday School Record*, 8, no. 91 (July 1920), 20).

63 Burns, *Sermons in Art*, 201.

64 *Aberdare Leader* (22 April 1905), 7.

65 *South Wales Daily News* (23 November 1904), 6; (3 December 1904), 6; (2 January 1905), 5; Eilir, 'The Religious Revival in Wales', *Western Mail*, pamphlet no. 3 (1905), 1; Awstin, 'The Religious Revival in Wales', *Western Mail*, pamphlet no. 3 (1905), 21.

66 *South Wales Daily News* (21 January 1905), 5.

67 *South Wales Daily News* (22 December 1904), 6.
68 Ibid., 6.
69 Evan Roberts wrote poetry both before and after the revival (Evan Roberts, [miscellaneous poetry], Calvinistic Methodist Archives, National Library of Wales, Aberystwyth, MSS, 25632; 25633; 25636; 25680; 25682).
70 *South Wales Daily News* (22 April 1905), 6.

Chapter 4

1 Prior to and during the revival, the Welsh press carried frequent reports of supernatural phenomena including angelic voices, ghosts, and strange lights in Merioneth. This helped to fuel a general ethos of curiosity and expectation regarding the spiritual stirrings in Wales and thus a particular interest in the revival visions. The years 1904–5 saw the greatest proliferation of visionary experiences, although the Apostolic Church continues to claim such experiences up to the present (*South Wales Daily News* (26 November 1904), 6; (10 December 1904), 4; (14 February 1905), 5; (9 February 1905), 4; (21 February 1905); 6, *North Wales Chronicle* (18 February 1905), 1).

2 The first article of the *Westminster Confession of Faith* (1647) states:

> it pleased the Lord, at sundry times, and in divers manners, to reveal himself, and to declare that his will unto his Church; and afterwards, for the better preserving and propagating of the truth, and for the more sure establishment and comfort of the Church against the corruption of the flesh, and the malice of Satan and of the world, to commit the same wholly unto writing; which maketh the holy scripture to be most necessary; those former ways of God's revealing his will unto his people being now ceased. ([Westminster Assembly], 19–20)

3 J. H. Merle D'Aubigné, *The Life and Times of Martin Luther*, translated by H. White (Chicago: Moody Press, 1950), 483.
4 H. Elvet Lewis, *With Christ among the Miners* (London: Hodder and Stoughton, 1906), 231.
5 Jonathan Edwards, *The Great Awakening*, edited by C. C. Coen, The Works of Jonathan Edwards (New Haven and London: Yale University Press, IV, 1972), 237.
6 Ibid.
7 W. T. Stead, *The Revival of 1905*, fourth edition (London: Review of Reviews Office, 1905), 54; Eleazar Roberts, 'The Revival, from a Welsh Point of View', *Monthly Treasury*, 6, no. 9 (September 1905), 198–9 (199).
8 Jessie Pen Lewis and Evan Roberts, *War on the Saints* (Leicester: Overcomer Office; London: Marshall Brothers, 1912), 115. Here, 'picture' should be understood in terms of a visual impression rather than in the full-fledged sense of, for example, a painting or drawing. It is impossible to know the extent to which the visions resembled pictures. Roberts and the other visionaries were not relating their experiences with the express purpose of demonstrating their correspondence to representational art. The paucity of

references to pictorial qualities, such as composition, line, tone, colour, and light is not, therefore, in itself an indication that the visions were not like pictures. That these accounts do not concern themselves with such qualities was probably because the visionaries' primary interest was in relating the purported meaning of their visions. This required the description of only those elements and their conjunctions which would make the meaning of the visions clear. If, as Susanne Langer implies, we always conceive of things in terms of universals, what Roberts 'saw' was a conjunction of symbols which had all the general or salient features of the objects they represented, rather than particular objects, in all their idiosyncratic detail. Indeed, all that Roberts needed to visualize in order to comprehend the meaning of the visions was the barest representation of the objects (Susanne K. Langer, *Philosophy in a New Key*, third edition (Cambridge, Massachusetts: Harvard University Press, 1969), 70).

9   There was the perceived danger that members of the congregations would imitate Evan Roberts's visionary experiences. The Revd Edward Morgan told his congregation that Roberts's visions should not be marvelled at, and implied that more men would receive them if they experienced greater spiritual sensitivity (Awstin, 'The Religious Revival in Wales', *Western Mail*, pamphlet no. 7 (1905), 1; *South Wales Daily News* (3 April 1905), 6).

10 Hugh McLeod, *Religion and the Working Class in Nineteenth-Century Britain*, Studies in Economic and Social History (London: Macmillan, 1984), 27.

11 Fredrick Morgan Davenport, *Primitive Traits in Religious Revivals* (London and New York: Macmillan and Co., 1905), 26–7.

12 This was a result of the training they had received at the Welsh denominational colleges, which, in attempting to equip the students with a higher standard of education to meet the requirements of a more educated congregation, had set them a syllabus that was too diverse and academic to be useful in their calling. Consequently, the graduates, inflated by a partial knowledge of the classics, philosophy, and science, often delivered opaque and ineffective sermons to a mystified congregation, with an affected bravura that was a pale reflection of the *hwyl* of the previous generation of preachers. There were, at the same time, some ministers whose claim to intellect and eloquence was justified, whose mental acumen and acquired culture had enabled them to inject weight and thoughtfulness into their preaching; if false oratory and ostentation had been the weakness of the former, the latter faced the peril of sterile academicism and emotional aridity. Some, however, managed to sustain the unity of knowledge and passion, but letters and unction did not in themselves guarantee God's blessing or an end to the spiritual and moral declension that characterized Wales at the turn of the century (J. Jones and J. Jones, 'Welsh Preaching', *Red Dragon*, 2 (1895), 428–36 (432–3)).

13 Edmund Jones, *A Relation of Apparitions of Spirits in the County of Monmouthshire and the Principality of Wales*, third edition (Newport: E. Lewis, 1813), ix.

14 Eifion Evans, *The Welsh Revival of 1904* (1969) (Bridgend: Evangelical Press of Wales, 1981), 41–2.

15 D. M. Phillips, *Evan Roberts the Great Welsh Revivalist and His Work*, second edition (London: Marshall Brothers, 1906), 164.

16 Phillips, *Evan Roberts a'i Waith*, 212. Roberts believed that the Holy Spirit revealed the

visions to him, but he did not explain what he considered to be the nature of the inspiration. To take the analogy of the inspiration of Scripture, for example, there are generally three views: mechanical inspiration, where the writer is thought to have produced a verbatim transcript of what God said to him, in such a way as to exclude the participation of his own mind, observations, influences, and manner of writing; dynamic inspiration, where what is written is the outpouring of an author whose mental and spiritual life has been so elevated by God as to enable him to perceive spiritual realities with greater perspicuity and depth; and organic inspiration, which Protestant evangelicals hold to be the correct view of inspiration, where

> the Holy Spirit acted on the writers of the Bible in an organic way, in harmony with the laws of their own inner being, using them just as they were, with their character and temperament, their gifts and talents, their education and culture, their vocabulary and style.

The application of these distinctions to the phenomenon of visions means that the mechanical view of their inspiration, in contrast to the organic, would preclude any consideration of the visionary's visualizing skills, style, choice and use of imagery, the influence of general visual experience, and the culture to which he or she belonged, for these could not have contributed to the form and content of the vision. The dynamic interpretation of inspiration, which in application to visions constitutes an uncertain middle ground between the two other views, would prove equally unfruitful, as it would be impossible to distinguish which elements of the spiritual illumination were direct impressions from God, and which were derived from a sanctified imagination. Roberts may well have held to the mechanical view with respect to both the revelation of Scripture and his visions, for he certainly believed that God had dictated to him the contents of a notebook he kept during a period of retreat from public appearances, known as 'The Seven Days of Silence' (Louis Berkhof, *A Summary of Christian Doctrine*, 1938 (Edinburgh: Banner of Truth Trust, 1978), 18; Awstin, 'The Religious Revival in Wales', *Western Mail*, pamphlet no. 5 (1905), 3–8).

17 Phillips, *Evan Roberts a'i Waith*, 212–14, 220, 221.
18 Ibid., 219.
19 Phillips, *Evan Roberts the Great Welsh Revivalist and His Work*, 237–8.
20 Phillips, *Evan Roberts a'i Waith*, 219. Roberts also fused the spiritual and the mundane in his choice of illustrations for public speaking (Awstin, 'The Religious Revival in Wales', *Western Mail*, pamphlet no. 4 (1905), 10).
21 Phillips, *Evan Roberts a'i Waith*, 221.
22 Ibid., 218.
23 Ibid., 215.
24 Ibid., 221. The Revd D. S. Jones of Bridgend saw a vision of a ball of fire descending from heaven upon the Church and interpreted it as fire coming from heaven to burn up the dross. The vision appears to conflate two successive images which formed part of the apostle John's vision, related in verses 8 and 10 of Revelation chapter 8: 'a great mountain

burning with fire was cast into the sea . . . a great star from heaven, burning as it were a lamp, and it fell upon the third part of the rivers, and upon the fountains of waters' (*South Wales Daily News* (3 February 1905), 6).

25 Phillips, *Evan Roberts the Great Welsh Revivalist and His Work*, 237–8.
26 *South Wales Daily News* (19 November 1904), 6.
27 Alasdair MacIntyre divided vision experiences into three categories, and defined them as follows:

> An external vision is one in which what appears appears as part of the environment and may be confused with the ordinary world of things and people. An imaginal vision is one in which what appears appears as an object of vision in some sense, but can be distinguished sharply from material objects. An intellectual vision is not a vision at all but a feeling of presence . . . these can be reduced to two classes: first, those visions which can properly be called such, that is, those where something is seen; and second, those where the experience is of a feeling-state or of a mental image, which are only called visions by an honorific extension of the term. (Alasdair MacIntyre, 'Visions', in *New Essays in Philosophical Theology*, edited by Anthony Flew and Alasdair MacIntyre, The Library of Philosophy and Theology (London: SCM Press, 1955), 254–60 (254–5))

28 Pen Lewis and Roberts, *War on the Saints*, 114.
29 Phillips, *Evan Roberts a'i Waith*, 215.
30 Ibid.
31 *Aberdare Leader* (10 December 1904), 5.
32 *North Wales Chronicle* (28 January 1905), 5; *South Wales Daily News* (26 November 1904), 6. Mary Jones was, in her own view, the female counterpart of Evan Roberts. Numerous accounts of her visions appeared in the press following the report that strange lights and a brilliant star accompanied her on journeys to chapel. On one occasion she saw a triangle of light with rounded corners, each side measuring five feet in length, filled with diamond lights of considerable brilliance. Her figurative visions included one of spiritual beings worshipping God with heads bowed, who later ascended into heaven. Another vision featured a group of young men singing hymns to Christ. After Christ departed, the figure of the devil appeared. Then a great storm of hail, smoke, and mist swept him from her sight (*Evening Express* (9 February 1905), 3; *North Wales Chronicle* (28 January 1905), 5; (11 February 1905), 6; (18 February 1905), 9).
33 Davenport, *Primitive Traits*, 233.
34 [Forward Movement], *Forward Movement Torch*, 7, no. 6 (January 1904), 68.
35 *South Wales Daily News* (26 November 1904), 6.
36 Ibid.
37 Phillips, *Evan Roberts a'i Waith*, 220.
38 In an example of the latter, 'Throw Out the Life-Line', the anthem of the revival, likened the sinner to a drowning man or woman to whom Christ casts the life-ring of salvation (Awstin, 'The Religious Revival in Wales', *Western Mail*, pamphlet no. 4 (1905), 24).

39 William Williams, 'Guide me, O Thou great Jehovah', *Union Hymnal*, no. 490.
40 Awstin, 'The Religious Revival in Wales', *Western Mail*, pamphlet no. 1 (1904), 5.
41 Preceding the vision Roberts felt that the chapel at which he was speaking was full of angels eager to crown him (Phillips, *Evan Roberts a'i Waith*, 219). A scene similar to Roberts's vision occurred in a dream experienced by a man at Abertillery. He saw a harvest field in which the 'radiant' corn owner offers him four 'full ripe ears of corn', which, the dreamer interpreted, signified that he had only four years to live (*South Wales Daily News* (24 February 1905), 7).
42 Henry Alford, 'Come, ye thankful people, come', *Union Hymnal*, no. 822.
43 G. G. Johnson, 'A Centenary Celebration for Pastor Daniel Powell Williams 1882–1982', *Riches of Grace*, 6, no. 51 (May 1982), 68–9 (69).
44 William Cowper, 'There is a fountain filled with blood', *Olney Hymns*, new edition (London: J. Johnson, 1797), no. 79.
45 Isaac Watts, 'When I survey the wondrous cross', *Hymns of Faith and Life* (Glasgow: James Maclehose and Sons, 1889), no. 130.
46 William W. How, 'It is a thing most wonderful', *Children's Hymn Book* (London: SPCK, [n.d.]), no. 161.
47 Pen Lewis and Roberts, *War on the Saints*, 82.
48 On one occasion students witnessed a vision of blazing light containing a cross and Christ crucified on it. On another, Christ appeared on the cross with arms outstretched, welcoming (*South Wales Daily News* (6 February 1905), 6; (21 February 1905), 6).
49 Awstin, 'The Religious Revival in Wales', *Western Mail*, pamphlet no. 2 (1905), 19.
50 Ibid.
51 John Harvey, *The Art of Piety: The Visual Culture of Welsh Nonconformity* (Cardiff: University of Wales Press, 1995), 62–3.
52 Awstin, 'The Religious Revival in Wales', *Western Mail*, pamphlet no. 1 (1904), 14.
53 Roberts wrote to the editor of the *Sunday Companion* in November 1904 with a vague enquiry regarding the production of revival picture-postcards and an artist who could put his visions on paper with a view to their wider dissemination. The editor suggested Noyes Lewis at the London Electrotype Agency as an artist who could do the work Roberts wanted. However, it does not appear that the postcards were ever made (Phillips, *Evan Roberts the Great Welsh Revivalist and His Work*, 198; *Evan Roberts a'i Waith*, 266–9).
54 Awstin, 'The Religious Revival in Wales', *Western Mail*, pamphlet no. 1 (1904), 7.
55 *South Wales Press* (22 December 1904), 7.
56 Harvey, *The Art of Piety*, 34–6.
57 [Anon.], '"What Hast Thou Done for Me?"', *Christian Age*, 57, no. 1, 478 (3 January 1900), 10.
58 The interaction of visual and verbal elements, which is likely to have comprised Roberts's experience at Newcastle Emlyn, continued to manifest itself in the way he was to recount the visions which he perceived during the revival. God explained the visions to him, either subsequently or simultaneously, in a propositional form. (This mode of vision disclosure is rooted in the biblical tradition, as exemplified in the apostle John's narrative of the apocalypse, for instance in Revelation 1 chapter 12, verse 20.) The only exceptions to this

were two visions: the first was a vision of darkness (see note 59); the other which Phillips referred to as the 'hidden vision', and Roberts considered to be a miracle. Roberts never revealed its contents, believing that it would be wrong to tell anyone until God gave him more illumination on the matter (Phillips, *Evan Roberts a'i Waith*, 214–15, 218).

59 While the majority of Roberts's visions, and those experienced by others, were figurative and interpretable, a few were obscure, abstract or symbolic. A room, in which Roberts was confined during a period of illness, during the lightest part of the day, started to darken until the whole interior was dark as night (Phillips, *Evan Roberts a'i Waith*, 214). A member of Ainon Baptist Chapel, Ystradgynlais declared that, at a Sunday morning prayer meeting, he saw a vision of dazzling glory in the gallery of the chapel (*South Wales Daily News* (1 December 1904), 6).

60 There was a steady demand for the book in Wales from 1688, four years after its original publication, when it was first published in Welsh ([Baptist Quarterly], '*Pilgrim's Progress*', Welsh and English', *Baptist Quarterly*, 1 (1922–3), 39–42 (39)).

61 Höltgen, *Aspects of the Emblem*, 164.

62 Quarles, *Emblems*, iii.

63 Phillips, *Evan Roberts a'i Waith*, 220.

64 Ibid., 214.

65 Geffrey Whitney, *A Choice of Emblemes and Other Devices, Leyden, 1586* (Amsterdam and New York: Da Capo Press, Theatrvm Orbis Terrarvm, 1969), 203.

66 Phillips, *Evan Roberts a'i Waith*, 216.

67 J. D. Douglas et al. (editors), *The Illustrated Bible Dictionary*, 3 vols. (Leicester: Inter-Varsity Press, 1980), I, 51.

68 Phillips, *Evan Roberts a'i Waith*, 214.

69 Huston Diehl, 'Graven Images: Protestant Emblem Books in England', *Renaissance Quarterly*, 39, no. 1 (Spring 1986), 49–66 (56).

70 Ibid., 57.

71 Elvet Lewis, *With Christ among the Miners*, 234.

72 Ibid., 233.

73 W. J. Adams, *Miracles of Today* (Stockholm: W. J. Adams, [1926]), 14.

74 Ibid., 21.

75 Ibid., 17.

76 Ibid., 15.

77 Ibid., 15.

78 *Llanelly Argus* (11 July 1914), 1.

79 *South Wales Press* (15 July 1914), 6.

80 Joseph Runzo, 'Visions, Pictures and Rules', *Religious Studies*, 13 (1977), 303–18 (305).

81 Ibid., 309.

82 Another example of inferential recognition occurred in the vision experienced by an old lady, mentioned above. She inferred the identity of each figure not from their physical appearance alone, but from the stark contrast between the distinguishing characteristics of the two. She visualized Satan as 'black and ugly', giving corporeality to the biblical description of his province of activity, 'the kingdom of darkness', and to his morally and

83 Phillips, *Evan Roberts a'i Waith*, 221.

84 D'Aubigné, *Luther*, 483.

85 Morgan W. Williams, 'The Cinema', *Treasury*, 1, no. 11 (November 1913), 214.

86 C. C. Dobson, *The Face of Christ* (London: Centenary Press, 1933), 7.

87 Thomas Heaphy, *The Likeness of Christ*, edited by Wyke Bayliss (London: David Bogue, 1880).

88 *Somerset and Wiltshire Journal* (4 February 1871), quoted in [Thomas Henry Thomas], 'Illustrated Lectures upon Art', [broadsheet of lectures], National Museum of Wales, Cardiff.

89 [Anon.], 'Priceless Portraits of the Master', *Christian Age*, 60, no. 1567 (18 September 1901), 203.

90 [Anon.], 'The Living Room', *Evangelical Magazine*, no. 70 (October 1887), 453–60 (457).

91 James Burns, *The Christ Face in Art* (London: Duckworth and Co., 1907), xviii.

92 H. Harris, in *New Dictionary of Theology*, edited by Sinclair B. Ferguson and David F. Wright (Leicester: Inter-Varsity Press, 1988), 386.

93 Heaphy, *Likeness of Christ*, 77–8; Burns, *The Christ Face in Art*, xvi.

94 Jeremy Maas, *The Light of the World* (London: Scolar Press, 1983), 128.

95 S. Andrews and Son, the owners of this venue, were collectors of paintings, some of which they loaned to the Museum and Art Gallery of the Free Public Library, Newport, opened on 15 August 1895 (*Johns's Newport Directory* (Newport: R. H. Johns, 1901), 142).

96 *South Wales Daily News* (19 July 1905), 6.

97 James Burns, *Illustrations from Art for Pulpit and Platform* (London: James Clarke and Co., 1912), 18.

98 Burns, *The Christ Face in Art*, 224.

99 Ibid., 240.

100 The occasion on which Christ spoke these words highlighted His desire that children should believe in Him, and for this reason, no doubt, it became the most extensively illustrated of Bible stories to appear in Welsh Nonconformist children's literature. In 1922 the *Treasury* published several articles for children based on the painting, together with a free monochrome reproduction in the July edition. The message of the picture was that 'Jesus and the children are "the Hope of the World." You, as boys and girls of to-day, are the nation's hope and the key to the future. We are looking to you for great things.' The sentiment reflected the almost idolatrous esteem that Nonconformists gave to children in the years immediately following the First World War. The young were the new generation, who would be responsible for the reconstruction of a new world-order and for repopulating the Church, which had been devastated by the loss of many of its leaders, and for the spread of the gospel throughout the nations (Watcyn M. Price, '"The Hope of the World"', *Treasury*, 10, no. 7 (July 1922), 110–12 (111); Watcyn M. Price, 'Children of Other Lands', *Treasury*, 10, no. 2 (February 1922), 31–2 (31)). The picture also evokes a popular hymn at the time which emphasized the international appeal of the gospel to children:

> Jesus died for all the children, all the children of the world;
> Red and yellow, black and white, all are precious in His sight,
> Jesus died for all the children of the world
> (*CSSM Choruses* (London: Scripture Union, CSSM, 1959), no. 232)

101 Stephen Jeffreys was a preacher whom Evans admires considerably, and his biography, *Stephen Jeffreys: Beloved Evangelist*, in which an account of the vision appears, is well known to the artist.

Chapter 5

1 Albert Rothenberg, *The Emerging Goddess* (Chicago and London: University of Chicago Press, 1979), 127.
2 Ibid., 1.
3 Evans, a talk on his life and work.
4 Ibid.
5 Ibid.; Nicholas Evans, *How's Life?*, BBC, Radio Wales (January 1986).
6 Phillips, *Evan Roberts the Great Welsh Revivalist and his Work*, 120–3; Walter J. Hollenweger, *The Pentecostals*, translated by R. A. Wilson, second edition ([London]: SCM Press, 1976), 178.
7 Awstin, 'The Religious Revival in Wales', pamphlet no. 1 (1904), 2.
8 The gift was manifest in the form of the contents of a notebook written during 'The Seven Days of Silence', and a prescience of how many people would be converted during the revival and what, where, and when he should preach (Awstin, 'The Religious Revival in Wales', pamphlet no. 4 (1904), 5; pamphlet no. 5 (1904), 4–5).
9 D. M. Lloyd-Jones, *Preaching and Preachers* (London: Hodder & Stoughton 1971), 224–7. Dabney believed that it was a serious 'wresting of Scriptures, to claim for the uninspired preacher that extraordinary inspiration, superseding the necessity for premeditation' (Robert L. Dabney, *Sacred Rhetoric; or, A Course of Lectures on Preaching* (1870) (Edinburgh: Banner of Truth Trust, 1979), 18).
10 C. G. Williams, 'A Study of Pentecostal Glossolalia and Related Phenomena', unpublished Ph.D. thesis, University College Cardiff (1978), 278–9.
11 Nicholas Evans, *A Kind of Singing*, BBC, Radio Wales (March 1982).
12 Ibid.
13 Ibid.
14 Hywel Harries, *Cymru'r Cynfas/Wales on Canvas* (1983), (Talybont: Y Lolfa, 1988), xi.
15 Evans, *A Kind of Singing*.
16 Ernst Kris and Otto Kurz, *Legend, Myth, and Magic in the Image of the Artist* (New Haven and London: Yale University Press, 1979), 48–9.
17 M. H. Abrams, *The Mirror and the Lamp* (1953) (Oxford: Oxford University Press, 1960), 191.
18 Frank Parker, 'Portrait of an Apostolic Artist', *Riches of Grace*, 3, no. 7 (July 1979), 123–4 (124).
19 Kris and Kurz, *Legend, Myth, and Magic*, 57.

20 Leon J. Wood, *The Holy Spirit in the Old Testament*, second edition, Contemporary Evangelical Perspectives (Michigan: Zondervan Publishing House, 1978), 41–3, 72–4.
21 U. Cassuto, *A Commentary on the Book of Exodus* (1951; first English edition) (Jerusalem: Magness Press, Hebrew University, 1967), 401–2.
22 J. Cynddylan Jones, *The Gift of Tongues* (Newport: W. Jones, 1877), 10.
23 Ibid., 9.
24 W. R. Jones, 'The Nine Gifts of the Holy Spirit', in *Pentecostal Doctrine*, edited by P. S. Brewster (Cardiff: P. S. Brewster, 1976), 47–61 (52).
25 Ibid., 50.
26 T. M. Barratt, quoted in Nils Bloch-Hoell, *The Pentecostal Movement* (Oslo: Universitetsforlaget; London: Allen & Unwin, 1964), 134–5.
27 John Russell Taylor, 'Nicholas Evans: Magic and Mystery', *Art and Artists*, 16, no. 186 (March 1982), 23–4 (23).
28 Harold Horton, quoted in C. G. Williams, 'Pentecostal Glossolalia', 13.
29 Frederick Dale Bruner, *A Theology of the Holy Spirit* (London: Hodder and Stoughton, 1970), 144.
30 Cynddylan Jones, *The Gift of Tongues*, 8.
31 Evans, *A Kind of Singing*.
32 Hollenweger, *The Pentecostals*, 11; C. G. Williams, 'Pentecostal Glossolalia', 223; Jim Davidson, *This Happy Gift of Tongues* (Aberdeen: Vine Publishing, 1985), 74.
33 W. J. Samarin, 'The Linguisticality of Glossolalia', *Hartford Quarterly*, 8, no. 4 (1968), 61.
34 Davidson, *This Happy Gift*, 32.
35 Evans and Evans, *Symphonies in Black*, 84.
36 An observation derived from accounts of initiation experiences of tongues-speaking recounted to the author by Pentecostals.
37 C. G. Williams, 'Pentecostal Glossolalia', 244–64.
38 Evans, a talk on his life and work; Harries, *Cymru'r Cynfas*, 28.
39 Hollenweger, *The Pentecostals*, 16.
40 Evans, a talk on his life and work.

Chapter 6

1 O. M. Edwards, *Hanes Cymru*, 2 parts (Caernarfon: Swyddfa Cymru, I, 1895), 9.
2 *Manchester Guardian* (13 April 1901), 9.
3 *Manchester Guardian* (1 January 1902), 3.
4 T. T. Lucius Morgan, 'The Future of Welsh Nonconformity', *Welsh Outlook*, 18, no. 3 (March 1931), 75–80 (75).
5 D. Wynne Evans, 'Studies in Iberic-Hebraic Eschatology, II', *Young Wales*, 7, no. 78 (June 1901), 121–5 (122–3).
6 Theophilus Evans, *A View of the Primitive Ages*, translated by George Roberts, Welsh edition, 1716, reprinted from American edition, 1834 (Llanidloes: John Pryse, [1864]), 19–20.

7 P. T. J. Morgan, 'The Abbé Pezron and the Celts', *Transactions of the Honourable Society of Cymmrodorion* (Session 1965), Part 2, 286–95 (291).

8 Glanmor Williams, *Religion, Language and Nationality in Wales* (Cardiff: University of Wales Press, 1979), 24–5.

9 E. T. Davies, *Religion and Society in the Nineteenth Century*, A New History of Wales, edited by Ralph Griffith, Kenneth O. Morgan, and J. Beverley Smith, (Llandybïe: Christopher Davies, 1981), 37.

10 Howell had referred to the parallels between Wales and Palestine as a particular instance of more general 'points of resemblance between . . . my own nation, the ancient British people, their land and their history'. In the late nineteenth and early twentieth centuries an astonishing identification was construed, between the Israelites and the Anglo-Saxons. The notion derived from several obscure Old Testament prophecies regarding Joseph's son Ephraim, whose descendants would become a 'multitude of nations', interpreted as the British Empire and America. Both nations had stakes in the lands to the north and west of Palestine, the former having been responsible for the liberation of Jerusalem in 1917, supposedly fulfilling a prediction to this effect. The event was seen as a prelude to the conversion of the Jews, the reunification of Israel and Judah, and the premillennial advent of Christ (Wynne Evans, 'Iberic-Hebraic Eschatology', 123; Denis Hanan and H. Aldersmith (eds.), *British-Israel Truth*, thirteenth edition (London: Covenant Publishing Co., 1926), vii, 209; A. J. Ferris, *Palestine: For Jew or Arab?*, second edition (London: Marshall Press, 1946), 35–6).

11 Arthur Penrhyn Stanley, *Sinai and Palestine*, new edition (London: John Murray, 1877), 102.

12 Richard Lovett (editor), *Welsh Pictures* (London: Religious Tract Society, [1892]); [Bible], *Y Bibl Darluniadol*, 2 vols. (London: Simpkin, Marshall and Co.; Caerleon: A. H. Hughes, 1844).

13 Both pictures are organized according to Claude Lorraine's (1600–82) landscape idiom, in which the spectator's eye is enabled to roam from the foreground, through the middle distance, into the background by means of a serpentine line.

14 W. F. H. Nicolaisen, Margaret Gelling, and Melville Richards, *The Names of Towns and Cities in Britain* (London: B. T. Batsford, 1970), 51.

15 Patricia Hanks and Flavia Hodges, *A Dictionary of First Names* (1990) (Oxford: Oxford University Press, reprinted 1991), vii, x–xiii. The list of names that Bunyan provided in his emblem book 'To learn children to spell a-right their names' are almost entirely biblical in origin (Bunyan, *A Book for Boys and Girls*, [vii]).

16 The names of chapels, Anthony Jones considers, also coincided with the development of the Nonconformists' confidence in their identity. As such, they became the placards of denominational and theological conviction (Anthony Jones, *Welsh Chapels*, 31, 101).

17 The Nonconformists' preference for Old Testament rather than Celtic names, which were popular in the eighteenth century, also reflects their desire to disaffiliate themselves from the pagan associations of Celticism in favour of a tradition more in accord with their religious convictions.

18 Urban chapels that did not adopt biblical place names took their titles from the locality, usually the district or street, in which they were situated. This follows the practice of the early, rural chapels which were often named after the villages in which they were located.

19 A. Morris, *History of Havelock Street Presbyterian Church, Newport, Mon., Jubilee Souvenir, 1846–1914* (Newport: W. Jones, 1914), 20.

20 [Calvinistic Methodist Church], 'Newport, Monmouthshire', *Treasury*, 1, no. 12 (December 1864), 372–3 (372).

21 Jahn was of the opinion that the windows 'appear to have been latticed'. If true, this feature would have provided the basis for a more substantial correspondence with those chapel windows that employed leading and glazing bars (John Jahn, *Archaeologia Biblica: A Manual of Biblical Antiquities* (Oxford: D. A. Talboys, 1836), 394).

22 [Anon.], *Scripture Illustrations*, 5 parts (London: Teape, 1824), 80.

23 Ernest Renan, *Histoire du Peuple d' Israël* (1887–94), 5 vols. (Paris, II, 1891), 142.

24 The Temple

> was one hundred and sixteen feet three inches long, to which must be added the pronaos, in the same way as St Paul, Covent Garden, nineteen feet four inches and a half more; giving a total length of one hundred and thirty five feet seven inches and a half long, by thirty-seven feet six inches broad, and fifty eight feet one inch and a half high. (John Kitto, *The Pictorial Bible: Being the Old and New Testaments*, standard edition, 4 vols. (London: Charles Knight, II, 1847), 273)

25 Anthony Jones, *Welsh Chapels*, 32.

26 Kitto, *The Pictorial Bible*, II, 270.

27 Augustin Calmet, *Dictionary of the Bible*, 3 vols. (London: J. J. and P. Knapton et al., 1732).

28 John Jones, *Scripture Antiquities: or, A Compendious Summary of the Religious Institutions, Customs, and Manners of the Hebrew Nation*, second edition (London: Seeley, 1821); [Anon.], *Scripture Illustrations*, III, 15.

29 Edwin Cone Bissell, *Biblical Antiquities: A Handbook*, Green Fund Book No. 5, (Philadelphia: American Sunday School Union, 1888), 291.

30 The Table of Shewbread was positioned on the north side of the Tabernacle, while the communion table was positioned centrally in front of the *sêt fawr*.

31 Bissell, *Biblical Antiquities*, 292.

32 John Kitto, *The Pictorial Sunday Book* (London and New York: London Printing and Publishing Company, 1855–6), 81.

33 Bezalel Narkiss, 'Tabernacle', in *Encyclopaedia Judaica*, 16 vols. (Jerusalem: Kettering Publishing House, XV, 1972), cols. 680–1.

34 The gospels record that the corresponding curtain in the Temple, which separated the Holy Place or sanctuary from the Holy of Holies, wherein the priests offered sacrifices for the sins of the people, was torn from top to bottom at the crucifixion (André Parrot, *The Temple of Jerusalem* (London: SCM Press, 1957), 95).

35 Calvin, *Institutes*, I, 134.

36 Kuyper, *Calvinism*, 226.

37 C. P. Francis, 'Notes on Bible Types and Shadows', *Riches of Grace/Cyfoes y Gras*, 8, no. 5 (May 1933), 216–18 (216).

38 *Evening Express* (5 April 1898), [3].

39 *The Times* (29 August 1893), quoted in Peter Stead, 'The Welsh Working Class', *Llafur*, 1, no. 2 (May 1973) 42–54 (52).

40 R. J. Barker, *Christ in the Valley of Unemployment* (London: Hodder and Stoughton, 1936), 13.

41 A. L. Lloyd, *Come All Ye Bold Miners: Ballads and Songs of the Coalfields*, first published 1952 (London: Lawrence and Wishart, revised edition, 1978), 221.

42 Ibid., 292, 31, 168.

43 Trevor Herbert (editor), *Bands: The Brass Band Movement in the 19th and 20th Centuries*, Popular Music in Britain (Milton Keynes and Philadelphia: Open University Press, 1991), 2, 39, 201.

44 Meurig Walters, 'Two Rhondda Poems', *Welsh Review*, 1, no. 2 (March 1939), 69; Josef Herman, *Related Twilights* (London: Robson Books, 1975), 100.

45 Michael Paul Driskel, 'Manet, Naturalism and the Politics of Christian Art', *Arts Magazine*, 60, no. 3 (November 1985), 44–54 (45).

46 The safety lamp is an exception, signifying not only the occupation and identity of the labourers but also the specific period in the history of mining technology to which it belongs, and the gaseousness and potential danger peculiar to coal- and iron-ore fields.

Chapter 7

1 Lee M. Edwards, 'The Heroic Worker and Hubert von Herkomer's *On Strike*', *Arts Magazine*, 62, no. 1, July 1981, 29–35 (29).

2 Henry Wallis, 'The Late M. Millet', *The Times* (23 January 1875), 12.

3 Linda Nochlin, *Realism*, Style and Civilization, edited by John Fleming and Hugh Honor (Harmondsworth: Penguin Books, 1971), 88.

4 Evan Williams, 'Picture Talks to Boys and Girls. "The Angelus," by J. F. Millet', *Baptist Record*, 3, no. 29 (May 1915), 14.

5 Griselda Pollock, *Millet* (London: Oresko Books, 1977), 42. During the nineteenth century Millet's paintings of peasants were often subjected to not only religious but also socio-political readings which went beyond the artist's intentions. Collins Baker complained:

> Sentimental commentators of Millet have perhaps strained the truth, introducing a moralising tendency into his resolute acceptance of the inevitability of life. They find his pictures doctrinal, reading into them their own gloomy propaganda. Thus his 'Vinedresser' and his 'Hoeman' are interpreted as types of industrial oppression, as symbols of betrayed humanity and degraded, downtrodden man.

Many critics considered that what facilitated the deconstruction of the painting into a moralizing or propagandist tract was, as Herbert described it, the 'dialogue between man and implacable fate' which Millet had established in his art. Herbert continued:

> [Millet] was essentially a pessimist who believed that fate and history were apolitical forces that kept the peasant in his weary place. However, the liberal reformers who commented upon his art believed that fate and history were weapons of established

authority, and therefore subject to challenge: the artist's dialectic between man and fate became the reformer's dialectic between man and oppressive social forces. (C. H. Collins Baker, *Jean François Millet: Painter of Labour*, first published as *Memorabilia*, no. 103 (1916) (London: Medici Society, [n.d.]), 8; Robert Herbert, 'Peasant Naturalism and Millet's Reputation', in *Jean François Millet* [exhibition catalogue] (London: Arts Council of Great Britain, 1976), 9–16 (11))

6   Burns, *Sermons in Art*, 19.
7   Ibid., 25.
8   Henry Naegely, *J. F. Millet and Rustic Art* (London: Elliot Stock, 1898), 74.
9   Burns, *Sermons in Art*, 27.
10 Ibid., 28–9, 31.
11 Ibid., 32–3. However, Herbert believed that the man's attitude did not signify prayer, and that he was playing with his hat while he waiting for the woman to finish. Given that Millet did not attend church, he saw the painting not as a celebration of the artist's own religious feelings, but as a statement about the strong association of women with religion (Herbert, 'Peasant Naturalism', 87).
12 Burns, *Sermons in Art*, 35.
13 W. S. Jones, 'Religion and Business', *Monthly Treasury*, 2, no. 5 (May 1901), 110–1 (111).
14 Hugh Price Hughes, *Ethical Christianity* (London: Sampson Low, Marston and Co., 1892), 29.
15 George Herbert, 'The Elixir', *Poems of George Herbert*, Red Letter Library (London: Blackie and Son, [n.d.]), 334–5.
16 John Ellerton, 'Behold us, Lord, a little space', *Union Hymnal*, no. 730.
17 R. W. Dale, *Laws of Christ for Common Life* (London: Hodder and Stoughton, 1884), 9.
18 Evan Williams, 'Picture Talks. "The Angelus"', 14.
19 Martin Luther, *Three Treatise* (Philadelphia: Fortress Press, 1960), 17.
20 Thomas Carlyle, *Past and Present*, The Works of Thomas Carlyle, 30 vols. (London: Chapman and Hall, X, 1897), 196, 200, 202.
21 John Linton, *The Cross in Modern Art* (London: Duckworth and Co., 1916), 6.
22 Albert Boime, 'Ford Madox Brown, Thomas Carlyle, and Karl Marx: Meaning and Mystification of Work in the Nineteenth Century', *Arts Magazine*, 56, no. 1 (September 1981), 116–125 (116). Those portions of the biblical text included in Brown's quotation are italicized in the following verses: '*Seest thou a man diligent in his business? he shall stand before kings*; he shall not stand before mean men' (Proverbs 22: 29); '*Neither did we eat any man's bread for nought; but wrought with labour and travail day and night*' (2 Thessalonians 3: 8); '*I must work* the works of him that sent me *while it is day: [for] the night cometh, when no man can work*' (John 9: 4); '*In the sweat of thy face shalt thou eat bread*, till thou return unto the ground; for out of it wast thou taken: for dust thou art, and unto dust thou shalt return' (Genesis 3: 19).
23 Carlyle, *Past and Present*, 202. In his sermonic description of the painting, Madox Brown expounded the characters' history, social circumstances, and personalities, praising the navvies: 'you will find them serious, intelligent men, and with much to interest in their conversation, which, moreover, contains about the same amount of morality and

sentiment that is commonly found among men in the active and hazardous walks of life' (Ford M. Hueffer, *Ford Madox Brown: A Record of His Life and Work* (London: Longmans, Green and Co., 1896), 194).

24 Herbert Furst, 'Christian Art Now', *Apollo*, 28 (December 1938), 277–81 (279).
25 W. R. Lambert, 'Some Working-Class Attitudes towards Organised Religion in Nineteenth-Century Wales', *Llafur*, 2, no. 1 (Spring 1976), 4–17 (10).
26 Jay Gee, '"Collier Jack": The Collier's Lot', *Children's Treasury*, 11, no. 7 (July 1914) 105–6 (105).
27 *South Wales Daily News* (11 March 1905), 5.
28 Reprinted in *Y Geninen* (1906), 127 (English translation from C. R. Williams, 'The Welsh Religious Revival, 1904–5', *British Journal of Sociology*, 3, no. 3 (September 1952), 242–59 (245)).
29 *South Wales Daily News* (16 December 1904), 5.
30 *South Wales Daily News* (23 November 1904), 6; (26 November 1904), 6; (28 December 1904), 6; Awstin, 'The Religious Revival in Wales', *Western Mail*, pamphlet no. 1 (1904), 16, 22.
31 The illustration earned its notoriety on account of the collier's response to Father Christmas's question 'Who am I to thank for it?' – 'God and Evan Roberts!' What was for many a 'blasphemous cartoon' appeared to some to suggest that Roberts was, with God, jointly responsible for the salutary results of the revival. The remarks in the following letter to the *Western Mail* are typical of the fervour of the denunciation:

> Had one of the clergy in one of our parish churches devoted his sermon yesterday to a graphic description of the ever Blessed Virgin Mother and . . . pointed out the benefits we may derive by her prayers and protection, what a loud cry of 'popery' would have been raised. But how many will be ready to accept the new creed set up by the 'Western Mail' A.D. December 26, 1904, proclaiming Evan Roberts (from some remote village) the new saviour of South Wales.

The collier's reply anticipated another controversy that a letter from Peter Price, a prominent Congregational minister, published in the *Western Mail* on 31 January 1905, began. Price fiercely argued that the revival was a manifestation not only of divine power but also of the conspicuous presence of human frailty in the form of Evan Roberts:

> I have come to the conclusion that there are two so-called Revivals going on amongst us. The one, undoubtedly, from above – Divine, real, intense in its nature, and Cymric in its form . . . But there is another Revival in South Wales – a sham Revival, a mockery, a blasphemous travesty of the real thing. The chief figure in this mock Revival is Evan Roberts, whose language is inconsistent with the character of anyone except that of a person endowed with the attributes of a Divine Being. (*Western Mail* (27 December 1904), 5); quoted in Awstin, 'The Religious Revival in Wales', *Western Mail*, pamphlet no. 7 (1905), 1, 2)

32 W. Percy Hicks, *Life-Story of Evan Roberts* (London: Charles H. Kelly, [n.d]), 73–4.

33 *South Wales Daily News* (22 December 1904), 6.
34 Awstin, 'The Religious Revival in Wales', *Western Mail*, pamphlet no. 1 (1904), 30.
35 Ibid.
36 For example:

> A miner . . . joins a 'seam' rather than a pit and, similarly, a member joins a Chapel rather than a denomination, though both really follow. A man cannot be a member of a 'seam' unless he is part of a specific coal mine, and a person cannot be accepted as a member of, say, a Presbyterian Church without at the same time being a Presbyterian. The miner cannot be moved from the 'seam' if there is work there; neither can a Nonconformist member lose his membership if he attends regularly, lives morally, and pays his dues. Both miner and the person have graduated to gain their membership. (D. Ben Rees, *Chapels in the Valleys* (Upton, Wirral: Ffynnon Press, 1975), 148, 151, 170–1)

37 Hilling, *Historic Architecture of Wales*, 165.
38 D. Gerwyn Thomas, *Welsh Coal Mines* (Cardiff: National Museum of Wales, 1979), 24.
39 W. Walford Moore, 'A Chapel in the Fossil Woods', *Sunday Magazine* (1889), 253–7, (254).
40 Anthony Jones, *Welsh Chapels*, 22–9.
41 *South Wales Daily News* (21 December 1904), 6; (29 December 1904), 6.
42 Josef Herman identified a comparison of the image of the miner with saints in religious icons. He recalls how once at Ystradgynlais, Breconshire, he saw a group of miners stepping on to a bridge: 'For a split second their heads appeared against the full body of the sun, as against a yellow disc – the whole image was not unlike an icon depicting the saints with their haloes' (Josef Herman, *The Early Years in Scotland and Wales* (Llandybïe: Christopher Davies, 1984), 21).
43 Evans, a talk on his life and work.
44 In his Fourth Discourse, Reynolds explained this aspect of the classical aesthetic with reference to Raphael's representation of the apostles in his cartoons:

> In all the pictures in which the painter has represented the apostles, he has drawn them with great nobleness; he has given them as much dignity as the human figure is capable of receiving; yet we are expressly told in the Scripture that they had no such respectable appearance; and of Paul in particular, we are told by himself that his bodily presence was mean. (Joshua Reynolds, *Discourses on Art* (London: Collier-Macmillan, 1969), 57–8)

45 Evans and Evans, *Symphonies in Black*, 106.
46 [Westminster Assembly], *Confession*, 68–73.
47 Ibid., 61–3.

Chapter 8

1 Robert Morgan, 'Word', in *On the Banks of the Cynon* (Todmorden, Yorkshire: Arc Publications, 1974), 15.

2 P. S. Brewster, *The Revolutionised Life* (London: Victory Press, [n.d]), 27; A. Greenway, 'Christian Separation', *Riches of Grace/Cyfoes y Gras*, 3, no. 1 (March 1929), 326–9; Alex Ferran, 'On Worldliness', *Riches of Grace*, 1, no. 12 (December 1977), 235–6. Commenting on the fourth tenet of the Apostolic Church's confession George Perfect wrote:

> our Church teaches a sanctification which means separation from the world and unclean habits. Although there may be some difference of opinion amongst the leaders on details, yet on such things as picture-theatres and smoking we are united, and are prepared to exercise discipline amongst our members and officers in regard to such things. (George Perfect, 'What Does the Apostolic Church Stand For?', *Herald of Grace*, 1, no. 1 (January 1941), 12–13 (12))

3 B. R. Wilson, *Sects and Society* (London: William Heinemann, 1961), 82.

4 See, for example, the biographies of Howard Carter (1891–1971) and William F. P. Burton (1886–1971) in Colin C. Whittaker, *Seven Pentecostal Pioneers* (Basingstoke: Marshall Pickering, 1983), 102, 115–17.

5 The idea, according to Robert Clarke (art teacher and lay preacher in the Elim Pentecostal Church), originated in the United States in the late 1950s (correspondence with the author, 12 June 1987; also George Canty, correspondence with the author, 1 June 1987).

6 Parker, 'Portrait of an Apostolic Artist', 123.

7 Ibid., 123–4.

8 Barthes, *Image – Music – Text*, 39, 46.

9 Paul Tillich, *Theology of Culture* (New York: Oxford University Press, 1964), 68–70, 74; Theodore M. Greene, 'Authentic Religious Art', *Liturgical Arts*, 28, no. 19 (1 August 1954), 13.

10 For a comparison of the salient differences between fundamentalism and liberalism see J. Gresham Machen, *Christianity and Liberalism* (Grand Rapids, Michigan: William B. Eerdmans Publishing Co., 1923); Ilico, 'Why Fundamentalism Will Not Do', *British Weekly* (29 December 1949), 6.

11 E. H. Gombrich, 'Image and Word in Twentieth-Century Art', *Word and Image*, 1, no. 3 (July–September 1985), 213–41 (221).

12 Edwyn Bevan, *Symbolism and Belief* (London: Allen and Unwin, 1938), 280.

13 Augustus Montague Toplady, 'Rock of Ages, cleft for me', *Union Hymnal*, no. 327.

14 Fairley, *Glossary of Terms*, 7.

15 Evans and Evans, *Symphonies in Black*, 74. In mining terminology the collective noun 'journey' was used to describe the line of drams that travelled the main road of the pit.

16 Christiane Sourvinou-Inwood, in *Lexicon Iconographicum Mythologiae Classicae*, 3 vols. (Zurich and Munich: Artemis Verlag, I, 1986), 212, 220, 222.

17 These examples can also be considered an example of what Panofsky called *pseudo-*

morphosis: 'the emergence of form A, morphologically analogous to, or even identical with, form B, yet entirely unrelated to it from a genetic point of view' (Erwin Panofsky, *Tomb Sculpture*, edited by H. W. Janson (London: Thames and Hudson, 1964), 25–7).

18 J. A. MacCulloch, *The Harrowing of Hell* (Edinburgh: T. and T. Clark, 1930) 253–4.

19 Evans is interested in the history of the Jewish Holocaust, and has made several paintings illustrating the plight of the Jews and their suffering. Photographs and film-footage of the appalling scenes of carnage, including the shallow graves into which the dead were slung by their executioners, have exerted an unconscious influence on the representation of Evans's semi-interred colliers (Evans and Evans, *Symphonies in Black*, 8; *Aberdare Leader* (13 May 1982), 8).

20 Vann, 'Out of the Darkness' (11).

21 Quoted in Michael Pollard, *The Hardest Work under Heaven* (London: Hutchinson, 1984), 48.

22 Philippe Ariès, *Images of Man and Death*, translated by Janet Lloyd (Cambridge: Massachusetts: Harvard University Press, 1985), 176.

23 Quoted in Helen Duckham and Baron Duckham, *Great Pit Disasters* (Newton Abbot: David and Charles, 1973), 159.

24 Philippe Ariès, *The Hour of Our Death*, translated by Helen Weaver (Harmondsworth: Penguin Books, 1983), 59–60.

25 John Calvin, *Commentary upon the Epistle of Saint Paul to the Romans*, edited by Henry Beveridge (Edinburgh: Calvin Translation Society, 1844), 134–5.

26 Halewood, *Six Subjects of Reformation Art*, 11.

27 Henry, *Exposition*, III, 314.

28 Höltgen, *Aspects of the Emblem*, 43.

29 Emblems for sin are rare. Bunyan emblematized sin in the form of a bee 'Whose Sweet [honey] unto many death hath been'. In the mining illustrations, a closer relationship is established between the nature of the concept and the subject adapted to typify it (Bunyan, *A Book for Boys and Girls*, 11).

30 *South Wales Daily News* (13 January 1905), 6. In associating sin with black, Nonconformity departed from the biblical tradition. In the Old Testament sin is symbolized by red: 'though your sins be as scarlet, they shall be as white as snow; though they be red like crimson, they shall be as wool' (Isaiah 1: 18). The connection between black and sin, other than casually by way of association with darkness, derives from the biblical custom of weaving sackcloth to signify penitence for sin (1 Kings 21: 27, Matthew 11: 21). The coarse material, which was black in colour (Revelation 6: 12), was also worn as a sign of mourning not only for sin, but also for the dead and for national and personal calamities.

31 [Forward Movement], *Forward Movement Torch*, 68; Phillips, *Evan Roberts a'i Waith*, 219–20.

32 R. Williams, 'The Gospel of Colours', *Children's Treasury*, 9, no. 9 (September 1912), 132–3 (132).

33 Ibid.

34 Here 'blacker' (Hebrew *chasak*) is used. It is the same word as employed by Micah in his rebuke of false prophets, denoting 'to become dark': 'Therefore night shall be unto you, that ye shall not have a vision; and it shall dark unto you' (Micah 3: 6). Further, in

Jeremiah's expression of sorrow over his people's continued captivity – 'I am black; astonishment hath taken hold on me' (Jeremiah 8: 21) – 'black' (Hebrew *gadar*: to be covered dark, found in Joel's apocalyptic image: 'the sun and moon shall be darkened' (Joel 3: 15)). *Gadar* is also used in Hebrew to mean 'to cause to mourn', as in 'I cause Lebanon to mourn for him' (Ezekiel 31: 15).

35 D. J. Williams, 'Shadows', *Colliery Workers' Magazine*, 1, no. 5 (May 1923), 117.

36 Here I have used the term 'polychrome' when contrasting the colour of *Entombed* with the later works in order to convey the sense that the later works are painted in one colour rather than that there is an absence of colour, which is the usual implication of the term 'black and white'.

37 Fred Licht, *Goya: The Origins of the Modern Temper in Art* (London: John Murray, 1980), 180.

38 Roman Catholicism held that this gulf between heaven and earth, God and man, could be bridged by a person's own efforts and 'works', and by baptism into the institution of the Church, a view fiercely refuted by the Reformers: 'if righteousness were in the law of works, our glorying were not excluded; but because it is of faith only . . . it bringeth nothing but a humble confession of need and want' (Calvin, *Commentary upon the Epistle of Saint Paul to the Romans*, 90).

39 Robert Morgan, 'The Donors', in *On the Banks of the Cynon*, 27–33 (27, 33); 'Years Ago', in *The Night's Prison* (London: Rupert Hart-Davis, 1967), 36.

40 Awstin, 'The Religious Revival in Wales', *Western Mail*, pamphlet no. 1 (1904), 10.

41 Phillips, *Evan Roberts the Great Revivalist and His Work*, 489, 503.

42 George Campbell Morgan, *The Gospel According to Luke* (New York: Fleming H. Revell Co., 1931), 273; J. C. Ryle, *Expository Thoughts on the Gospels: Luke*, 1858, 2 vols. (Edinburgh: Banner of Truth Trust, II, 1986), 479.

43 Ruskin, *Works*, XIV, 61–6.

44 Wilson, *Sects and Society*, 111.

Appendix 1

1 Both poems are taken from the archives of the Welsh Industrial and Maritime Museum, Cardiff.

Appendix 2

1 [Calvinistic Methodist Church], 'Should Christians Attend Theatres?', *Monthly Treasury*, 7, no. 10 (October 1906), 224–7 (224–5).

2 H. Elwyn Thomas, *Pulpit Talks*, 67–9.

3 [Baptist Union of England and Wales], 'The "Church" in the Theatre', *Baptist Record*, 2, no. 15 (July 1896), 9–10 (10).

4 *South Wales Daily News* (30 January 1905), 5.

5 S. M. Berry, 'From the Centre', *The Congregational Magazine*, 11, no. 2 (February 1929),

17–18 (18). Biblical dramas with titles such as 'Ruth and Naomi' and 'Esther for Queen' were performed, mostly in Welsh, by amateur dramatic groups in the chapels in the decade leading up to the First World War (Delwyn Jones, Bedlinog, transcript of recorded interviews with south Wales miners, interviewed by Alun Morgan (10 September 1973), South Wales Miners' Library, Swansea, ref. DJ/113/3,5–7).

Appendix 3

1 Quoted by Eilir in Awstin, 'The Religious Revival in Wales', *Western Mail*, pamphlet no. 1 (1904), 2.
2 D. Ben Rees, *Wales: The Cultural Heritage* (Ormskirk: G. W. and A. Hesketh, 1981), 71.
3 Awstin, 'The Religious Revival in Wales', *Western Mail*, pamphlet no. 6 (1905), 24, 26.
4 David Edwards, *The Welsh Pulpit* (London: T. Fisher Unwin, 1864), 41.
5 Edward Russell in Awstin, 'The Religious Revival in Wales', *Western Mail*, pamphlet no. 6 (1905), 2.

Appendix 4

1 [Apostolic Church], *The Apostolic Church: Its Principles and Practices* (Pen-y-groes: Apostolic Church, 1937), 185–218; George Perfect, 'What Does the Apostolic Church Stand For?', *Herald of Grace*, 1, no. 1 (January 1941), 12–13 (12).
2 Frank Parker, 'What We Stand For', *Riches of Grace*, 1, no. 4 (April 1977), 70–7 (71).
3 T. W. Walker, 'The Baptism of the Holy Spirit', in *Pentecostal Doctrine*, edited by P. S. Brewster ([Cardiff]: P. S. Brewster, 1976), 27–37 (34). The purposes for which the baptism and gifts of the Spirit are still to be sought, it is contended, are the Church's continual need of power and equipment for evangelism (ibid., 27), edification, guidance, protection, worship, the confirmation of the gospel, and the demonstration of the power of God to men (W. R. Jones, 'The Nine Gifts of the Holy Spirit', in *Pentecostal Doctrine*, 47–61).
4 T. N. Turnbull, *What God Hath Wrought* (Bradford: Puritan Press, [1959]), 14.
5 Frederick Dale Bruner, *A Theology of the Holy Spirit* (London: Hodder and Stoughton, 1970), 38–9; Charles G. Finney, *Lectures on Revivals of Religion* (London: Thomas Tegg, 1838), 102–3.
6 Bruner, *Theology of the Holy Spirit*, 44.
7 Eifion Evans, *The Welsh Revival of 1904* (1969) (Bridgend: Evangelical Press of Wales, 1981), 31.
8 *South Wales Daily News* (1 October 1904), 6; (3 October 1904), 6.
9 Pen Lewis and Roberts, *War on the Saints*, 284.
10 D. P. Williams experienced tongues-speaking in the revival, but 'because of the variety of supernatural manifestations at the time very little attention was given to this new phenomenon' (Turnbull, *What God Hath Wrought*, 18). During the revival, gypsies on the mountainside at Trecynon were reported as singing and praying to God in a 'strange

tongue' (*Aberdare Leader* (19 November 1904), 4), while in north Wales it was reported that some men and women who knew little Welsh were able to pray fluently in it (*North Wales Chronicle* (31 December 1904), 7).
11 Turnbull, *What God Hath Wrought*, 13.

Select Bibliography

Adams, W. J., *Miracles of Today* (Stockholm: W. J. Adams, [1926]).
Alexander, Archibald B. D., *Christianity and Ethics* (London: Duckworth and Co., 1914).
Allchin, A. M., *Ann Griffiths*, Writers of Wales, edited by Meic Stephens and R. Brinley Jones (Cardiff: University of Wales Press, Welsh Arts Council, 1976).
Andrews, C. F., *Christ and Labour* (London: SCM Press, 1923).
[Anon.], 'Christianised Culture', *Christian Pictorial*, 1, no. 23 (3 August 1893), 360–1.
[Anon.], 'John Ruskin's Teaching', *Christian Pictorial*, 14, no. 363 (8 February 1900), 294–5.
[Anon.], *Scripture Illustrations*, 5 parts (London: Teape, 1824).
[Anon.], 'The Mystery Painting: The Shadow of the Cross', *Perilous Times*, no. 154 (January 1912), 340.
Awstin, 'The Religious Revival in Wales', *Western Mail*, pamphlets nos. 1–7 (1904–5).
Ariès, Philippe, *The Hour of Our Death*, translated by Helen Weaver (Harmondsworth: Penguin Books, 1983).
Ariès, Philippe, *Images of Man and Death*, translated by Janet Lloyd (Cambridge, Massachusetts: Harvard University Press, 1985).
Arnold, Matthew, *On the Study of Celtic Literature* (London: Smith, Elder and Co., 1867).
[Baptist Union of England and Wales], 'The Laocoon of Life', *Baptist Record*, 14, no. 8 (March 1928), 18.
Baker, C. H. Collins, *Jean François Millet: Painter of Labour*, first published as *Memorabilia*, no. 103 (1916) (London: Medici Society, [n.d.]).
Barker, R. J., *Christ in the Valley of Unemployment* (London: Hodder and Stoughton, 1936).
Barthes, Roland, *Image – Music – Text*, translated by Stephen Heath, Fontana Paperbacks (Glasgow: Collins, 1977).
Barthes, Roland, *S/Z*, translated by Richard Miller (London: Jonathan Cape, 1975).
Bath, M., *Speaking Pictures: English Emblem Books and Renaissance Culture*, Longman Medieval and Renaissance Library (London and New York: Longman, 1994).
Bevan, Edwyn, *Holy Images: An Inquiry into Idolatry and Image Worship in Ancient Paganism and in Christianity* (London: George Allen, and Unwin, 1940).
Bevan, Edwyn, *Symbolism and Belief* (London: Allen and Unwin, 1938).
[Bible], *Bibl yr Addoliad Teuluaidd*, annotated by Peter Williams (Bangor: Evan Ingram, [1878]).
[Bible], *Y Bibl Darluniadol*, 2 vols. (London: Simpkin, Marshall and Co.; Caerleon: A. H. Hughes, 1844).
Bissell, Edwin Cone, *Biblical Antiquities: A Handbook*, Green Fund Book No. 5, (Philadelphia: American Sunday School Union, 1888).

Bloch-Hoell, Nils, *The Pentecostal Movement* (Oslo: Universitetsforlaget; London: Allen and Unwin, 1964).

Boime, Albert, 'Ford Madox Brown, Thomas Carlyle, and Karl Marx: Meaning and Mystification of Work in the Nineteenth Century', *Arts Magazine*, 56, no. 1 (September 1981), 116–25.

Breese, C. E., *Welsh Nationality* (Caernarfon: Welsh National Press Co., 1895).

Brewster, P. S., 'The Seven-Fold Work of the Holy Spirit', in *Pentecostal Doctrine*, edited by P. S. Brewster, ([Cardiff]: P. S. Brewster, 1976, 9–24).

Briggs, M. S., *Puritan Architecture* (London and Redhill: Lutterworth Press, 1946).

Brown, John, *Argraphiad Newydd o Eiriadur Beiblaidd* (London: William Mackenzie, [n.d.]).

Brown, Kenneth D., *A Social History of the Nonconformist Ministry in England and Wales 1800–1930* (Oxford: Clarendon Press, 1988).

Bruner, Frederick Dale, *A Theology of the Holy Spirit* (London: Hodder and Stoughton, 1971).

Buchanan, James, *Analogy Considered as a Guide to Truth, and Applied as an Aid to Faith* (Edinburgh: Johnstone, Hunter and Co., 1864).

Bulman, H. F., *Coal Mining and the Coal Miner* (London: Methuen and Co., 1920).

Bunyan, John, *The Pilgrim's Progress* (London: W. Johnston, 1770).

Burns, James, *The Christ Face in Art* (London: Duckworth and Co., 1907).

Burns, James, *Illustrations from Art for Pulpit and Platform* (London: James Clarke and Co., 1912).

Burns, James, *Sermons in Art by the Great Masters* (London: Duckworth, 1908).

Calmet, Augustin, *Dictionary of the Bible*, 3 vols. (London: J. J. and P. Knapton, 1732).

Calvin, John, *Commentary upon the Epistle of Saint Paul to the Romans*, edited by Henry Beveridge (Edinburgh: Calvin Translation Society, 1844).

Calvin, John, *Institutes of the Christian Religion*, translated by Henry Beveridge, 3 vols. (Edinburgh: Calvin Translation Society, 1845).

[Calvinistic Methodist Church], 'Christian Culture – Private and Public', *Monthly Treasury*, 5, no. 59 (November 1898), 253–4.

[Calvinistic Methodist Church], 'How a Painter Can Preach', *Monthly Treasury*, 4, no. 2 (February 1903), 126.

Campbell, R. J., *The New Theology* (London: Chapman and Hall, 1907).

Carlyle, Thomas, *Past and Present*, The Works of Thomas Carlyle, 30 vols. (London: Chapman and Hall, X, 1897).

Cassuto, U., *A Commentary on the Book of Exodus* (Hebrew University, Jerusalem: Magness Press, first published in Hebrew, 1951; first published in English, 1967).

Charles, Thomas, *An Exposition of the Ten Commandments by Way of Question and Answer* (Bala: R. Saunderson, 1805).

Clark, Kenneth, *Blake and Visionary Art* (Glasgow: University of Glasgow Press, 1973).

Cope, Gilbert, *Symbolism in the Bible and Church* (London: SCM Press, 1959).

Cross, Joseph, *Sermons of Christmas Evans* (Philadelphia: Leary and Getz, 1857).

Crouch, Joseph, *Puritanism and Art: An Enquiry into a Popular Fallacy* (London: Cassell and Co., 1910).

Dabney, Robert L., *Sacred Rhetoric: or, A Course of Lectures on Preaching* (1870) (Edinburgh: Banner of Truth Trust, 1979).

Dale, R. W., *Laws of Christ for Common Life* (London: Hodder and Stoughton, 1884).

Davenport, Fredrick Morgan, *Primitive Traits in Religious Revivals* (London and New York: Macmillan and Co., 1905).

Davies, David, *Sacred Themes and Famous Paintings* (London: Alexander and Shepheard, 1885).

Davies, E. T., *Religion and Society in the Nineteenth Century*, A New History of Wales, edited by Ralph Griffith, Kenneth O. Morgan, and J. Beverley Smith (Llandybïe: Christopher Davies, 1981).

Davies, E. T., *Religion in the Industrial Revolution in South Wales* (Cardiff: University of Wales Press, 1965).

Davies, Evan, *Revivals in Wales* (London: John Snow, 1859).

Davies, J. Gynoro, *Flashes from the Welsh Pulpit* (London: Hodder and Stoughton, 1889).

Dayton, Donald W., *Theological Roots of Pentecostalism*, Studies in Evangelicalism no. 5 (Metuchen and London: Scarecrow Press, 1987).

Diehl, Huston, 'Graven Images: Protestant Emblem Books in England', *Renaissance Quarterly*, 39, no. 1 (Spring 1986), 49–66.

Dixon, A. C., *Present Day Life and Religion* (London: S. W. Partridge and Co., [n.d.]).

Dobson, C. C., *The Face of Christ* (London: Centenary Press, 1933).

Downes, Robert P., *Pure Pleasures* (London: Charles H. Kelly, 1895).

Drummond, A. L., *The Church Architecture of Protestantism* (Edinburgh: T. and T. Clark, 1934).

Duckham, Helen, and Baron Duckham, *Great Pit Disasters* (Newton Abbot: David and Charles, 1973).

Edwards, David, *The Welsh Pulpit* (London: T. Fisher Unwin, 1864).

Edwards, Jonathan, *The Great Awakening*, edited by C. C. Coen, The Works of Jonathan Edwards (New Haven and London: Yale University Press, IV, 1972).

Edwards, Ness, *The Industrial Revolution in South Wales* (London: Labour Publishing Co., 1924).

Edwards, R. D., 'The Collier's Lamp', *Treasury*, 2, no. 1 (January 1914), 9.

Edwards, Thomas Charles, *The Epistle to the Hebrews* (London: Hodder and Stoughton, 1888).

Evans, Christmas, *The Allegories of Christmas Evans*, translated by R. E. Williams (Aberdare: G. M. Evans, 1899).

Evans, Christmas, *Sermons, on Various Subjects*, translated by J. Davies (Beaver: William Henry, 1837).

Evans, E. W., *The Miners of South Wales* (Cardiff: University of Wales Press, 1961).

Evans, Eifion, *Daniel Rowland and the Great Evangelical Awakening in Wales* (Edinburgh: Banner of Truth Trust, 1985).

Evans, Eifion, *The Welsh Revival of 1904* (1969) (Bridgend: Evangelical Press of Wales, 1981).

Evans, Gwynfor, and Ioan Rhys, 'Wales', in *Celtic Nationalism*, edited by Owen Dudley Edwards, Gwynfor Evans, Ioan Rhys and Hugh MacDiarmid (London: Routledge and Kegan Paul, 1968), 211–98.

[Evans, Nicholas], *How's Life?*, BBC, Radio Wales (January 1986).

[Evans, Nicholas], in *It's Never Too Late*, BBC, (July 1983), [transcript], 47–57.

[Evans, Nicholas], *A Kind of Singing*, produced by Mark Owen, BBC, Radio Wales (March 1982).

Evans, Nicholas, [a talk on his life and work], Aberystwyth Arts Centre (July 1983).

Evans, Nicholas, and Rhoda Evans, *Symphonies in Black* (Talybont: Y Lolfa, 1987).

Evans, Theophilus, *A View of the Primitive Ages*, translated by George Roberts, Welsh edition, 1716, reprinted from American edition, 1834 (Llanidloes: John Pryse, [1864]).

Evans, W., *History of Welsh Theology* (London: James Nisbet and Co., 1900).

Fairbairn, Patrick, *The Typology of Scripture: Viewed in Connection with the Entire Scheme of Divine Dispensation*, 2 vols. (Edinburgh: Clark, 1847).

Fairley, William, *Glossary of Terms Used in the Coal-Mining-Districts of (First) South Wales, (Second) Bristol and Somersetshire* (London: Colliery Guardian, 1868).

Fairley, William, *Practical Observations on the South Wales Coal Field* (London: W. M. Hutchings, Colliery Guardian Office, [1868]).

Fawcett, T., *The Symbolic Language of Religion* (London: SCM Press, 1970).

Fingeston, Peter, 'Toward a New Definition of Religious Art', *College Art Journal*, 10, no. 2 (Winter 1951), 131–46.

Finney, Charles G., *Lectures on Revivals in Religion* (London: Thomas Tegg, 1838).

Fletcher, Ifan Kyrle, 'The Appreciation of Art in Wales', *Welsh Outlook*, 14, no. 10 (October 1927), 264–5.

Foster, Addison P., 'The Types of Scripture', *Homiletic Quarterly*, 1 (1877), 8–24.

Forsyth, P. T., *Christ on Parnassus* (London: Hodder and Stoughton, [n.d.]).

Forsyth, P. T., *Religion in Recent Art* (London: Hodder and Stoughton, 1901).

Garvan, Anthony, 'The Protestant Plain Style Before 1630', *Journal of the Society of Architectural Historians*, 9, no. 3 (October 1950), 5–13.

Gee, Jay, '"Collier Jack." The Collier's Lot', *Children's Treasury*, 11, no. 7 (July 1914), 105–6.

Ginswick, Jules (editor), *Labour and the Poor in England and Wales 1849–1851*, 8 vols. (London: Frank Cass, III, 1983).

Gombrich, E. H., 'Image and Word in Twentieth-Century Art', *Word and Image*, 1, no. 3 (July–September 1985), 213–41.

Goodman, Felicitas D., *Speaking in Tongues: A Cross Cultural Study in Glossolalia* (Chicago and London: University of Chicago Press, 1972).

Gray, Douglas, 'Art and Coal', in *Coal: British Mining in Art 1680–1980*, [exhibition catalogue] (London: Arts Council of Great Britain, 1982), 7–42.

Greenway, A., 'Christian Separation', *Riches of Grace/Cyfoes y Gras*, 3, no. 1 (March 1929), 326–9.

Gwyther, Cyril E., 'Sidelights on Religion and Politics in the Rhondda Valley 1906–26', *Llafur*, 3, no. 1 (Spring 1980), 30–43.

Halewood, William H., *Six Subjects of Reformation Art: A Preface to Rembrandt* (Toronto, Buffalo and London: University of Toronto Press, 1982).

Harries, Hywel, *Cymru'r Cynfas/Wales on Canvas* (1983), new bilingual edition (Talybont: Y Lolfa, 1988).

Harvey, John, *The Art of Piety: The Visual Culture of Welsh Nonconformity* (Cardiff: University of Wales Press, 1995).

Heaphy, Thomas, *The Likeness of Christ*, edited by Wyke Bayliss (London: David Bogue, 1880).

Henry, Matthew, *An Exposition of the Old and New Testaments*, 3 vols. (London: Thomas Parkhurst, I, 1704).

Herbert, Robert, 'Peasant Naturalism and Millet's Reputation', in *Jean François Millet*, [exhibition catalogue] (London: Arts Council of Great Britain, 1976), 9–16.

Hicks, W. Percy, *Life-Story of Evan Roberts* (London: Charles H. Kelly, [n.d.]).

Hilling, John B., *The Historic Architecture of Wales: An Introduction* (Cardiff: University of Wales Press, 1976).

Hodge, Charles, *Systematic Theology* (1871–3), 3 vols. (Grand Rapids, Michigan: William B. Eerdmans Publishing Co., II, 1986).

Hollenweger, Walter J., *The Pentecostals*, translated by R. A. Wilson, second edition ([London]: SCM Press, 1976).

Höltgen, Karl Josef, *Aspects of the Emblem: Studies in the English Emblem Tradition and the European Context*, Problemata Semiotica, 2 (Kassel: Edition Reichenberger, 1986).

Hood, Edwin Paxton, *Christmas Evans: The Preacher of Wild Wales* (London: Hodder and Stoughton, 1881).

Hood, Edwin Paxton, *The Vocation of the Preacher* (London: Hodder and Stoughton, 1886).

[House of Lords], *Commissioners on the Employment and Condition of Children in Mines and Manufactories* ([London]: [House of Lords], [1842]).

Hughes, Henry, in 'Y Diwygiad a'r Weinidogaeth', *Y Geninen*, 24, no. 2 (February 1906), 127–32.

Hughes, Hugh Price, *Ethical Christianity* (London: Sampson Low, Marston and Co., 1892).

[Hymnal], *Victorian Hymns*, second edition (London: Kegan Paul, Trench and Co., 1887).

[Hymnal], *Well-Known Revival Hymns* (London: Christian Herald, [n.d.]).

Jahn, John, *Archaeologia Biblica: A Manual of Biblical Antiquities* (Oxford: D. A. Talboys, 1836).

Jenkins, David, and Moses Powell, *Life from the Dead: Being the History of the Entombed Colliers in the 'Tynewydd Pit'* (Cwmavon: Griffith and Sons, [c.1877]).

Jenkins, W., 'The Welsh Renaissance II', *Wales*, 2 (1895), 444–8.

Jenner, Henry, *Christ in Art* (London: Methuen and Co., 1906).

Jobson, F. J., *Chapel and School Architecture* (London: Hamilton, Adams Co., 1856).

John, A. H., *The Industrial Development of South Wales* (Cardiff: University of Wales Press, 1950).

Jones, Anthony, *Welsh Chapels* (1984) (Cardiff and Stroud: National Museum of Wales and Alun Sutton Publishing, 1996).

Jones, Edmund, *A Relation of Apparitions of Spirits in the County of Monmouth and the Principality of Wales*, third edition (Newport: E. Lewis, 1813).

Jones, G. Hartwell, 'The Celtic Renaissance and How to Forward It', *Y Cymmrodor*, 42 (1930), 111–28.

Jones, Henry, 'Art and Life', *Welsh Outlook*, 2, no. 4 (May 1915), 168–72.

Jones, Ieuan Gwynedd, 'The South Wales Collier in Mid-Nineteenth Century', in *Victorian South Wales – Architecture, Industry and Society*, Seventh Conference Report (London: Victorian Society, 1971), 34–51.

Jones, J. Cynddylan, *The Gift of Tongues* (Newport: W. Jones, 1877).

Jones, J. Cynddylan (editor), *The Welsh Pulpit Today* (London: Hodder and Stoughton, 1885).

Jones, J., and J. Jones, 'Welsh Preaching', *Red Dragon*, 2 (1895), 428–6.

Jones, John, *Scripture Antiquities: or, A Compendious Summary of the Religious Institutions, Customs, and Manners of the Hebrew Nation*, second edition (London: Seeley, 1821).

Jones, J. R. Kilsby, 'Characteristics of Welsh Preaching', in *Echoes from the Welsh Hills*, by David Davies (London: Alexander and Shepheard, 1883).

Jones, M. E. (editor), *Sermons by Young Welsh Ministers*, Yspryd yr Oes (Zeitgeist) Series no. 1 (Mold: Yspryd yr Oes Co., 1905).

Jones, Owen, *Some of the Great Preachers of Wales* (London: Passmore and Alabaster, 1885).

Jones, P. Mansell, 'Welsh Industrial Landscapes', *Welsh Outlook*, 18, no. 6 (June 1931), 154–6.

Jones, Ronald P., *Nonconformist Church Architecture* (London: Lindsey Press, 1914).

Jones, Thomas, 'Coal-Mining Terms', *Bulletin of the Board of Celtic Studies*, 8, no. 3 (November 1936), 208–24.

Joshua, Seth, [sermon notes], Calvinistic Methodist Archives, National Library of Wales, Aberystwyth (April 1907), MS, HZ/1/17/4.

Kitto, John, *The Pictorial Bible: Being the Old and New Testaments*, standard edition, 4 vols. (London: Charles Knight, II, 1847).

Kitto, John, *The Pictorial Sunday Book* (London and New York: London Printing and Publishing Company, 1855–6).

Kris, Ernst, and Otto Kurz, *Legend, Myth, and Magic in the Image of the Artist* (New Haven and London: Yale University Press, 1979).

Kuyper, Abraham, *Calvinism* (London: Sovereign Grace Union, [n.d.]).

Lambert, W. R., *Drink and Sobriety in Victorian Wales c.1820–c.1895* (Cardiff: University of Wales Press, 1983).

Lambert, W. R., 'Some Working-Class Attitudes towards Organised Religion in Nineteenth-Century Wales', *Llafur*, 2, no. 1 (Spring 1976), 4–17.

Leighton, Frederic, *Addresses Delivered to the Students of the Royal Academy* (London: Kegan Paul, Trench, Trübner and Co., 1896).

Lewis, H. Elvet, *With Christ among the Miners* (London: Hodder and Stoughton, 1906).

Lewis, Jessie Pen, and Evan Roberts, *War on the Saints* (Leicester: Overcomer Office; London: Marshall Brothers, 1912).

Lindley, Kenneth, *Chapels and Meeting Houses* (London: John Baker, 1969).

Linton, John, *The Cross in Modern Art* (London: Duckworth and Co., 1916).

Lloyd, A. L., *Come All Ye Bold Miners: Ballads and Songs of the Coalfields*, first published 1952 (London: Lawrence and Wishart, revised edition, 1978).

Lovett, Richard (editor), *Welsh Pictures* (London: Religious Tract Society, [1892]).

Luther, Martin, *Three Treatise* (Philadelphia: Fortress Press, 1960).

Maas, Jeremy, *The Light of the World* (London: Scolar Press, 1983).

MacCulloch, J. A., *The Harrowing of Hell* (Edinburgh: T. and T. Clark, 1930).

MacIntyre, Alasdair, 'Visions', in *New Essays in Philosophical Theology*, edited by Anthony Flew and Alasdair MacIntyre, The Library of Philosophy and Theology (London: SCM Press, 1955), 254–60.

Mathews, Thomas F., 'Tillich on Religious Content in Modern Art', *Art Journal*, 27, no. 1 (Fall 1967), 16–19.

McLeod, Hugh, *Religion and the Working Class in Nineteenth-Century Britain*, Studies in Economic and Social History (London: Macmillan, 1984).

Moore, Albert C., *Iconography of Religions* (London: SCM Press, 1977).

Moore, Robert, *Pitmen, Preachers and Politics* (Cambridge: Cambridge University Press, 1974).

Morgan, Edward, *John Elias: Life, Letters and Essays*, first published as *Memoir of John Elias* (1844) and *Letters Essays and Other Papers* (1847) (Edinburgh: Banner of Truth Trust, 1973).

Morgan, J. Vrynwy, *The Welsh Revival 1904–5* (London: Chapman and Hall, 1909).

Morgan, P. T. J., 'The Abbé Pezron and the Celts', *Transactions of the Honourable Society of Cymmrodorion* (Session 1965), Part 2, 286–95.

Morgan, Robert, *My Lamp Still Burns* (Llandysul: Gomer Press, 1981).

Morgan, Robert, *On the Banks of the Cynon* (Todmorden: Yorkshire, Arc Publications, 1974).

Morris, J. H., and L. J. Williams, *The South Wales Coal Industry 1841–1875* (Cardiff: University of Wales Press, 1958).

Naegely, Henry, *J. F. Millet and Rustic Art* (London: Elliot Stock, 1898).

Nicolaisen, W. F. H., Margaret Gelling, and Melville Richards, *The Names of Towns and Cities in Britain* (London: B. T. Batsford, 1970).

Nixon, John, *Explosions in Coal Mines* (Cardiff: Chronicle Office, 1867).

Nochlin, Linda, *Realism*, Style and Civilization, edited by John Fleming and Hugh Honor (Harmondsworth: Penguin Books, 1971).

Owen, John, *The Works of John Owen*, edited by William H. Goold, 16 vols. (Edinburgh: T. and T. Clark, XIV, 1862).

P., 'Revival at Abertillery, Monmouthshire', *Treasury*, 16, no. 189 (September 1879), 172–3.

Parker, Frank, 'Portrait of an Apostolic Artist', *Riches of Grace*, 3, no. 7 (July 1979), 123–4.

Phillips, D. M., *Evan Roberts a'i Waith* (Dolgellau: E. W. Evans, 1912).

Phillips, D. M., *Evan Roberts the Great Welsh Revivalist and His Work*, second edition (London: Marshall Brothers, 1906).

Phillips, Thomas, *The Welsh Revival* (London: James Nisbet, 1860).

Praz, Mario, *Studies in Seventeenth Century Imagery* (Rome: Edizioni di Storia e Letteratura, 1964).

Price, Watcyn M., '"The Hope of the World"', *Treasury*, 10, no. 7 (July 1922), 110–12.

Quarles, Francis, *Emblems, Divine and Moral*, new edition (London: John Bennet, 1834).

Rawnsley, H. D., 'The Danger of the Pernicious Picture', in *The Church and Life of Today* (London: Hodder and Stoughton, 1910), 77–90.

Rees, D. Ben, *Chapels in the Valleys* (Upton, Wirral: Ffynnon Press, 1975).

Rees, T. Mardy, *Welsh Painters, Engravers, Sculptors 1527–1911* (Caernarfon: Welsh Publishing Co., 1912).

Rees, Thomas, *History of Protestant Nonconformity in Wales*, second edition (London: John Snow and Co., 1883).

Rees, Thomas, *Miscellaneous Papers: Subjects Relating to Wales* (London: John Snow, 1867).

Roberts, Eleazar, 'The Revival, from a Welsh Point of View', *Monthly Treasury*, 6, no. 9 (September 1905), 198–9.

Roberts, Evan, [miscellaneous poetry], Calvinistic Methodist Archives, National Library of Wales, Aberystwyth, MSS, 25632; 25633; 25636; 25680; 25682.

Rosman, Doreen, *Evangelicals and Culture* (London: Croom Helm, 1984).

Rothenberg, Albert, *The Emerging Goddess* (Chicago and London: University of Chicago Press, 1979).

Rowland, Daniel, *Eight Sermons upon Practical Subjects* (London: Thomas Davies, 1774).

Runzo, Joseph, 'Visions, Pictures and Rules', *Religious Studies*, 13 (1977), 303–18.

Ruskin, John, *Academy Notes*, The Works of John Ruskin, edited by E. T. Cook and Alexander Wedderburn, Library Edition (London: George Allen, XIV, 1903–5).

Ruskin, John, *Modern Painters*, The Works of John Ruskin, edited by E. T. Cook and Alexander Wedderburn, Library Edition, 5 vols. (London: George Allen, II, 1903–5).

Sharrock, Roger, 'Bunyan and the English Emblem Writers', *Review of English Studies*, 21, no. 82 (April 1945), 105–16.

Simonin, Louis, *Mines and Miners; or, Underground Life*, translated by H. W. Bristow (London: William Mackenzie, 1868).

Smith, David R., 'Towards a Protestant Aesthetic: Rembrandt's *1655 Sacrifice of Isaac*', *Art History*, 8, no. 3 (September 1985), 290–302.

South Wales Arts Association, Minutes (June 1895–October 1919), Glamorgan County Archives, Cardiff, D/D SWA 1–4.

Sprague, W. B., *Lectures on Revivals of Religion*, second edition (Glasgow: Collins, 1833).

Spurgeon, Charles Haddon *John Ploughman's Pictures: More of his Talks* (London: Passmore and Alabaster, 1890).

Stanley, Arthur Penrhyn *Lectures on the History of the Jewish Church*, second edition, 2 vols. (London: John Murray, II, 1863).

Stanley, Arthur Penrhyn, *Sinai and Palestine*, new edition (London: John Murray, 1877).

Stead, Peter, 'The Welsh Working Class', *Llafur*, 1, no. 2 (May 1973), 42–54.

Stead, W. T., *The Revival of 1905*, fourth edition (London: Review of Reviews Office, 1905).

Thomas, H. Elwyn, *Pulpit Talks to Young People* (London: H. R. Allenson, 1900).

Thomas, H. R., *Art: Viewed from a Moral and Spiritual Aspect* (Llanelli: Guardian Office, 1919).

[Thomas, T. H.], 'Illustrated Lectures upon Art', [broadsheet of lectures], National Museum of Wales, Cardiff.

Thompson, David M. (editor), *Nonconformity in the Nineteenth Century* (London: Routledge and Kegan Paul, 1972).

Tillich, Paul, *Theology of Culture* (New York: Oxford University Press, 1964).

T.J.P., 'The Colliery Explosion in Monmouthshire', *Treasury*, 14, no. 160 (April 1877), 73–5.

Trimen, Andrew, *Church and Chapel Architecture* (London: Longman, Brown, Green and Longmans, 1849).

Trumbull, H. Clay, *Border Lines in the Field of Doubtful Practices* (London: Hodder and Stoughton, 1899).

Turnbull, T. N., *What God Hath Wrought* (Bradford: Puritan Press, [1959]).

Turner, Christopher B., 'Religious Revivalism and Welsh Industrial Society: Aberdare in 1859', *Llafur*, 4, no. 1 (1984), 4–13.

Vann, Philip, 'Nicholas Evans', *Arts Review*, 37, no. 18 (13 September 1985), 454.

Vann, Philip, 'Out of the Darkness', *Artist*, 100, no. 11 (November 1985), 8–11.

Walters, Meurig, 'Two Rhondda Poems', *Welsh Review*, 1, no. 2 (March 1939), 69.

Watson, Thomas, *The Ten Commandments*, revised edition, first published as part of *A Body of Practical Divinity* (1692), (Edinburgh: Banner of Truth Trust, 1965).

Watts, Isaac, *A Guide to Prayer: or, A Free and Rationale Account of the Gift, Grace and Spirit of Prayer* (1715), fifth edition (London: Emmanuel Matthews, 1730).

Watts, Isaac, *The Holiness of Times, Places, and People under the Jewish and Christian Dispensations* (London: Hett and Brackstone, 1738).

Webber, F. R., *A History of Preaching in Britain and America*, 3 vols. (Milwaukee: Northwestern Publishing House, 1955).

[Westminster Assembly], *Westminster Confession of Faith* (1646) (Glasgow: Free Presbyterian Publications, 1976).

White, James F., *Protestant Worship and Church Architecture* (New York: Oxford University Press, 1964).

Whitney, Geffrey, *A Choice of Emblemes and Other Devices, Leyden, 1586* (Amsterdam and New York: Da Capo Press, Theatrvm Orbis Terrarvm, 1969).

Whittaker, Colin C., *Seven Pentecostal Pioneers* (Basingstoke: Marshall Pickering, 1983).

Wilkins, Charles, *Buried Alive* (London: Houlston and Sons, 1877).

Williams, C. G., 'A Study of Pentecostal Glossolalia and Related Phenomena', unpublished Ph.D. thesis, University College Cardiff, 1978.

Williams, C. R., 'The Welsh Religious Revival, 1904–5', *British Journal of Sociology*, 3, no. 3, (September 1952), 242–59.

Williams, D. J., 'Shadows', *Colliery Workers' Magazine*, 1, no. 5 (May 1923), 117.

Williams, Evan, 'Picture Talks to Boys and Girls. "The Angelus," by J. F. Millet', *Baptist Record*, 3, no. 29 (May 1915), 14.

Williams, Evan, 'Picture Talks to Boys and Girls. "Hope," by G. F. Watts', *Baptist Record*, 3, no. 28 (April 1915), 15.

Williams, Glanmor, 'The Idea of Nationality in Wales', *Cambridge Journal*, 7, no. 3 (December 1953), 145–58.

Williams, Glanmor, *Religious Language and Nationality in Wales* (Cardiff: University of Wales Press, 1979).

Williams, Norman, 'The Senghenydd Colliery Disaster', *Glamorgan Historian*, 6 (1969), 148–59.

Williams, R., 'The Gospel of Colours', *Children's Treasury*, 9, no. 9 (September 1912), 132–3.

Wilson, B. R., *Sects and Society* (London: William Heinemann, 1961).

Wood, Leon J., *The Holy Spirit in the Old Testament*, Contemporary Evangelical Perspectives, second edition (Grand Rapids, Michigan: Zondervan Publishing House, 1978).

Woodhead, Abraham, *Concerning Images and Idolatry* (Oxford, 1698).

Wright, Barbara, 'Nicholas Evans', *Arts Review*, 30, no. 18 (September 1978), 490.

Index

Page references in italic type denote illustrations

Adams, W. J. 75–6
aesthetic theory 55–6
aestheticism 47, 55
Alexander, Archibald 47
Alford, Henry 66
allegory 23, 50, 160
   visions as 65–6, 71
   see also emblems; symbol(s); symbolism
Anabaptists 60
angels, representation 77
Anglican churches 19, 20, 103
   Llanfair Caereinion Mynafon Church *17*
Apostolic Church 3, 89, 140, 168, 184n1
   see also Evans, Nicholas; Williams, Daniel P.
architecture *see* chapel(s)
Ariès, Philippe 151
Arnheim, Rudolf 155
Arnold, Matthew 46, 47
art
   Nonconformity in 19th and early 20th century 45–58
   Pentecostals and 140
   Reformation tradition and *see* Reformation tradition
   relationship between religion and 2–3, 45, 54–7, 159
   see also religious art
   used in preaching 44, 49–54, 57–8, 120–1, 135, 140, 158–9
   Welsh 3, 54–7, 158
Art Journal 80
Arts and Crafts Movement 133
Awstin 87, 131

Baker, H. Collins 195n5
Baptist Record 165
Baptists 3
   chapels *104, 107, 108, 110, 112*
Barker, R. J. 114
Barratt, T. B. 90

Barthes, Roland 39, 141, 171n5
Bell, Clive 55
Bevan, Edwyn 143
Bibl Darluniadol, Y 97–100, *99, 100, 101, 102,* 117
Bibl Yr Addoliad Teuluaidd 69
Bible
   centrality to Nonconformity 1, 59, 160
   image of God in New Testament 11–14
   invisibility of God in Old Testament 6–10
   and visions 59, 61–5
   see also biblical
Bible dictionaries 77, *106,* 108
biblical
   associations of mining 38
   in Evans's paintings 3, 4–5, 115–18, 141–59, 160–1
   nature of emblems 3
   in Staniforth's 'The Religious Revival' 131
biblical antiquities, visual representation of 7–10, *8, 9,* 106–13, *106, 107, 108, 110, 112*
biblical illustration 50, *51,* 68, *69,* 70, 76, 83, 84, 97–100, *99, 100, 101, 102, 110*
biblical texts 70, 135
Bissell, Edwin, *Biblical Antiquities 109,* 111
blackness 158
   landscape 155–7
   and sin 152–5
Braque, Georges 118
Brown, Ford Madox, *Work 122,* 123, 134, 138, 142
Bruner, F. D. 168
Bryson, Norman 171n5
Bucer, Martin 172n19
Buchanan, James 27
Buchholz, F. 3
Bunyan, John

   A Book for Boys and Girls 24, 193n15, 200n29
   Pilgrim's Progress 20, 21, 23, 29, 71
Burns, James 38, 50–1, 53, 56, 81, 84, 85, 86, 120–1
Burton, William F. P. 199n4

Caine, Hall 57
Calmet, Augustin, *Dictionary of the Bible 106,* 108
Calvin, John 13, 16, 23, 113, 151, 152, 172n19
Calvinism 6, 15, 20, 113
   prohibition on representation of God 42, 68
Calvinistic Methodism 3, 84
   chapels *15,* 103
   see also Children's Treasury; Monthly Treasury; Trysorfa y Plant
Canty, George 199n5
Caravaggio 155
Carlyle, Thomas 123, 139
Carracci, Annibale *69*
Carter, Howard 199n4
catacombs 80, 135
Caunter, Hobart, *Illustrations of the Bible by Westall and Martin* 50, *51*
chapel
   architectural features
     communion table 111, *112*
     pulpit *15, 108, 110,* 111, *112*
     sêt fawr 15, 110, 111, 133
     window glass 19, 20
   centrality of the Word 160
   developmental phases 6
   early 14–20, 26, 113, 158, 160
   names 102–3, 144
   19th and early 20th century 19, 100–13, 131–5
   parallels between Tabernacle, Temple and Chapel 100–13, *104, 107, 108, 110, 112*

Reformation theology in
14–20, *15*, *16*, *17*, 160
structure paralleled in colliery
2, 131–5
chapels
Alfred Place Baptist,
Aberystwyth *112*
Baptist, Newtown *104*
Bethel Welsh Baptist,
Aberystwyth *107*, *108*, *110*
Capel Beilheulog, Gwenddwr,
Brecon 18
Capel Mair, St Clears, Carms. *132*
Capel Newydd, Llŷn 18
Four Crosses Calvinistic
Methodist *15*
Havelock Street Presbyterian,
Newport, Mons. *103*, *105*
Maesyronnen, Glasbury, Rads.
16, 18
Mynydd Newydd Colliery,
Forest Fach 134–5, *136*
Peniel, Tremadog *106*
charismata 86, 87–8, 90–4, 168–9
cherubim, representation 10, 21,
77
chiaroscuro 155
children's literature 37–8, 51, 77,
85, 177n54, 190n100
Collier Jack serial 34–5, 36–7,
40, 124–5
emblem books 24–5, 28
Children's Treasury 34
Christ
emblems of 21
representation and visions of
1904–5 revival 63–4, 67–86
representation as miner 36–7,
38–44, 131
representation in New
Testament and Reformed
thought 11–14
theophany, in story of fiery
furnace 40
Christian Age 70
Christian culture 45–9, 158
Clarke, Robert 199n5
coal-mining *see* mining
collieries, relationship between
chapels and architecture of
2, 131–5
community, miners/Israelites
114–18, 142
congregation, importance in
Nonconformity 14–16,
166–7

congregational singing 166
Congregationalism 3, 10, 124
chapels *16*, 18
connotation, visual theory of
applied to Evans's paintings
4–5, 135–9, 141–59
applied to Staniforth's 'The
Religious Revival' 131
conversion 166
imagery 65–7
Copping, Harold, *The Hope of the
World* 84–5, *Plate 2*
Cotman, John Sell, *Snowdon 101*
Cowper, William 14, 50, 67
culture
continuity between biblical
societies and Nonconformity
3–4
Pentecostalism and 140
Welsh, and religion 54–7, 158

Dabney, R. L. 191n9
Davenport, Fredrick 60
Davidson, Jim 91
Davies, David 42, 50, 51, 125–6, *126*
Davies, E. T. 97
death and mortality
hymns 65
paintings of Nicholas Evans
140–59, 161
definitions
biblical 3
religious 3
devil, imagery and visions of
1904–5 revival 59, 63–4, 71,
77–80, 154
Diehl, Huston 21, 74
Dissenters 14, 23, 134
Diwygiwr, Y 124
Dobson, C. C. 80
Downes, Robert 46, 53
drama, Nonconformity and 48,
49, 57, 164–5
dreams 7
Driskel, Michael 117

Early-Church Fathers 10, 24
Edwards, J. H. 95–6
Edwards, Jonathan 59
Edwards, O. M. 95
Edwards, R. D. 37–8
Edwards, Thomas Charles 11
Elias, John 1, 2
Ellerton, John 121–2
emblem books 20–5, 52, 53,
152–3, 158

19th century 3, 24–5, 50, 51,
158
visions and 60, 71–4, *72*
emblems 2
cherubim as, of angelic nature
10, 21
Evans's paintings 3, 38–43, 117,
135, 158, 161
of labour 119–25
persistence into 20th century
25
pictures as 44, 49–54, 119–25,
131, 135, 158
sermonic 23, 26–38, 43–4, 60,
131, 153, 156
of sin 153
see also miner(s); mining; visions
emotion, incitement of 166
engravings 70
topographic 97–100, *99*, *100*,
101, *102*, 117
Evangelical Magazine 81
Evans, Benjamin (1816–66) 34
Evans, Benjamin (1844–1900) 34
Evans, Christmas 1, 27, 28–9,
30–2, 35, 38, 42
Evans, Nicholas 4–5
biblical nature of painting 3,
4–5, 115–18, 141–59, 160–1
divine inspiration 86, 87, 88,
89–94, 140
identification of miners with
Israelites 115–18
mining and mortality in 140–59
work / worship in later
paintings 135–9
paintings
All Out – End of Shift 116,
117
Ashes to Ashes 141, 156
The Broken Rope 143, 144–5,
144
*Candle-Men Carrying Out Dead
150*
Claustrophobia 138
Coalface 150
Coalface (2) 123, 138–9
Coalface 1920s 150
Coalface – Tight Squeeze 149, *150*
The Dignity of Labour 138
Early Mining 138
Ecce Homo 157
Entombed – Jesus in the Midst 2,
3, 4, 38–44, 85–6, 135, 136,
141, 143, 145–6, 149, 154,
157, 160–1, *Plate 1*

INDEX

Journey to the Far End 146–7, *146*
The Last Bond 143, 145, 147–9, *147*, 150
Miners Approaching Workplace 138
Pit Closure – Miners Coming Up for the Last Time 92, 145, 147–9, 150, 151, Plate 5
A Place of Refuge 143–4
Standing a Post 135–8, *137*
Strike – Gleaners on Slag Heap 116–17, *116*
Transport to the Far End 146–7, *146*
'The Trumpet Shall Sound' – Resurrection! 141
Underground Chapel during 1904 Revival 137, 139
The Water-Hole 118
Women Coal Carriers 117
Evans, Rhoda 170n4
Evans, Sydney 57, 73, 153
Evans, Theophilus, *Drych y Prif Oesoedd* 96
Evans, Wynne 96
Evening Express 56, 71, 74, *75*, 114, 116, *127*, 128

Finney, Charles G. 26, 168, 169
Fletcher, Ifan Kyrle 55
formalism 55
Forward Movement Torch 64
Frith, William, *The Road to Ruin* 52
Fry, Roger 55
Furst, Herbert 124

Gee, Jay 34–5, 36–7, 40, 124
Genedl Gymreig, Y 126
George, Philip 170n4
Ginzberg, Eli 41
God
 Evans's paintings as images made by 88, 91, 93
 representation in Reformation tradition 6–25
  emblem books 20–5
  image in New Testament 11–14
  invisibility in Old Testament 6–10
  meeting house and 14–20
gold-mining, emblem 30
Gombrich, E. H. 23, 143
Gospel Ship, The Plate 4

Gowing, Lawrence 170n4
Gurevich, Vladimir 177n50
Gwerinwr, Y 124
Gwlad Canaan; Ar Gynllun Gogledd a Deheudir Cymru i Blant 97, *98*, 100

Halewood, William 152
Hanks, Patricia 102
Harries, Hywel 170n4
Heaphy, Thomas 80, 81–2
Heemskerck, Maerten van 152
hell
 Evans's paintings 145–9, 161
 visions 62
Henry, Matthew 7, 10, 21, 39, 50, 173n34, 177nn50, 52, 178n1
Herbert, George 121
Herbert, Robert 195n5, 196n11
Herman, Josef 117, 118, 156, 198n42
Hicks, Percy 128
higher-critical theology 49, 61, 81, 113
Hilling, John 132
Hodge, Charles 6
Hodges, Flavia 102
Holiness Movement 168
Höltgen, Karl 21
Holy Spirit, baptism of 87–8, 89, 168–9
 see also inspiration, divine
homiletic tradition
 Evans's paintings in 3, 38–44, 143–58 *passim*, 160–1
 sermonic emblems 23, 26–38, 43–4, 60, 131, 153, 156
 see also preaching
How, William, bishop 67, 68
Howell, Archdeacon 97
Hughes, Daniel 47
Hughes, Henry 126–7
Hughes, Hugh Price 121
Hunt, William Holman
 The Awakening Conscience 53
 The Light of the World 42, 50–1, 83, 85
 The Scapegoat 157
 Shadow of Death 42, 149
hwyl 166
hymns 14, 23–4, 37, 43, 50, 60, 93, 96, 144, 166
 and labour 121–2
 visions of 1904–5 revival 65–8
Ibbetson, Julius Caesar 125

iconographic tradition 171n5
 relationship of Evans's paintings to 4, 38, 41, 42, 85, 136
icons 10, 158, 198n42
Ifold, Cyril 156
Illustrated London News 124, 125
image, Nonconformity and 1–2, 160–1
Impressionism 54
Independents *see* Congregationalism
inspiration, artistic 87–94
inspiration, divine 4, 60, 86, 140
 Old Testament 89–90
 painting and preaching 87–8
 parallels between speaking in tongues and artistic inspiration 90–4
 Pentecostal theology 168–9
instrumentality, and divine/artistic inspiration 88, 91, 93
interpretative tradition 4, 71, 171n5
iron-ore mining, as emblem 30–2, 35
Israelites
 Christians as antitype of 19
 miners as 2, 113–18
 see also Wales/Israel correspondence

Jahn, John 194n21
Jeffreys, Stephen 75–6, 191n101
Jenkins, W. 54
Jewish Holocaust 200n19
John Ploughman's Pictures 25
Jones, Anthony 106, 193n16
Jones, D. Gwynfryn 47–8
Jones, D. S. 186n24
Jones, David 46–7
Jones, Edmund 61
Jones, H. W. 181n29
Jones, J. Cynddylan 90, 91
Jones, John, *Scripture Antiquities* 107, *108*
Jones, Mary ('Welsh Seeress') 64, *79*
Jones, W. R. 90
Joshua, Seth 102
judgement
 imagery of 73, 156
 paintings of Nicholas Evans 141, 145–9, 156, 157, 161

Keswick Convention 168
Kitto, John 9, 106, 111, *112*

Kris, Ernst 87, 89
Kurz, Otto 89
Kuyper, Abraham 47, 113

Lambert, W. R. 124
Laocoön 53
Last Judgement (c.1000) *147*, 148–9
Laud, William, archbishop 13
Le Rolle, H., *The Nativity* 38, *39*
Leighton, Frederic 53–4
leisure pursuits, Nonconformity and 48, 57
Lewis, H. Elvet 59, 135
Lewis, Jessie Pen 168
Lewis, Noyes 188n53
Lhermitte, Léon, *Christ Visiting the Poor* 84, 85
Licht, Fred 155
light
  Evans's paintings 155
  safety lamp as emblem 37–8, 42–3
  visions 62–3, 72–3
lighthouse as emblem 28–9
Linton, John 123
Lorraine, Claude 193n13
Lovett, Richard, *Welsh Pictures* 97–100, *99*, *100*
Luther, Martin 59, 79, 122

Maas, Jeremy 83
MacIntyre, Alasdair 187n27
McLeod, Hugh 60
maritime images *22*, 23–4, 29–30, Plate 4
Martin, John 50, *51*
meeting-house 6, 14–20, 26, 113, 160
  see also chapel
memento mori 149–52, 162
metaphors 160
  biblical 73, 79, 144
  homiletic tradition 1, 28, 34, 37, 42–3, 113, 158
  hymns 24, 43, 65, 67, 144
  visual 43, 152, 153
Methodism 103
  Primitive 60
  Wesleyan 168
  see also Calvinistic Methodism
Michelangelo
  David 138
  Last Judgement 146–7
Millet, Jean François, *The Angelus* 51, 119–21, *120*, 122, 125, 131, 135, 136, 142

Mills, John 166
Mills, Richard 166
miner(s)
  Christ represented as 31–2, 36–7, 38–43
  death and 149–52
  as emblem of saint and sinner 2, 30–43, 118, 119, 125–31, 142, 158, 161, 162
  as Israelites 2, 113–18
mining
  death and mortality 140–59
  as emblem in painting 38–44, 161
  as emblem in sermons 30–8, 160
  Nicholas Evans and 4–5, 161
  relationship to Nonconformity 2, 33–4, 119
  see also Evans, Nicholas
mining disasters
  Aberfan disaster (1966) 176n39
  death/judgement 141, 144–5, 149, 151, 156
  Evans's paintings 4, 141, 144–5, 149–51, 156
  see also Evans, Nicholas, paintings, *Entombed*
  miners and heroism *124*, 125
  poetry and ballads 162–3
  sermonic emblems 35–7
Montgomery, James 67
Monthly Treasury 52
More, Henry 22–3, 143
Morgan, Edward 185n9
Morgan, Lucius 96
Morgan, Robert 155–6
Morris, Caleb 102
Morris, William 133
mortality *see* death and mortality
music 49, 59, 114–15
  congregational singing 166
  songs 90, 114–15

Naegely, Henry 120–1
national cultural revival, and art/religion 54–7, 95, 158
Newman, John Henry 37
newspaper illustration 38, 56, *75*, *124*, 127–31, *127*, *128*, *130*, 135, 136, 142, 145
Nicholls, Chag. W. 129
Nochlin, Linda 119
novel, Nonconformity and 48, 57
Old Testament worship
  parallels between Tabernacle, Temple and chapel 100–13

Reformation tradition and invisibility of God 6–10
visual elements
  Ark of the Covenant 9, *108*, 112
  Holy of Holies *8*, 10, 14, 111, 112, 113
  Mercy Seat 9, 10, 14, *108*
  Table of Shewbread 111, *112*
  Temple 7, 9–10, 11, 12, 24, 45, 100–13
  see also Tabernacle
Only True Likeness of Our Saviour 81, *82*
Owen, John 10, 14
Owens, Priscilla 23–4

Panofsky, Erwin 199n17
Parry, Joseph 166
Pentecostalism 4, 114
  baptism of the Spirit 88, 168–9
  divine inspiration 87, 88, 90–4, 140
  visions 2, 75–6, 85, 86
  see also Apostolic Church
Perfect, George 199n2
Petts, John, *The Cage 148*, 149
Pezron, Paul 96
Phillips, D. M. 61, 63, 64–5
Picasso, Pablo 118, 142
picture-postcards of 1904–5 revival 70
Piero della Francesca, *Resurrection of Christ* 145–6
pit
  as ossuary 150–1
  sermonic emblem 31–7, 147, 160
  visions of 1904–5 revival 62
plaques, ornamental *71*
Plotinism 88, 90
poetry 49, 57, 90, 155–6
  commemoration of mining disasters 162–3
posters, 'broad and narrow way' 23, 25, Plate 3
preaching 1
  art used in 44, 49–54, 57–8, 120–1, 135, 140, 158–9
  divine inspiration 87–8
  identification of Old Testament and contemporary worlds 113–14
  Reformers' reliance on 13–14

INDEX

visions as 60, 69–71
see also homiletic tradition; sermon illustrations
Presbyterian Church of Wales *see* Calvinistic Methodism
Price, Peter 197n31
Prideaux, *Pictorial Bible 110*
Primitive Methodists 60
pseudo-morphosis 200n17
Puritans 6, 7, 10, 13, 20, 23, 70, 102
  representation of God 81, 84

Quakers 60
Quarles, Francis, emblem books 20, 21, *22*, 23–4, 26, 28, 29, 42, 50, 53, 72–3, *72*, 144, *153*, 158

Raphael 198n44, *Christ on the Cross, with the Virgin, John, Jerome and Mary Magdalene* 136
Rees, D. Ben 131
Reformation 3, 168
Reformation tradition
  and visual representation 6–25, 45, 74, 160
    death/sin 151–2
    emblem books 20–5
    image of God in New Testament 11–14
    invisibility of God in Old Testament 6–10
    worship 14–20
  of work 122
refuge, image of 143–4
religion/art, Nonconformity and relation between 2–3, 45, 54–7, 159
religious, definition 3
religious art
  emblems of labour 119–25
  Evans's paintings as 4–5, 85–6, 135–59, 161
  Nonconformist 1, 4–5, 158–9, 161
  and visions 68–85
  Welsh 3, 54–7, 158
religious drama 164–5
religious revivals 41, 87, 168
  1859 Irish 64
  1904–5 in Wales 3, 4, 95, 96, 113, 169
    and culture 56–7
    emblems 37–8
    mining/miner and 2, 37, 126–31, 135, 142, 153, 156

music 166
  visions 58, 59–86, 87, 95, 154, 167
Rembrandt 151, 152, 155
  Christ Preaching the Remission of Sins 130, 131, 145
  'The Return of the Prodigal Son' 152
Renaissance art 119, 148, 151, 152
  inspiration 88, 89–90
  interpretative tradition 171n5
Reynolds, Joshua 198n44
Rhys, Ernest 95, 97
Riches of Grace 89, 140
Roberts, Evan 34, *56*, 57, 154, 156, 166, 169, 197n31
  divine inspiration 87–8
  visions 59, 60–74, 79–80
rock, emblem *22*, 24
Roman Catholicism 80, 201n38
  churches 19, 103
  imagery 7, 10, 11, 13, 21, 42, 68, 119, 177n50
  visionary tradition 59
  worship 15
Rothenberg, Albert 87
Rowland, Daniel 1, 27, 30
Runzo, Joseph 76
Ruskin, John 51, 55, 56, 157
Rutter, Frank 55

safety lamp as emblem 37–8, 42–3
saint/sinner, miner as *see under* miner(s)
Salomon, Herman, *Christus* 83, 84
Samarin, W. J. 91
Sandby, Paul 125
science, new 113
Scripture Illustrations 108
seafaring images *22*, 23–4, 29–30, Plate 4
sermon illustrations 23, 26–38, 43–4, 60, 113
  art used in preaching 44, 49–54, 57–8, 120–1, 135, 140, 158–9
  emblems from everyday life 26–30
  industrial emblems 2, 30–8, 131, 153, 156
  see also homiletic tradition
Sharrock, Roger 20, 173n30
Simonin, Louis 32–3, *33*
sin, associations with blackness and coal 151–5, 157, 158
singing, congregational 166

sinner/saint, miner as *see under* miner(s)
social gospel 49, 84, 85, 121, 158
songs 90
  Christian consciousness 114–15
South Wales Daily News 60, 64, 83, 128–9, *128*
spiritual conflict, visions and representations 63–5, 71, 73, 74, 77–80, *78*
spiritual gifts 86, 87–8, 90–4, 168–9
sport, Nonconformity and 48, 57
Sprague, W. B. 26
Spurgeon, Charles Haddon 25
Staniforth, J. M. *56*, 71, 125, *127*, 128
  'The Religious Revival' 38, 129–31, *130*, 135, 136, 139, 145
  'A Result of the Revival. Then and Now' *56*, 128
Stanley, Arthur Penrhyn 11, 97
Sunday Magazine 134, *136*
symbol(s), symbolism
  Entombed – Jesus in the Midst as 86, 143
  judgement 156
  labour 117, 131
  miner 118
  in Nonconformity 113, 160
  see also allegory; emblems; typology

Tabernacle 19, 45
  divine inspiration for construction 89–90, 94
  Nonconformist visualization 7–10, *8*
  parallels between chapel and 100–13, *107*, 144
  as type 11, 12
Tabula Cebetis 23
Tarrant, Margaret 177n54
Taylor, John Russell 170n4
theatre, Nonconformity and 48, 49, 57, 164–5
Thomas, H. Elwyn 48, 164, 165
Thomas, H. R. 183n62
Thomas, John *15*, *17*, 77, 81, *82*, *132*
Thomas, Nathaniel 34
Thomas, Thomas Henry 80–1, 84, 125–6, *126*, 129
  'Mary Jones and the Devil' *79*
Thomas, W. Gerwyn 134

Tillet, Ben 114
Tillich, Paul 142, 143
tongues, speaking in *see* spiritual gifts
Toplady, Augustus 24, 72, 144
Torrey, R. A. 169
transi 150, 153
Treasury 80, 103, 190n100
Trysorfa y Plant 8, *9*, 78
Turin Shroud 80
Turnbull, T. N. 168
typology 11, 18, 19, 22, 157, 160
    miners/mining 4, 113–14, 118, 135, 158

Uhde, Fritz von 85

Vann, Philip 150, 170n4
Veil of Veronica 80, 81
Villalpandus, John-Baptist *106*, 108
visionary tradition 59–60
    biblical 7, 61–5
    Evans's paintings in 2, 4, 85–6, 87, 140
    hymnological tradition 65–8
visions 160
    Island Place Mission Hall, Llanelli 75–6, 83, 85, 86
    1904–5 revival 58, 59–86, 87, 95, 154, 167
    and religious pictures 68–85
visual artefacts 1, 6, 70, *71*
visual representation
    Nonconformity 1–2, 6, 160–1
    see also under Reformation tradition

Wales/Israel correspondence 27–8, 43, 94, 95–118, 131
    and Evans's paintings 2, 141–2, 157
    historic, linguistic and topographic parallels 95–100
    miners/Israelites 113–18
    names 102
    Tabernacle, Temple and chapel 100–13
wall pictures/artefacts 70, *71*
Wallis, Henry 119
Walters, Meurig 117
Watson, Thomas 7
Watts, G. F. 54–5, 183n56
    Hope 52, 53
Watts, Isaac 18, 67–8
Welsh art/culture, and religion 3, 54–7, 158
Welsh Outlook 55
Welsh Pictures 97–100, *99*, *100*
Wesley, Charles 43
Wesleyan Methodism 168
Westall, Richard 50
Western Mail 60, 74, 87, 125, 128, 129, 197n31
Whale, J. S. 15
White, F. C. 183n62
whiteness, meeting-house 19–20, 158
Whitney, Geffrey 20, 73
Wilenski, R. H. 55
Williams, Cyril 88
Williams, Daniel P. 34, 66–7, 202n10
Williams, Evan 53, 119–20, 121, 122

Williams, Glanmor 97
Williams, Iona 54, 55, 158
Williams, R. 154
Williams, Watkin H. 34
Williams, William, Pantycelyn 65
Williams, William, of Wern 27
Wither, George 20
Woodshed, Abraham 13
Word, the
    Nonconformist emphasis on and visualization of 1–2, 160
    Reformation tradition 13, 15–16, 20–5
work/worship 43, 119–39
    colliery and chapel 131–5
    emblems of labour 119–25
    miners redeemed 125–31
    in paintings of Nicholas Evans 135–9
worship
    art as 93, 140
    democratization 166–7
    New Testament 11–14
    theological expression in early Nonconformist meeting-house 14–20, 26
    see also Old Testament worship; Tabernacle; work/worship
Wright, Barbara 170n4

Zinzendorf, Nicolaus Ludwig von 70
Zwingli, Ulrich 172n19